Deleuze and the City

D1610570

Deleuze Connections

'It is not the elements or the sets which define the multiplicity. What defines it is the AND, as something which has its place between the elements or between the sets. AND, AND, AND – stammering.'

Gilles Deleuze and Claire Parnet, *Dialogues*

General Editor
Ian Buchanan

Editorial Advisory Board

Keith Ansell-Pearson
Rosi Braidotti
Claire Colebrook
Tom Conley

Gregg Lambert
Adrian Parr
Paul Patton
Patricia Pisters

Titles Available in the Series

Visit the Deleuze Connections website at
www.euppublishing.com/series/delco

Deleuze and the City

Edited by Hélène Frichot, Catharina Gabrielsson and Jonathan Metzger

EDINBURGH
University Press

Edinburgh University Press is one of the leading university presses in the UK. We publish academic books and journals in our selected subject areas across the humanities and social sciences, combining cutting-edge scholarship with high editorial and production values to produce academic works of lasting importance. For more information visit our website: www.edinburghuniversitypress.com

Edinburgh University Press Ltd
The Tun – Holyrood Road
12(2f) Jackson's Entry
Edinburgh EH8 8PJ

Typeset in 10.5/13 Adobe Sabon by
Servis Filmsetting Ltd, Stockport, Cheshire,
and printed and bound in Great Britain by
CPI Group (UK) Ltd, Croydon CR0 4YY

A CIP record for this book is available from the British Library

ISBN 978 1 4744 0758 8 (hardback)
ISBN 978 1 4744 0760 1 (webready PDF)
ISBN 978 1 4744 0759 5 (paperback)
ISBN 978 1 4744 0761 8 (epub)

Contents

Acknowledgements

The editors would like to thank all the contributors to *Deleuze and the City*, our copy-editor David Kelly, and Carol Macdonald at Edinburgh University Press. Jean Hillier, also a contributor to this book, has offered invaluable advice throughout the editorial process. We are indebted to our inspirational colleagues, patient families and kind friends who have offered support and advice throughout the planning and editing of this book. This book project was supported by the Formas funded Strong Research Environment 'Architecture in Effect', and by the research project 'Transversal Writing' funded by Vetenskapsrådet (The Swedish Research Council).

List of Illustrations

What a City Can Do

Hélène Frichot, Catharina Gabrielsson and
Jonathan Metzger

This book rests on a conviction that philosophy is crucially important not only for advancing knowledge of how cities work, but also for allowing us to envisage new forms of urban life in a more sustainable future. The present volume, while strangely belated in an era obsessed by cities, is therefore a timely addition to the *Deleuze Connections* series. Whether expressed implicitly or explicitly, established through references scattered across their writings, the city is ever-present in both the independent and collaborative work of Félix Guattari and Gilles Deleuze. If the city and philosophy share the same contingent birth, are reciprocally produced and remain mutually dependent (Deleuze and Guattari 1994: 43; Beistegui 2012: 18–19), it seems only fit that what we know as the city today – the flows of bodies, forces and matter, the overheated centres, the sprawls and the margins – would generate a thinking such as theirs: a challenge to the very notion of form or iden-tity, including that of philosophy itself. In fact, if what the city primarily generates is a non-philosophy, making that which we call philosophy possible (Deleuze and Guattari 1994: 218), it may perhaps also generate a non-city, an 'outside' to the city that can no longer be envisaged as the wilderness beyond, nor as external forces confronting the (now digital) city walls, but as the element of struggle that stirs trouble on the city's striations from within.

Following the ethos of Deleuze and Guattari, with this compilation we aim to dispel the old question of what the city *is*, asking instead what it can *do*. In the first instance it imposes its boundary lines everywhere, transforming the world into centres or peripheries in an increasingly rigid segmentarity (Deleuze and Guattari 1987: 212). There are com-plicated distinctions between town, city, *polis* and the State apparatus – none of which are privileged, all of which are somehow co-constitutive – but there is no evolutionary progression between them: each city has its own plane of consistency, its own located histories and specificities. The city, any-city-whatever, is situated amid mental, social and environmental ecologies that serve as witness and backdrop to emergent subjectivities, collective enunciations, continuously heterogeneous and confused admixtures of the natural and the cultivated. Across the writings of Deleuze and Guattari, the city is conjured up in all its contradictions, a near ubiquitous milieu, enfolded in global capitalism, but also contingent, geographically secured and marked by distinctions. Constituted by complexes of forces, encounters and relations, the city is a machinic assemblage, and neither smooth nor striated nor even holey space can exhaust the many points of passage, entry and egress its dynamic system entails.

What we argue for here are primary matters of concern when it comes to assessing contemporary urban situations. To consider the subject of cities today we must think beyond the logic of forms identified with the urban fabric, even beyond the more fluid socio-ecological approaches to the city, both serving as platforms for dominant notions of 'urban sustainability'. Any such coding carries the related insistence of ever more virulent forms of neoliberal market capitalism, what Guattari has called Integrated World Capitalism and what Maurizio Lazzarato characterises as the relation between machinic enslavement and social subjection (Lazzarato 2014). The ramifications of what 'matters' in urban situations intensify when we consider how violence and disease have contributed to the planning and occupations of cities, past and present, and how both wealth and poverty are outcomes of cities, generating intensities and voids, processes of eviction and segregation. The city is embroiled and co-opted and co-constituted with diverse and dynamic, affirmative and negative, relations and compositions, and whether through acts of planning or the absence of planning, through acts of terrorism or under the guise of the protection of a population, these processes are channelled through collective political imaginations that emerge from and forge the city in its actual and virtual existence.

Considering the city along these trajectories is greatly informed by the work of Deleuze and Guattari. Indeed, we would argue that a Deleuzian approach is indispensible for the project of 'rethinking the epistemology of the urban', recently advocated by Brenner and Schmid as 'an open-ended interplay between critique (of inherited traditions of urban theory and contemporary urban ideologies), epistemological experimentation (leading to the elaboration of new concepts and methods) and concrete research (on specific contexts, struggles and transformations)' (Brenner and Schmid 2015: 161). Engaging with concepts situated within an ontology of immanence, defined by multiplicities, events and becomings, we have asked authors to especially consider *assemblage, haecceity, affect* and *multiplicity*, and more generally the processes of *coding, de-* and *re-territorialisation* of entities ongoing in and through urban settings. Together, these concepts and loci of concern serve as a loose framework that articulates the chapters of this book, that in extending from the explicit references to 'the city' in Deleuze and Guattari's writings follow their philosophical project closely.[1]

From Urban Conditions to Sustainable Cities

Thinking today what a city can do is to engage, explicitly or not, with the inexorable process of diversification and specialisation that followed upon the postmodern 'rediscovery' of the city in the 1980s. Postmodernism was obsessed with defining 'urban conditions' as part of a project of redefining the status of knowledge, power, culture and politics with the advent of a new mode of technological and late-capitalist globalisation. With the shift from topographical to topological thinking, however – as illustrated, for instance, by reorientations in cultural geography (Murdoch 2006) – the neat progression of historical epochs signalled by the prefix 'post' has become obsolete. Deleuze has been enormously influential in this reorientation by way of the impact of his transcendental empiricism and through the 'geophilosophy' elaborated in collaboration with Guattari. In his extended essay *The Three Ecologies* (2000), Guattari stresses the ecological effects of concepts, values and ideas on the material built environment. Urging us to think transversally across three ecological registers – mental, social and environmental – Guattari emphasises the necessity to confront our enslavement in global capitalism. In reconfiguring the sharp distinctions between economy, society and nature imposed by 'sustainable development' policy-makers, this is not only a call for trans- or interdisciplinary thinking, but a radical undermining of such categories. In a postscript to this compilation, 'For an Urban Machinic Ecology', Gary Genosko elaborates further on the significance of Guattari's understanding of cities as mega-machines composed of overlapping human and non-human entities and relations. Deleuze and Guattari are of central importance for the 'ecological turn' in the humanities and social sciences, and their call to think complexity and for complex thinking remains a challenge (Herzogenrath 2009), especially within an empiricist and policy-driven field like urban planning.

The massive amount of research conducted today in the name of sustainable urban development, resilient cities and 'smart cities growth' proceeds from a point of departure that is remarkably similar to the ontology devised by Deleuze and Guattari, but with a notable absence of their criticality. While research on urban metabolism, for instance, conceives cities as complex forms of self-organisation, constituted as adaptive networks that are linked across temporal and spatial scales in non-linear ways, it is frequently marked by an inability to seriously consider issues of power, politics and agency that unavoidably emerge when investigating notions of sustainability. An oversimplified path of evolution from postmodern urban conditions to our present-day discourse on sustainable cities, accompanied by a shift from a socio-cultural to a technical-scientific explanatory basis, has impacted on how cities are currently explained, described and projected. The greater challenge of understanding the city as material-semiotic conundrum requires that a precarious position be taken up between modes of subjectification and machinic enslavement, which cannot be grasped within a technical-scientific paradigm nor exclusively as socio-cultural phenomena. A number of chapters in this volume offer resistance to any attempt at a one-dimensional pinning-down of 'the urban', such as those performative reductionisms produced by orthodox Marxism, technocratic managerialism or neoliberal capitalism and its profit-based motivation.

With *Deleuze and the City*, we hope to show how the geophilosophy of Deleuze and Guattari is a matter of urgent concern for urban planners, architects, philosophers, geographers and spatial thinkers addressing the topic of sustainable cities today. As elaborated in Janet McGaw's chapter 'Imagining Portland's Future Past: Lessons from Indigenous Placemaking in a Colonial City', the non-linear and contradictory passages of urban development always constitute 'holey stories' of entangled smooth migrations and spatial striations. Colonial histories and ways of living, like those presently dominating places like Portland, Australia, tend to ignore any such transversal connections at their own peril, McGaw adds, in the face of unfolding ecological crises. Further problematising the conventional maintenance of borders between nature and culture, Jean Hillier suggests that the bacteria *Treponema pallidum* – better known as syphilis – actually planned the city of Melbourne. In her chapter 'Deterritorialising the Face of the City: How *Treponema pallidum* Planned Melbourne', Hillier challenges Melbourne's heritage planners to rethink the historical folding-together of the planes of reference of health/medicine, town planning and moral purity which contributed to stratifying Melbourne as the city it has become today. Addressing the dominant discourse on urban development, merging policy-making with real-estate interests, Hélène Frichot and Jonathan Metzger demonstrate in 'Never Believe that the City Will Suffice to Save Us! Stockholm Gentri-Fictions' how the best intentions with respect to producing sustainable cities can quickly devolve into stratagems for marketing urban neighbourhoods, and take issue with the very assumption that the city is the environment-world that will save us, the human species, from ourselves.

Machinic Assemblages and Schizoanalysis

The conception of cities as machinic assemblages is key for identifying the powerful role cities play in Deleuze and Guattari's writings. It seems we cannot avoid this term when addressing the dynamic, messy, perpetually self-differentiating complex of becoming-city, nor when we attempt to capture the diagrammatic forces of urban environments. The term assemblage (*agencement*) has become paramount in social science research that ventures to go beyond the standard categorisations (Farías and Bender 2009), perhaps even to the point of exhaustion, and thus Guattari's explanation serves as a useful reminder:

> Deleuze and I forged the concept of 'arrangement' [*agencement*] which originally belonged to the domain of scientific logic. It's a broader, more all-encompassing notion because it doesn't only designate an unconscious formation, but also relates to imaginary representations, to language chains, to economic, political, aesthetic, microsocial etc. semiotics. Compared to 'complex' it is a notion whose comprehension is weaker, but whose extension is greater, enabling categories of diverse origins not to be excluded from the 'complex' field, which in turn graft onto other concepts like 'machine'. Thus we speak of 'machinic arrangements' for eventual association with 'collective arrangements of enunciation'. (Guattari 1995b: 40–1)

Importantly, Deleuze and Guattari have no claims to universality – they see their concepts as tools. With respect to importing *agencement* as an organisational concept into the social field, however, Guattari argues that it 'might help to configure the situation, to come up with cartographies capable of identifying and eluding certain simplistic conceptions concerning class struggle' (Guattari 1995b: 43). In superseding the typologies in post-Marxist thought – whether it's the city or the factory that constitutes the privileged site of political struggle – *agencement* brings forth the open-ended dynamics of power relations everywhere, in any spatio-temporal configuration. Reverting to the precise conceptual significance in the work of Deleuze and Guattari thus endows us with a sharper thinking tool than working with assemblage as a blurred label for complex arrangements. Notably, addressing the city in terms of *agencement* is also to address the State-apparatus, bearing in mind the distinction between *nomos* and *logos* that Deleuze and Guattari discuss with respect to processes of territorialisation. The *nomos* is the vague expanse around the city, the pre-urban countryside, steppes or mountains – a special kind of distribution without division or shares (Deleuze and Guattari 1987: 380). *Nomos* is set in distinction to *logos*, the urban form, *polis* or town, which organises the cultivation of the earth, striating pre-urban landscapes so that another opposition, between farmers and nomads, fleetingly emerges. These are asymmetrical movements, addling a desire to bring in simple oppositions, but it's never a question of striated cities and smooth steppes or seas, for the city can be smoothed and the steppes and sea striated. In noting, for instance, that it is the 'city that creates agriculture, without going through small towns' (Deleuze and Guattari 1987: 430), they articulate an approach that is by now widely accepted among urban pre-historians: there are no straight lines, neither in words nor in things, and many means of becoming-city. Emphasising the non-linear and reciprocal effects of specific *agencements*, generated through unforeseeable combinations, Deleuze and Guattari complicate notions of polarisation, centrality, order or progression through the lens of schizoanalysis.

The potential of schizoanalysis for assessing the contemporary city is explored by Marc Boumeester and Andrej Radman in 'The Impredicative City, or What Can a Boston Square Do?' Analysing the conceptual content of a photographic montage, they argue that any life-form, and specifically the *city*-life-form, is always a figuration in continuum in relation to action, perception and environment that cannot be captured by conventional architectural or geometrical models. Ignacio Farías and Stefan Höhne place emphasis on the liberatory potentials of city life in 'Humans as Vectors and Intensities: Becoming Urban in Berlin and New York City' with their discussion on how mass-transit passengers and tourists are inserted into the urban 'machinosphere'. For them, it entails a production of subjectivities that reconfigures one of the most long-standing promises of the city: that of becoming someone else. In a similar vein, Louise Beltzung Horvath and Markus Maicher examine the phenomenon of immersive urban online gaming in their contribution 'Rethinking the City as a Body without Organs', describing the players' alternations between realities that in the process endow mundane places and ordinary things with new significance. Related to Deleuze and Guattari's concept of the *Body without Organs*, the authors argue that the silent productions of affects and intensities within such commercial games generate both 'movements towards liberation from the organism, as well as new logics of capture' (p. 34).

Capitalist Flows and Political Confrontations

Capitalism holds a special place in the continuous heterogeneity that is the city, unsettling and advancing the role normally attributed to cities as sites for capitalist accumulation and modes of exploitation. Generating and constituting flows of desire, capitalism is a 'very special kind of delirium' (Deleuze and Guattari 2001) with uncertain limits and origins. Deleuze and Guattari assert that although the town anticipates capitalism it does not create it, and may even ward it off: instead it is the State-form 'that gives capitalism its models of realization'. But the relation to the town is a reciprocal one, and what is realised is 'an independent, worldwide axiomatic that is like a single City, megalopolis, or "megamachine" of which the States are parts, or neighborhoods' (Deleuze and Guattari 1987: 434–5).

Faced with a globalised, urbanised world embedded in capitalism, conventional lines of distinctions dissolve with the expansion of territorialising forces, even perhaps to the point of a 'planetary urbanization' (Merrifield 2013; Brenner 2014). This territorialisation is also an inverted movement, however, as shown by Catherine Malabou. Drawing on Deleuze, she points out the uncanny parallel between neoliberal capitalism and the organic constitution and neurological workings of the brain (Malabou 2008). Stressing our 'neuronal self' as a socio-historic construction, created through a continuous exchange between biological and socio-economic factors, confers on the urban environment the role as mediator for a cognitive and affective capitalism, a producer of subjectivities at the level of the non-conscious. In their contribution 'Laboratory Urbanism in Schladming', Magnus Eriksson and Karl Palmås reflect on how current forms of urban practices and spatial remodelling respond to such inner workings of capitalism. Adopting a small Austrian ski resort as their object of study, the authors explore the emergence of a 'laboratory urbanism' that focuses on both engineering and harnessing the creativity of pre-individual potentiality and affect.

This current emphasis on affect and space has a precursor in the loosely knit CERFI research group, in which both Guattari and Deleuze were engaged in the early 1970s, as outlined by Sven-Olov Wallenstein in 'Genealogy of Capital and the City: CERFI, Deleuze and Guattari'. CERFI staged an encounter between psychoanalysis, social movements and political activism, leading to what Daniel Defert has called 'one of the most interesting log books from the ideological crossings of those times' (p. 117). Wallenstein's intellectual contextualisation of CERFI's work, particularly as regards the influential urban theories of Henri Lefebvre, suggest that the reconceptualisation of cities in terms of networks and modes of territorialisation – so pertinent for the thinking of Deleuze and Guattari – proceeds from this concrete setting. The central topic of the STATE-apparatus capture vis-à-vis the potential for a specifically urban democracy reappears in Mark Purcell's provocative contribution, 'Urban Democracy Beyond Deleuze and Guattari'. Although he finds the revolutionary potential of cities to be implicit in Deleuze and Guattari's thinking, Purcell argues that their outline is insufficient to give us a real grasp of the problem at hand and that we cannot do without Henri Lefebvre to decipher the real significance of an urban democracy. Conversely, Maria Hellström Reimer demonstrates how addressing cities in terms of flows and networks produced through processes of desire and capital in 'Cut-Make-and-Trim: Fast Fashion Urbanity in the Residues of Rana Plaza' carries profound political implications. In joining the dots between a 'sustainable' shopping mall in Sweden and the disastrous collapse of Rana Plaza – one of the largest sweatshops in Dhaka – Hellström Reimer critically interrogates Western urban consumerism and raises difficult questions about consequences, responsibilities and guilt.

Eruptions of Violence, Poverty and Hope

As we write, the Islamic State (IS) is threating the ancient city of Palmyra, apparently intent on the organised destruction of cultural artefacts that contribute to the histories and lives of cities old and new. The destruction of cultural monuments in an attempt to undermine the symbolic value vested in cities is not a new phenomenon and constitutes only one expression of 'urbicide'. Rather than targeting urban inhabitants one by one, the destruction of cities instead takes broad aim at the diffuse urban environment, in effect reducing the specific livelihood of urban inhabitants by degrading the habitability of their environmental milieu. These extreme forces of urban destruction, associated with warfare and terrorist attacks – whether targeting the symbolic values of architecture, the civic infrastructures of hospitals and marketplaces, the liveability of residential areas or bodies themselves – have their counterpart in the more insidious and daily expressions of urban violence. Through their propagation in populist media, the risk of natural disasters – whether real or imagined – combines with reports of gang violence and organised or drug-related crime in forming an 'ecology of fear' (Davis 1999) that furthers the interests of market-driven urbanisation. The increasing non-liveability of great cities like London, due to unprecedented speculation in real estate, constitutes violence at the very core of the city as *civitas*, a place for collectivity and coexistence. And while processes of gentri-fication, displacement, exclusion and segregation are met with protest movements and urban uprisings across the world, the relationship is asymmetrical in so far as we also witness the forging of a dangerous and hardened machinic assemblage of state control, increased surveillance and police brutality.

As demonstrated by Ronnen Ben-Arie in his chapter 'The Haifa Urban Destruction Machine', 'urbicide' is a flexible concept used to frame the many different forms urban destruction may take. Taking Haussmann's Paris as a point of departure, he identifies planning as one such mode of destruction, entangled with economic and military interests. Centred on the neoliberal rehabilitation of downtown Haifa, he demonstrates how the 'creative destruction' of capitalism merges with nationalist forces in reshaping urban spaces and subjectivities. The machinic destruction of the city's identity in the past is also shat-tering the identity of its former inhabitants, leading to a very particular kind of 'homelessness'. This theme is elaborated in Michele Lancione's chapter 'The City and the "Homeless": Machinic Subjects', building on his anthropological research of homeless people in Turin. Undesired, unseen, but in practice constitutive for the city, Lancione analyses the relationship between homelessness and urban space, conceptualised as a 'vitalist mechanosphere'.

The pertinence of the topic is actualised by the increasing numbers of beggars in European cities, due to the influx of so-called EU migrants who seek a temporary refuge from the inexorable poverty in their home countries. A stark manifestation of the uneven geography of capital-ist development, it furthermore reveals how categories of proximity and distance are annihilated in urban space. The nomadic, rather than migrant, existence of these transnational beggars is a reminder of how the figure of the nomad, in Deleuze and Guattari, is far from a simple configuration of freedom. From an outset of trauma and urban crime, Catharina Gabrielsson re-addresses the concept of the nomad from a material base of historic and economic coordinates in her chapter 'Folded Ground: Escape from Cape Town'. Exploring the desert as a potential exteriority to the city and of nomad thought as a means to confront the ubiquity of urban striations, Gabrielsson outlines a ground of sameness and consistency, defined by fragile and non-linear connections. The notion of 'losing oneself' through following lines of flight is wrought with tensions and violence, pointing to the crucial terms of social cohesion.

These approaches to the city as a site of violence, poverty and despair have their counter-image in the short essay that serves as an opening to *Deleuze and the City*. Taking as her point of departure that every city is dominated by a certain affectivity, Fredrika Spindler's contribution, 'Becoming-Other: New Orleans from a Deleuzian Perspective', presents New Orleans as a site for belonging precisely through its promise of perpetual change. Whether instituted by cultural or natural processes of transformation, the city in her account constitutes a complex weaving of ecologies with hybrid enunciations. Rather than providing a portrait of New Orleans, she addresses the city as haecceity: not as an image but as an affective assemblage that through an enfolding of spaces and temporalities dissolves the outlines of the subject, becoming-other to itself.

What a City Can Do

In commissioning the chapters in this book, we encouraged authors to commence from the middle, to quite simply 'start where you are!' (Gibson-Graham 2011: 2). Following Deleuze and Guattari, we believe that commencing from the midst of things 'with an eye on changing and transforming the existing orders, working towards "the diminishing of their power"' (Guattari 2011: 17) is what makes critique and socio-political articulations possible. Thus the chapters in this book commence from concrete problems, or from what Alfred North Whitehead calls 'occasions', to lay the stress on processes of becoming in and of a city. In asking authors to cite placenames and locate a port of departure, we hoped to emphasise minor locales, shrinking towns, forgotten neighbourhoods, mundane suburbs and unglamorous cities, as well as any radical revisions that might be brought to bear on the hegemonic vision of global cities and their connections. But we've come to realise that in some instances a point of departure *par le milieu* means departing less from the material relations of an environment-world than from a conceptual construct, a historical moment where 'Something will happen. Something is already happening' (Deleuze and Guattari 1987: 152).

In the penultimate essay included in this compilation, 'Sociability and Endurance in Jakarta', AbdouMaliq Simone takes us on a journey through Jakarta in ways that aptly illustrate the limitations of Eurocentric notions of what constitutes an urban life. He conjures up the new formations of collective life that, barely discernible, potentially carry the seed of 'alter[ing] the social arrangements and subjective experiences of being in the city' (p. 224). Emphasising the dynamics of doing and undoing social and material formations, Simone draws on Deleuze's figure of the *missing people* in arguing that sociality is always yet to be completed. There is always something that 'keeps people going', quite apart from utility-based goals or necessities, processes of desire or lines of flight. Conceptualising cities as circling, as constant *goings-on*, would seem to postpone the question of our final liberation or oppression. And surely schizoanalysis always proceeds from a *hic* – 'here is' – and goes on to destabilise any such claim, opening a space for 'it' (and any form of 'I') to become-otherwise. Thereby, any seemingly self-given object is placed under erasure, pushing it 'towards its complexification, its processual enrichment, towards the consistency of its virtual lines of bifurcation and differentiation, in short towards its ontological heterogeneity' (Guattari 1995a: 61). Schizoanalysis and the city: *hic* urbanity. And thus we proceed.

Note

1. All chapters in this book are original and previously unpublished works that have been revised following peer-review by the editors and in some instances by expert external reviewers.

References

Beistegui, M. de (2012) *Immanence: Deleuze and Philosophy*. Edinburgh: University of Edinburgh Press.

Brenner, N. (ed.) (2014) *Implosions/Explosions: Towards a Study of Planetary Urbanization*. Berlin: Jovis

Brenner, N. and Schmid, C. (2015) 'Towards a new epistemology of the urban?', in *City*, 19 (2–3): 151–82

Davis, M. (1999) *Ecology of Fear: Los Angeles and the Imagination of Disaster*. New York: Vintage Books.

Deleuze, G. and Guattari, F. (1987) *A Thousand Plateaus: Capitalism and Schizophrenia*, trans. B. Massumi. Minneapolis: University of Minnesota Press.

Deleuze, G. and Guattari, F. (1994) *What Is Philosophy?*, London: Verso.

Deleuze, G. and Guattari, F. (2001) 'Capitalism: a very special delirium', in C. Kraus and S. Lotringer (eds), *Hatred of Capitalism*. New York: Semiotext[e].

Farías, I. and Bender, T. (2009) *Urban Assemblages: How Actor-Network Theory Changes Urban Studies*. London: Routledge.

Gibson-Graham, J. K. (2011) 'A feminist project of belonging for the anthropocene', in *Gender, Place, and Culture*, 18 (1): 1–21.

Guattari, F. (1995a) *Chaosmosis: An Ethico-Aesthetic Paradigm*, trans. P. Bains and J. Pefanis. Sydney: Power Publications.

Guattari, F. (1995b) *Chaosophy*. Los Angeles: Semiotext(e) Foreign Agents Series.

Guattari, F. (2000) *The Three Ecologies*, trans. I. Pindar and P. Sutton. London: Athlone.

Guattari, F. (2011) *The Machinic Unconscious: Essays in Schizoanalysis*. Los Angeles: Semiotext(e) Foreign Agents Series.

Herzogenrath, B. (ed.) (2009) *Deleuze/Guattari and Ecology*. Basingstoke: Palgrave Macmillan.

Lazzarato, M. (2014) *Signs and Machines: Capitalism and the Production of Subjectivity*. Los Angeles: Semiotext(e).

Malabou, C. (2008) *What Should We Do with Our Brain?*, New York: Fordham University Press.

Merrifield, A. (2013) *The Politics of the Encounter: Urban Theory and Protest under Planetary Urbanization*. Athens: University of Georgia Press.

Murdoch, J. (2006) *Post-Structuralist Geography: A Guide to Relational Space*. London: Sage.

Chapter 1

Becoming-Other: New Orleans from a Deleuzian Perspective

Fredrika Spindler

It must be said, as an inevitable starting point: to each city, there is at least one dominating affectivity. In that of Stockholm, clear-cut, cool lines, hyperborean skies and the tranquil, rooted earthiness of the colours, the whole conditioned by a naturally circumscribed sea, are at work. In that of Paris, the apparent busy-ness and speed are belied by its fundamental assurance, its unshakeable belief in its own identity and fate; here it is grandeur, elegance and power, never mind a certain shabbiness and decline. Different in every way is that of Rio de Janeiro, where identity perpetually both undermines and transgresses itself. In Rio, even the most confident colonial grandeur is constantly shattered by its own underground: that which it has destroyed but which nevertheless is always more alive than ever; that which determines it in being its own perpetual other.

The examples would be countless, the differences and variations inexhaustible. However, among the many cities there is at least one that refuses any strict determination, or rather that exists in nothing but its own self-transformation. In New Orleans, in the swamps and marshlands of Louisiana nurtured by the moving beds of the Mississippi River, neither history nor actual ground is reliable: shifts occur by the moment – when not by devastating hurricanes and flash floods, popular movements, failing infrastructure or simple corruption, there will always be the ongoing subversion of its languages, its rewriting of its past and its present, its future always unwritten since catastrophe, death and destruction are built into its *topos*. Yet it is there, always, illegitimate by essence but shrugging off every intimidation, as well as every attempt at classification or identification. New Orleans is (and by no means simply) other – other-than-everything, but also other-than-itself, overcoming itself always before having become-itself: its mode is no other than that of ongoing deterritorialisations and displacements that are as geological and topological as they are cultural and linguistic, but which must also be understood as necessary betrayals, discardings, transformations and losses, of itself just as much as of those who come within its orbit.

Rather than attempting to define New Orleans – by its histories, its languages or its various cultures – this brief reflection concerns something that might be understood as the opposite of all of the above, namely the ways in which this moving ground shapes and moulds, but also undoes, those that it encounters. In other words, what it might be to be affected by New Orleans, moved by the city as one moves around and in it, is adopted and rejected by it as it escapes all attempts at domestication: a becoming-New-Orleans conditioned by one's own necessary becoming-other, becoming-disappeared, becoming-dissolved, understood as the possibility of becoming the subject of one's own haecceities.

Perhaps it is at dawn and at dusk that New Orleans first offers itself in its paradoxicality: as immobile movement, going nowhere but expanding and contracting by subtle fluctuations of breath. Here, all is suspended, a body without organs characterised by absolute fullness and saturation, but that at the same time moves and shifts as it subjects itself to leakage, connections that cannot come to a stop. It is at these moments that the complexity of the smells can be perceived – garbage and alcohol, the burned electricity of the streetcars, the foods that no longer know their origins but only what they have become through annexation, theft and new couplings. Wafts from the river and the sudden, intoxicating fragrance of blossoming magnolia, jasmine, honeysuckle and dogwood that are lost before they can be identified, the one drifting into the other, overpowering and surrendering taking place at the same time. Differentiation is continuously at play: as darkness turns into light, light into darkness, each and every element – shards of sound melting into one another like multiple whisperings of long-lost languages, the scents commingling – also blends in with the bodies that sense them all or partially, consume them, are devoured, altered, suddenly populated by them in movements so swift that they have always already taken place. Here, different and contradictory speeds pursue their own courses – a quickening of the heartbeats, the lungs inhaling and exhaling at a suddenly slower, deeper pace, the whole a fluidity that can be measured only by humidity and heat, everything deliquescing yet obstinately material and real.

What, exactly, is it that makes one become other – other than a simply acting Self, other than a First Person pronoun – an other where the I is refused as much as the We, in favour of an indeterminate it, they, perhaps altogether missing a proper pronoun? What is the process in which one becomes something that is infiltrated but also infiltrates, becoming both the dense materiality of the ageless live oaks and the epiphytic Spanish moss that as a ghostly yet perfectly live webbing is spun around its branches? Here, where the shadow is a friend but the sun relentlessly victorious, there is a joint undoing-becoming thriving on its own exaggeration, exhilaration always bearing death within itself. Language, not least, subjects itself to its own overcoming: whereas English, French and Spanish might consider themselves as royal and dominant – major languages by definition – they are also continuously imbued with, penetrated and overtaken by countless dialects from Senegal and Mali, the languages of slaves and stolen lives. That which has been oppressed, forced and raped has persisted, resisted and made its way through back doors and underground paths, turning into minor languages whose sonorities, idioms and tears echo furiously in every major language word, making them foreign to themselves. The same purported major tongues are twisted out of joint in their Creole and Cajun-becomings, while both Portuguese and Vietnamese intonations are coloured by a Caribbean lilt. And in all of them, under them, leaking out from them, are the whispering, hissing sounds of the Choctaw and the Houmas, rendering Tchopitoulas the most New Orleans of arteries.

Through intervention, friction and invention, the very foundations of language here are undermined, set in motion, liquefied even as with the instant introduction of the pre- or suffix 'eaux' to signal its New Orleansian claim. Geaux Saints!, Pho Bistreaux, and even the sinister Preaux Life sticker: playfully yet deadly serious, everything is tinted with a darkness that is not only tropical but historical and supra-historical at the same time, old as the swamps, powerful as voodoo. All is continuously lost, just as all is continuously reinvented through its own absolute limit; Catholicism turning into black magic, municipal buildings suddenly into ruins, hole-in-the-wall food places into gastronomic sanctuaries – and even bourgeoisie, identity's strongest foothold, belies the haughty grandeur of its mansions by turning them into reckless explosions of Mardi Gras transgression, while the unforgiving, non-domesticated force of tropical vegetation takes over seemingly carefully manicured yards.

Being in New Orleans is becoming something else: being inhabited by memories belonging to others, patterns of speech infiltrated by idioms foreign to one's tongue, bodily movements and changes of density as swift as streets that suddenly cave in, houses that are discovered to have leaning walls. These are leakages that always go both ways, thereby creating a continuous porosity, a sustainability of frailty that only resists by ongoing motion. Groundlessness is New Orleans' ground, destabilisation its mode of persisting and insisting, both for itself and for those who – not seldom inadvertently – come to stay. Perhaps it is precisely this destabilisation, this moving ground where shifts have always occurred before they are even noticed, that also makes its temporality that of 'what happened?' – famously said to be the temporality of the novella, temporality of every crack-up and inevitable transformation, where whatever happened has been effectuated in the body long before it comes to mind. Hence, it is as starkly contrasting with a New York's cosmopolitan and fast-paced 'what happens next?' tempo of realisation and quest for fulfilment, as from the monumentalist contentment of any European city's perennial 'this has always been'. Far from any realisation, and as far from conservation, what New Orleans generates in those who become with it is the affectivity of bewilderment, of loss in motion, of the loss having always already been consummated but also already partly forgotten – its edges softened by the new, that has already happened, taken place within the body that moves to a previously unknown beat, displacing the centre of gravity to the in-between of the internal and external.

Chapter 2

Humans as Vectors and Intensities: Becoming Urban in Berlin and New York City

Ignacio Farías and Stefan Höhne

One of the longest-standing and greatest promises of the city has been that it would allow one to become someone else. It bears the prospect of new forms of experience and pleasures as well as different ways of belonging and being with. This notion not only lies at the centre of early narrations of modern urbanity stretching from Baudelaire and Poe to Musil's 'Man without Qualities'. It also forms one of the central entry points of many patrons in the field of urban studies, such as Tönnies, Weber or Simmel. And indeed, as these scholars and their heirs emphasised, throughout history urban settings have served as powerful machines for producing countless new subjects, such as priests, merchants, the modern bourgeois, the *flâneur*, the foreigner, the homeless or the slum dweller. Moreover, the urban also allowed for the emergence of new forms of collective subjectivity, often brought about by new urban environments and dense agglomerations of human bodies. Over the last century or so, intellectuals theorised these urban populations via a variety of concepts, such as the mob, the masses, the pack or the multitude, each carrying specific moral and political connotations as well as implicit judgements. Around 1900, for example, with the densification of population in the western metropolises, a new collective subject came into focus, referred to by Le Bon (1896), Tarde ([1890] 1968), Freud (1922) and others as 'the crowd'. This new form of urban collectivity became both feared and detested, as well as glorified as a potential agent for social change. In their efforts to grasp the specific characteristics and agencies of these collective forms of urban subjectivity, it is striking that thinkers only rarely paid attention to the infrastructural dimension as a fundamental condition of possibility to bring a mass into being. Where they did so, such as in the writings of early urban sociologists focusing on the street (e.g. Whyte 1943), these infrastructures were predominantly understood as representations or results of dynamics such as social fragmentation or population shifts (Tonkiss 2005: 70). While assigning these materialities a rather secondary status, scholars tended to stress rather large-scale economic forces, such as new accumulation regimes of capital and shifting modes of production. To borrow a distinction made by Deleuze and Guattari in *Anti-Oedipus* (2004), the infrastructural settings of the urban have been mainly addressed as theatres, not as factories of the social.

In recent years, however, urban theory's conceptual repertoires have been significantly transformed and expanded, especially by the irruption of what has been generally called 'assemblage thinking' (McFarlane and Anderson 2011). Breaking with the long-standing Durkheimian postulate that the social can only be explained by means of the social (Durkheim [1890] 1982), this perspective draws attention to the constitutive role of materialities in forming the urban, such as technologies, infrastructures and 'nature' (Farías and Bender 2009; Höhne 2012). One of the most inspiring theorists aiming to introduce Deleuzian thought and especially assemblage theory into social studies, Manuel DeLanda, observes, 'Social entities like cities, for example, composed of entire populations of persons, networks and organizations, can hardly be conceptualized without a physical infrastructure of buildings, streets and various conduits for the circulation of matter and energy, defined in part by their spatial relations to one another' (DeLanda 2006: 94). By engaging with the concept of assemblage developed by Deleuze and Guattari it becomes possible to productively address these multiple relations and entanglements between such heterogeneous entities as territories, affects, technologies, discourses, materialities and bodies.

While this approach is opening a space for thinking the city differently, the relationship between urban assemblages and humans, especially in the context of modes of singular and collective subjectivities and desubjectifications, has remained under-theorised, as though the radical relationality of assemblage thinking has simply superseded the question of what is human. The early formulations of assemblage thinking, such as the Actor-Network Theory of the 1980s and 1990s in particular, apply the deflationary notion of human and non-human actants (Latour 1988). When assemblage thinkers turn to humans, they address the multiple and often conflict-laden processes of composing humans as subjects, which involves processes of subjectification achieved through diverse apparatuses such as schools, media and police. A fascinating example is Robbins and Sharp's (2006) study of the production of what they call 'turfgrass subjects' in North American cities, in which they trace how the chemical industry, local communities and the lawn itself *interpellate* (Althusser 2006) homeowners as lawn-caring subjects.

It is as though both these perspectives on the role of human subjectivities in the urban have manoeuvred us into a conceptual quagmire. They lead to one of only two rather poor options: we could either focus on new individual or collective subjects in the tradition of the classical urban studies outlined by Weber, Tönnies or Simmel, paying little regard to the material and technological dimensions of what we call 'the urban'; or we could focus on them as mere 'subject effects' of how machinic assemblages, actor-networks or apparatuses, are organised, dismissing the capacities and becomings of human individuals and populations in urban settings. We would thus be dealing with two asymmetrical understandings: the first which conceives of human individuals and populations as unfolding fully independently of the socio-material arrangements shaping the actual; and a second that reduces the human to a place to be filled, a script to be performed or a version to be enacted, neglecting their generative capacity to actually enter relationships and become things that surpass and undo the assemblages interpellating them as subjects.

Building on Deleuze and Guattari's work, we propose a different approach to the *becoming urban* of human individuals and populations by taking into account what the urban condition does to subjects and subjectivities. Accordingly, we begin this chapter by discussing the two key issues at stake: the city as a type of circulation and ultimately as a machinosphere,[1] that is the urban condition as a zone of proximity to the plane of consistency; and urban desubjectivation as a particular form of becoming multiple, indifferent, imperceptible. We further elaborate on this by reflecting on two types of urban situations, in which highly codified subjects constituted in striated modular spaces and interpellated by precise scripts of action – in one case the tourist, in the other the mass-transit passenger – suddenly become something else: urban vectors and urban intensities. In doing so, we aim to overcome the idea of urban subjectivity as a fixed property or attribute of either individuals or populations and instead foreground forms of urban individuation by haecceities. Becoming urban thus involves a micropolitical opening towards new compositions, futures and worlds.

Cities, Circulation and Urban Becomings

Let's be very explicit about this: Deleuze and Guattari are not good at thinking the urban. Their rather passing observations on the historical emergence of the city emphasise its state-like configuration as a centre of power against which nomadic war machines are often directed. Furthermore, both states and cities are highly striated spaces and entangled in a variety of ways. While sometimes being in competition, they more often act as complementary forces and can align themselves with powerful apparatuses that are central to the implementation of power, sovereignty and capitalist modes of production (Deleuze and Guattari 1987: 484–90). But those authors do point to a fundamental difference that would distinguish the city from the state. Whereas the state becomes a powerful apparatus by bounding a territory, keeping it from deterritorialized flows and producing a striated, quantified space, the city does so by functioning as a node in a network of flows, as an apparatus of capture and redistribution of deterritorialised circulations. The state revolution and the urban revolution thus represent two fundamentally distinct forms by which power becomes stabilised and centred, and they cannot be thought of as phases in a historical progression.

The idea that the city 'exists only as a function of circulation and of circuits' (Deleuze and Guattari 1987: 432) has also been taken up by Manuel DeLanda (2006) to explain the emergence of capitalism, and is consistent with the bulk of research in urban studies about global cities and networks. However, our contention is that the idea of the city as an apparatus of capture in economic networks contributes little to an understanding of urban life, an analytical limitation that Deleuze and Guattari seem to recognise: '[D]ifferences are not objective: it is possible to live striated on the deserts, steppes, or seas; it is possible to live smooth *even* in the cities, to be an urban nomad' (1987: 482, our emphasis). This is insufficient, however. As Amin and Thrift have pointed out, 'smooth displacements require the machinery of placement (instruments, metrics, labourers) [. . .] To think otherwise is to court ontological disaster' (2002: 82). Indeed, as we would like to show in this chapter, machinic assemblages producing urban circulations are key settings for smooth, nomadic and molecular becomings.

To begin, we need to go back to Deleuze and Guattari's emphasis on urban circulations, though with two slight but crucial amendments: first, the key circulations shaping the urban condition are not just between urban settlements but also within them; second, such circulations involve not just capital, goods, energy or information, but also humans. This is indeed one of the oldest sociological insights about urban life: 'the vast casual and mobile aggregations which constitute our urban populations are in a state of perpetual agitation, [. . .] and in consequence the community is in a chronic condition of crisis' (Park and Burgess 1925: 22).

For the reformist thinkers of the Chicago School, this condition of crisis involved the perils of anomy, instrumental reason and moral decay. It is the peril of the Hobo, who is 'always on the move, but he has no destination, and naturally never arrives [. . .] not only a "homeless man", but a man without a cause' (Park and Burgess 1925: 158–9). Despite their normative undertones, these early observations on the urban condition capture very well the most fundamental feature of the constant circulation of humans, namely its capacity to deconstruct identities, roles, ties, its capacity to anonymise, to make indifferent, imperceptible, to flatten.

Indeed, circulation is not simply a matter of transportation, but is about states of transition, liminal states; not simply a movement from an origin to a destination, but also a movement in-between subjectivities, temporalities and modes of existence. If we agree to think the city as a decentred socio-material formation enacted in multiple overlapping urban assemblages (Farías 2009a), thinking circulation as an urban condition requires grasping the plane of immanence in between urban assemblages, redrawing the city as a machinosphere, not a meta-assemblage of assemblages but their unformed juxtaposition. The city, we could say, 'is the Planomenon, or the Rhizosphere [. . .] It is the abstract Figure, or rather, since it has no form itself, the abstract Machine of which each concrete assemblage is a multiplicity, a becoming, a segment, a vibration' (Deleuze and Guattari 1987: 252).

Now we can go back to an old Deleuzian hypothesis: bringing human bodies into circulation is a crucial factor for allowing forms of both singular and collective subjectivity to become. But what kind of becomings are brought about in urban circulations? How are individual and collective subjectivities made and unmade? What are the implications for the urban everyday and its promises and struggles to become someone (or rather something) else?

Differently from subjectivation processes primarily structured by hegemonic power and apparatuses of knowledge and oriented to produce docile subjects, Deleuze and Guattari allow us to unveil processes of de- and resubjectivation occurring at the interstices of machinic assemblages and based on becomings: animal, intense, molecular, imperceptible, minoritarian. Indeed, 'all becoming is a becoming-minoritarian' (Deleuze and Guattari 1987: 291). It involves a molecular involution of 'man', as a molar, majoritarian category, the subject of enunciation. But it is neither a metamorphosis into a different entity – since 'a becoming lacks a subject distinct from itself' (238) – nor a regression into a de-differentiated state. It is rather a creative exploration of the subject's own forms, organs, functions, in order to extract those elements that are closest to what the subject is becoming. Becoming is a micropolitical exploration of the subject's particles entering zones of ontological proximity with other beings. It involves situated processes in which it is uncertain what belongs to which subject, where the boundaries between the human and non-human lie, when one becomes imperceptible.

Becoming urban, we propose, involves a molecular involution of subjects occurring in vectorial spaces between and within urban assemblages. This is also what de Certeau (1984) alludes to in his classic description of urban space as shaped by 'vectors of direction, velocities, and time variables [. . .] composed of intersections of mobile elements' (117). It also echoes Delgado's (1993) characterisation of the urban and more specifically the street as a BwO (Body without Organs), 'a whirl-wind that never rests, self-centred, asignifying, articulated in a thousand different ways . . . a body just bones, flesh, skin, musculature, an entity that can only be occupied by the intensities that circulate through it, that cross it in all directions' (190, our translation). In that vectorial space, shaped by movements, trajectories and transits, the users of public space have no fixed identity. Instead Delgado describes passers-by as beings on a threshold: 'they are not what they were, but haven't yet assumed a new role. [...] The passer-by is always absent, in something else, with the head somewhere else, that is, literally, in trance' (119, our translation). Becoming urban is thus not simply becoming someone or something else, but rather becoming imperceptible, indifferent, anybody and everything. 'The imperceptible is the immanent end of becoming' (Deleuze and Guattari 1987: 279), it is entering the urban machinosphere, the undifferentiated plane connecting all assemblages and strata.

As we will show, such becomings can be observed within two paradigmatic urban transient populations, the tourists and the passengers, who are in many ways the emblematic subjects of the modern urban everyday. They populate the machinic assemblages created to render the city a site of circulation. It is this collective being in circulation, however, that allows for radical involution of subject positions, as well as for new and potentially nonconformist subjectivities to emerge. As we discuss drawing from two scenarios we encountered in our work, inside these highly ordered machinic assemblages, situations occur that not only threaten the functionality of the whole apparatus, but also allow for urban becomings. These might be minoritarian, ephemeral and short lived, but they nevertheless hint at a central element of urban assemblages: that circulation can unleash becomings, affects and desires disrupting the assemblages within which they pass.

Subject Involutions: Tourists into Vectors

From its emergence in the nineteenth century, the tourist has been constructed as a highly homogeneous and hegemonic subject position inscribed in the countless assemblages shaping tourist destinations and the tourist industry. The term first entered an English dictionary in 1800 to designate 'a person who makes a tour, specially for pleasure' (Boorstin 1987: 85). Such an understanding was useful to distinguish the figure of the tourist from that of others closely associated with circular travel, such as merchants and pilgrims, for whom travel was a burden and even a risk endured in pursuit of economic or religious ends (Urbain 1991). Similarly, the Grand Tours of young members of the European elites in the seventeenth and eighteenth centuries around the capitals of continental Europe had primarily educational and socio-political purposes. It was only towards the end of the eighteenth century, as Grand Tour travellers began to shorten their travels, follow established routes and skip the systematic learning of the language and culture of the visited countries (Towner 1985) that these came to be described as tourists, not travellers. The distinction was crucial: if travel was to designate the exclusive and heroic activity of a serious and respectful observer, and even discoverer, of the world, the tourist could only be understood as a bad traveller: a superficial and hedonist figure travelling for the sake of it, privileging image over language, spectacle over dialogue, and rushing through the largest possible number of places to collect pictures and fake reproductions (Urbain 1991). It was only with the massification of vacations in the twentieth century that the tourist acquired a more positive connotation, for whereas the vacationer travels just to find repose and refuge in monotonous places, such as the seaside (the location of immobility and repetition par excellence), the tourist, in contrast, would be the one who moves constantly, always to a new place seeking, ironically or not, difference and authenticity.

   The central role such figurations of the tourist play in contemporary tourism might indeed explain the big effort put into deconstructing and decentring the tourist in contemporary tourist studies. From the abstract critique of the tourist as a Eurocentric, male, white and middle-class figure to the empirical exploration of the apparatuses involved in the production of playfully interested tourist subjectivities, the bottom-line argument is that the tourist is a 'subject effect' of powerful discourses, visual imaginaries, spatial arrangements, infrastructures, services, devices, etc. Interestingly, tourist assemblages rely on dual subjectification processes, by which both tourists and tour guides are co-produced.

This embraces not only what happens on guided tours or in tourist groups with a clear distribution of roles, but also the touring practices of families, couples, friends and singles, who tour and guide themselves in improvised ways. The tourist thus is not just inscribed as an ideal user of tourist artefacts and services, but is also interpellated by the guide as a subject with a specific set of interests, preferences and values.

Examples of this can be found in contemporary English- and German-language guided tours on the history of the Berlin Wall, which present, perform and interpret the division of the city in significantly different ways: in German-speaking tours, the Wall functions as the signifier of the division of the German nation (*us*), while Otherness is sought on the East side of the Wall, less in political history and more in details of everyday life. English-speaking guided tours frame the history of the Wall as part of European and world political history. They elaborate on the political opposition between the Allies and the Soviets and thereby project a quite different Other, reaching beyond Germany to the whole Soviet bloc. More importantly, whereas the German tourist these tours enact is a political subject seriously concerned with historical objectivity and the contradictory implications of German history for the present, the imagined English-speaking tourist is more interested in enjoying a powerful but straightforward story (Farías 2008).

One could and certainly should produce a much more complex account of the ways in which different tourist apparatuses interpellate individuals in very specific ways; the case of contemporary touring practice in Berlin is merely one example among many. But engaging in that task should not lead us to overlook the dynamics of desubjectification that can be observed in most touring practices in cities, whether in guided tours or in self-guided explorations, whether walking or in bus tours. Indeed, to the extent that touring practices in cities involve putting human bodies in circulation, they also open up spaces for the *involution* of tourist subjectivities and becoming urban, that is to say multiple, indifferent, imperceptible.[2]

Walking in walking tours at times facilitates such becomings. While tourist guides usually walk in front of the group, intent on leading the way and keeping to schedule, tourists don't always follow the guide's route and pace, lingering, separating from the group and merging into the stream of passers-by. During the walking from one place to the next, tourists engage with the city as a vectorial space, in which bodies in circulation are only connected by the direction, velocity and rhythm of their movements. Thus, even in walking tours, walking involves on occasion entering a zone of proximity with the city as a machinosphere, not simply advancing from place A to place B, but moving in-between points, in-between identities, in-between assemblages, and engaging with the city as a plane of immanence. Indeed, it is particularly interesting to observe how tour guides work to counteract these urban becomings and to maintain the situational frame of the tour, addressing these urban vectors as tourists with the aid of technical devices (loudspeakers, flags, etc.) and staging techniques. The situational boundary between walking and touring, between transiting urban space and visiting tourist attractions, is indeed the subject of careful performances by many tourist guides, which might involve suddenly stopping at a given point, looking silently at a site, waiting for the group to gather, and surprising the audience with some counter-intuitive opening remark such as 'Now we are standing outside Berlin', when the spot is in what is today the city centre, or 'From here we can enter Hitler's bunker', while all that the group can see is a parking lot (Farías 2008). In walking tours one encounters often a movement between two modes of urban existence: tourists becoming urban vectors, individualised only by their trajectories, speeds and pauses, and then again being interpellated as tourist subjects, defined by material semiotic relationships to bounded objects, tourist attractions.

Another example of such moments of desubjectification, in which the city too becomes destratified smooth space, can be daily observed in the route 100 and 200 double-decker buses that cross Berlin's city centre (Farías 2009b). These two lines are something of an insider tip for tourists unwilling to pay for standard bus tours, as they pass by the same set of tourist attractions viewed on such tours. Instead of an economic investment, tourists need, however, to make major performative investments in order to assemble and experience the touristic city. The help of maps, guidebooks or local friends might be enlisted to connect sites with names and other information, thereby co-producing tourists and tourist attractions. But such investments are often too costly, so that after a few minutes in circulation tourists slump back in their seats into dazed and unresponsive states of silent indifference and liminality, devoid of intentionality or desire while the city passes by. Rather than a collection of sights, the city emerges here as a continuous landscape, as a whole without parts – or better, a 'Body without Organs' (BwO), which is not simply empty, but surfaces as a plane of immanence, in which vectors, qualities and entities can enter into new affective relationships and produce new assemblages. In a sense, this is precisely what the destination becomes when experienced lying back in one of these buses. The city is taken away from its attractions: organic and stratified entities of tourism. However, what remains is the opposite of a placeless space or 'non-place' (Augé 1995). The destination, stripped of its organs, becomes a plane of intensity, a plane on which urban elements emerge as intensive singularities, breaking with representation and expressing the complex relations and connections that make up the destination. Indeed, it is not uncommon to see tired and silent tourists who, while looking out through the window, experience some kind of revelation that sets them off conveying to their partners the insights just won.

Tourism and especially tours could be rightly described as apparatuses of capture, stratification and subjectification, producing a striated space and docile subjects. But such a description would overlook the power of circulation to unleash processes of desubjectification, enabling human bodies to enter a destratified plane shaped by the movement and rest, the speed and slowness of destratified bodies, a field of vectors and particles intersecting in new ways, becoming something else. The latter point will be emphasised in more detail in the following sections.

Infrastructural Desires: Passengers into Intensive Affects

The second story we discuss is about affects and eroticisms in mass transportation experiences in the aftermath of the opening of New York City's subway system in 1904. The inauguration of the subway represented a cumulative moment in a specific governmental paradigm that can be described as governing through circulation. During the nineteenth century, the implementation of urban infrastructures like modern sewer systems, gas pipes, telegraphs and capsule pipelines allowed goods and information to circulate in the city and beyond – manifesting the new economic, social and political orders of the liberal city. Despite these efforts, the elites of New York were still concerned by the increasing congestion in the streets and tenement slums as well as the cultural and economic stagnation of their dwellers. Eventually, they came to the conclusion that it was the population itself that had to be brought into circulation. Installing a gigantic circulatory machine would aid the resolution of the ubiquitous congestion, which brought the city to the edge of collapse. This shift towards understanding the urban population as liberal subjects transformed the idea of good governance into what Foucault (2007) termed 'apparatuses of security'; he characterised the main role of these as 'organizing circulation, eliminating its dangerous elements, making a division between good and bad circulation, and maximizing the good circulation by diminishing the bad' (2007: 34).

Thereafter, the primary task of a good urban administration was to create a city that ensured the orderly circulation of its subjects, in the process fostering prosperity, health and social cohesion (Boutros and Straw 2010). Doing so would undermine the reprehensible and dangerous forms of circulation such as smuggling, vagrancy and the spread of disease. Good circulation was efficient, safe and reliable, and required diligent monitoring and control by the state apparatus (Aradau and Blanke 2010). Realising this liberal idea of rule called not only for political and educational efforts, but also for the implementation of socio-technical solutions that would allow for the control and freedom of the subjects via infrastructural provisions. This was achieved through, for example, public lighting or sanitation, which made for a healthier, safer and cleaner city and allowed its residents a certain kind of freedom and liberty (Joyce 2003). In the case of the subway too, these liberal forms of politics required mobilising both the subjects and the structure of city. However, the success of the subway not only rested on appealing to the hopes and dreams of the people for a better life, but also on addressing their fears and controlling their perceptions and interactions. This was achieved by recoding and sanitising the realms below the street and enforcing strategies of police control, and also by implementing specific aesthetic strategies and behavioural *scripts* (Akrich 1992) within its material components, such as lighting, gates or seating arrangements.

When the system finally opened on 27 October 1904, these strategies for controlling the behaviour of the passengers were time and again undermined by the strong affects and deviant practices generated in reaction to the new experience of collective speed and the oddity of travel underground. Already on the first run, the mayor of New York got carried away at the controls, speeding the train up to a dangerous velocity and refusing to hand over to a professional motorman, which resulted in a turbulent ride for the guests of honour and caused minor injuries when the mayor accidentally activated the emergency brake. This, however, was nothing compared to the evening opening to the public, when many more passengers than anticipated flooded the system, causing chaos, riots and behaviour in ways that eyewitnesses described as 'subway madness' (Hood 2004). According to the *New York Times* (1904), countless euphoric teenagers took over entire cars and started to flirt, sing and fool around.

In the following months and years, these new forms of collective affect and eroticism in the subway tunnels below New York were celebrated in numerous songs as well as dances and movies (Fitzpatrick 2009). The so-called *Subway Songs* especially, sold as sheet music to play at home, gained instant popularity (Stalter 2011). With titles such as 'Come Take a Ride Underground' (1904) and 'Subway Glide' (1907), they combined catchy waltz tunes and slang with juicy stories of love and lust. Their primary subject was a random encounter of two strangers amid the subway passenger throng, which then unfolded as a romantic or erotic situation. This infrastructural eroticism also becomes apparent in the very first movie ever made about the New York subway, titled *Two A.M. in the Subway* (1905). In this screen sequence lasting less than a minute, the lewd conduct of some passengers draws the attention of two policemen. They witness how a woman gathers up her dress and presents her silk stockings to her fellow travellers. This for the time highly obscene behaviour eventually results in the intervention of the authorities. Such sources show that, quite similar to the situation in the then newly implemented elevators, these anonymous encounters of circulating bodies in a high-tech setting seemed prone to becoming affectedly and sexually charged. The new experience of being in close contact with other anonymous bodies of any colour, gender and age, all willingly undergoing the turbulence of machinic circulation, also found its way into one of the most remarkable products of popular culture at that time: the 'Subway Express Two-Step'. This dance, which was immensely popular in the months after the opening of the subway, imitated the vibrations of riding in a train, and re-enacted the moments of unintentional physical contact as a result of harsh stops and rapid accelerations as highly pleasurable experiences.

These depictions of the subway as a highly affect-laden though morally ambiguous setting can be read as a sign of its *liminal* quality. In the eyes of the early subway passengers, the subterranean spaces of circulation appear as oddly removed, deprived of any clear attribution as either public or private. It is this ambivalence and anonymity amid transient populations of passengers which opens up new and experimental forms of being together and allows for moments of transgression and intimacy. Far removed from the traditional moral authorities of the family or the church, the new subterranean settings of the subway presented an under-coded space available for the realisation of desires and affects as hitherto unknown forms of 'being with'.

However, the erotic affects and intensities emerging in the subway might at first glimpse seem to be indicators of precisely those barbaric, irrational and antisocial qualities that thinkers such as Tarde, Freud or Le Bon attributed to the crowd. Instead, we would suggest understanding these intensities and desires not just as an irrational regression but rather as a transcendence of dominant moral codes and subjectivities. In the sense that Deleuze and Guattari differentiate between merely 'becoming undifferentiated' as molar masses from the perspective of an elite gaze and 'becoming imperceptible' as molecular intensities beyond established forms of subjectivity, it is the latter that becomes tangible here. As such, the machinic assemblages of circulation allowed for experimenting with new subjectivities which transgressed the classical subject orders and moral codes of the nineteenth century, such as self-composure, shame and inwardness. The subway served as a vehicle for the unfolding of new, and post-bourgeois, modes of subjectivity. Enabled by high densities of heterogeneous bodies and complex machineries of de/territorialisation, these ambiguous subjectivities were thus seen as capable of undermining hegemonic schemes of subjectivation inscribed into the subway network and its components. The fact that these schemes become temporarily overwritten by the strong desires of the people reveals that the 'circulation of affects within the machinic assemblage' (Deleuze and Guattari 1987: 260) functions as a destabilising force, resulting in the conflict of different ideas of what the subject of an infrastructure should be. In the chaotic events surrounding the line's opening day and the new collective affects unfolding in its aftermath, we can see various new forms of intersubjective modes of being and intensive affects emerging and being negotiated, sometimes as the result of the imposition of police force.

Conclusions

As Deleuze once pointed out in relation to structuralism, assemblage thinking 'is not at all a form of thought that suppresses the subject, but one that breaks it up and distributes it systematically, that contests the identity of the subject, that dissipates it and makes it shift from place to place, an always nomad subject, made of individuations, but impersonal ones, or of singularities, but preindividual ones' (2004: 190). In this chapter, we have explored the impersonal individuations and pre-individual singularities associated with the urban circulation of passengers and tourists. In doing so, we show the involution of stratified subjects and, moreover, how and to what extent this entails becoming not just someone but some*thing* else. Becoming urban, we have argued, involves first becoming a vectorial movement and then becoming an intensive affect. In both cases, the individuality of these becomings is not given by the subject or the substance that is touring or desiring, but by specific vectorial qualities (a certain speed, a certain direction, a certain force) or affective relations (desire, eat, pollute, etc.).

Becoming urban thus involves becoming a haecceity, which is to become an individual quality, a time, a degree: 'A degree of heat, an intensity of white, are perfect individualities [. . .] They are haeccities in the sense that they consist entirely of relations of movement and rest between molecules and particles, capacities to affect and be affected' (Deleuze and Guattari 1987: 261). More importantly, becoming urban involves in consequence an openness for new combinations of said qualities, velocities, times, intensities: 'There are only haeccities, affects, subjectless individuations that constitute collective assemblages [. . .] Nothing subjectifies, but haeccities form according to compositions of nonsubjectified powers or affects' (1987: 266).

Drawing from our two stories, we thus propose an alternative understanding of the potentiality of the urban to ground action for alternative urban worlds and subjectivities beyond subjects. In order to become something else, to unleash alternative forms of movement, thought and desire, of sociality and the commons, we need to first become urban, vectors, intensities. Desubjectivation, deterritorialisation and asociality, that is the plane of consistency, become thus an obligatory point of passage for opening up other possibilities, enabling recombinations, reinventing the social and becoming something else.

We conclude by pointing to AbdouMaliq Simone's (2010) similar argument that, in cities where infrastructures fail, people themselves become infrastructures. In such moments, people's selves, bodies and situations become the media through which locations, resources and stories are connected, creating opportunities for everyday survival. Interestingly, when people become infrastructure, 'the value of an individual existence rests less in the elaboration of a "meaningful" life or coherent story [. . .]. What is important is an individual's ability to be "hooked in" to different daily scenarios, dramas, networks, and affiliations that provide a constant set of alternatives' (2010: 126). People become links for new urban compositions that involve not just them but a collective, opening up connections, opportunities, possibilities for everyone else involved.

Notes

1. We are following here Amin and Thrift (2002), who use Deleuze and Guattari's concept of a *mechanosphere* to describe the city as a forcefield or a plane of consistency. We note, however, that the term 'mechanosphere' is unfortunate as it builds on the idea of a mechanism, precisely what the plane of consistency is freed from: 'This is not animism, any more than it is mechanism; rather, it is universal machinism: a plane of consistency occupied by an immense abstract machine comprising an infinite number of [machinic] assemblages' (Deleuze and Guattari 1987: 256). Hence we propose speaking of *machinosphere*.

2. These insights allow a positive reading of the non-human analogies frequently used to disparage tourists: flocks of sheep, pack of hounds, tourist hordes, viruses. Instead of criticising such symbolic homologies produced by elites to distinguish themselves from the masses, we should take them seriously – and not as structuralist analogies, but as forms of subjectless becomings. Indeed, they all point to a key feature of circulating transient population: becoming a multiplicity. As such, tourists also have capacities to expand, propagate, multiply that are based on contagion between heterogeneous terms.

References

Akrich, M. (1992) 'The de-scription of technical objects', in W. E. Bijker and J. Law (eds), *Shaping Technology/Building Society: Studies in Sociotechnical Change*. Cambridge, MA: MIT Press, pp. 205–24.

Althusser, L. (2006) 'Ideology and ideological state apparatuses (notes towards an investigation)', in A. Sharma and A. Gupta (eds), *The Anthropology of the State: A Reader*. Oxford: Blackwell, pp. 86–111.

Amin, A. and Thrift, N. (2002) *Cities: Reimagining the Urban*. Cambridge: Polity.

Aradau, C. and Blanke, T. (2010) 'Governing circulation: a critique of the biopolitics of security', in M. Larrinaga and M. G. Doucet (eds), *Security and Global Governmentality: Globalization, Governance and the State*. London: Routledge, pp. 44–58.

Augé, M. (1995) *Non Places: Introduction to an Anthropology of Hypermodernity*. New York: Verso.

Boorstin, D. (1987) *The Image: A Guide to Pseudo-Events in America*. New York: Atheneum.

Boutros, A. and Straw, W. (2010) 'Introduction', in A. Boutros and W. Straw (eds), *Circulation and the City*. Montreal: McGill-Queen's University Press, pp. 3–22.

de Certeau, M. (1984) *The Practice of Everyday Life*. Berkeley: University of California Press.

DeLanda, M. (2006) *A New Philosophy of Society: Assemblage Theory and Social Complexity*. London and New York: Continuum.

Deleuze, G. (2004) 'How do we recognize structuralism?', in G. Deleuze, *Desert Islands and Other Texts, 1953–1974*, ed. D. Lapoujade. New York: Semiotext(e) pp. 170–92.

Deleuze, G. and Guattari, F. (1987) *A Thousand Plateaus*. London and New York: Continuum.

Deleuze, G. and Guattari, F. (2004) *Anti-Oedipus*. London and New York: Continuum.

Delgado, M. (1993) *El animal público. Hacia una antropología de los espacios urbanos*. Barcelona: Anagrama.

Durkheim, E. ([1890] 1982) *The Rules of Sociological Method*, ed. S. Lukes. New York: Free Press.

Farías, I. (2008) 'Touring Berlin. Virtual Destination, Tourist Communication and the Multiple City'. PhD dissertation. Berlin: Humboldt Universität zu Berlin.

Farías, I. (2009a) 'Introduction: decentering the object of urban studies', in I. Farías and T. Bender (eds), *Urban Assemblages: How Actor-Network Theory Changes Urban Studies*. London: Routledge, pp. 1–24.

Farías, I. (2009b) 'The reality of urban tourism: framed activity and virtual ontology', in I. Farías and T. Bender (eds), *Urban Assemblages: How Actor-Network Theory Changes Urban Studies*. London: Routledge, pp. 209–28.

Farías, I. and Bender, T. (2009) *Urban Assemblages: How Actor-Network Theory Changes Urban Studies*. London: Routledge.

Fitzpatrick, T. (2009) *Art and the Subway: New York Underground*. Piscataway, NJ: Rutgers University Press.

Foucault, M. (2007) *Security, Territory, Population: Lectures at the Collège de France, 1977–78*, ed. M. Senellart. Basingstoke: Palgrave Macmillan.

Freud, S. (1922) *Group Psychology and the Analysis of the Ego*. London: International Psycho-analytical Press.

Höhne, S. (2012) 'An endless flow of machines to serve the city – infrastructural assemblages and the quest for the machinic metropolis', in D. Brantz, S. Disko and G. Wagner-Kyora (eds), *Thick Space: Approaches to Metropolitanism*. Bielefeld: Transcript.

Hood, C. (2004) *722 Miles. The Building of the Subways and How they Transformed New York*. Baltimore: Johns Hopkins University Press.

Joyce, P. (2003) *The Rule of Freedom: Liberalism and the Modern City*. London: Verso.

Latour, B. (1988) 'Mixing humans and nonhumans together: the sociology of a door-closer', *Social Problems*, 35 (3): 298–310.

Le Bon, G. (1896) *The Crowd: A Study of the Popular Mind*. New York: Macmillan Co.

McFarlane, C. and Anderson, B. (2011) 'Thinking with assemblage', *Area*, 43 (2): 162–4.

New York Times (1904) 'Things seen and heard along the Underground', *New York Times*, 28 October, p. 7.

Park, R. E. and Burgess, E. W. (1925) *The City: Suggestions for the Investigation of Human Behavior in the Urban Environment*. Chicago: University of Chicago Press.

Robbins, P. and Sharp, J. (2006) 'Turfgrass subjects: the political economy of urban monoculture', in N. Heynen, M. Kaika and E. Swyngedouw (eds), *In the Nature of Cities: Urban Political Ecology and the Politics of Urban Metabolism*. London: Routledge, pp. 110–28.

Simone, A. M. (2010) *City Life from Jakarta to Dakar: Movements at the Crossroads*, London: Routledge.

Stalter, S. (2011) 'The subway crush: making contact in New York City Subway songs, 1904–1915', *Journal of American Culture*, 34 (4): 321–31.

Tarde, G. ([1890] 1968) *Penal Philosophy*. Montclair, NJ: Patterson Smith.

Tonkiss, F. (2005) *Space, the City and Social Theory: Social Relations and Urban Forms*. Cambridge: Polity Press.

Towner, J. (1985) 'The Grand Tour: a key phase in the history of tourism', *Annals of Tourism Research*, 12: 297–333.

Urbain, J.-D. (1991) *L'idiot du voyage. Histoires de touristes*. Paris: Librairie Plon.

Whyte, W. F. (1943) *Street Corner Society: The Social Structure of an Italian Slum*. Chicago: University of Chicago Press.

Chapter 3

Rethinking the City as a Body without Organs

Louise Beltzung Horvath and Markus Maicher

The world around you is not what it seems. It's happening all around you. They aren't coming. They're already there.

Ingress

The forgotten, the invisible and the virtual of the city lie below, above and beyond the actualised streets, doors, parks and canalisations. Michel de Certeau spoke of the 'ghost of the city' (de Certeau et al. 1998: 136) to express what more there is than the mere material appearances of the city: the imaginary, the past, and one could add the rise of the digital era, which is radically changing the city as we know it. The digital impregnation of the material with codes and programs (Batty 1997) has given rise to claims that the city of flesh and stone (Sennett 1994) is turning into a city of bits and pixels (Mitchell 1996), or that a virtual and a real city exist side by side and need to be reconciled (Ruby 2001: 65). Beyond these claims of paradigmatic shifts, we see how new communication technologies have changed how we communicate, express ourselves and perceive our surroundings (Buchanan 2010: 4). 'Multiple realities [are] brought into being' (Graham et al. 2013: 465) when experiences are digitally mediated, enhanced or even replaced. This changes our notions of place, location, distance and intimacy and hence allows for ambivalent urban practices, between liberation and continuous (self-)surveillance.

Location-based games are an example of new, seemingly non-signifying practices in the city: those outside the game do not grasp the importance certain places attain or how structures of the city are recoded. The 'thrill' lies in their alteration of reality; they perforate the borders between gameplay and everyday life (Hulsey and Reeves 2014: 390 f.). Presently, the game *Ingress*, released by the Google start-up company Niantic Labs in 2012, is among the most popular with more than eight million downloads. The mobile phone game transforms the world into a war zone in which two parties have to fight for world domi-nance. For this, they have to conquer certain landmarks called 'portals' in the urban landscape and connect them to each other to build 'fields'. The storyline is constantly developed further without any definite end. The portals constantly switch from one faction to the other and yet it mobilises thousands of people who coordinate actions across countries and continents and spend hours walking through the cities for a fight that literally takes place as bodies move across the city leaving digital traces (Andersen 2014). For the second anniversary of the game in December 2014, Niantic Labs released figures illustrating the game's success: *Ingress* agents walked 127 million kilometres and they created more than three million portals in over two hundred countries (Beltzung 2015).

These emergent virtual cartographies do not find representations in mappings and thought-images of the city, which stick to an idea of the city as composed of streets, buildings, directions and locations, of struc-tures and significations. Those who plan the city, however, are not those who write it. They are the *Wandersmänner*, as de Certeau calls them:

> These practitioners make use of spaces that cannot be seen; their knowl-edge of them is as blind as that of lovers in each other's arms [. . .] The networks of these moving, intersecting writings compose a manifold story that has neither author nor spectator, shaped out of fragments of trajecto-ries and alterations of spaces: in relation to representations, it remains daily and indefinitely other. (de Certeau 1984: 93)

The moving writings of digital realities in urban games can be under-stood as silent productions of affects and intensities that we will discuss with reference to the complex concept of the Body without Organs (BwO). The BwO is an 'object of construction, a practice' (Bonta and Protevi 2004: 62) that frees desire from capture within apparatuses (of the state, the city) and allows for intensities to flow into new directions. Constructing the BwO correlates to a new geography and cartography of flows, thus what follows is a sketch to (re)conceptualise the city as a BwO populated by intensities rather than as a functionalistic organism.[1] We want to strengthen the understanding of the BwO as an opportu-nity to rethink the city as made up of practices that oscillate between stratification and destratification, between capture and liberation of flows. The concept of the BwO allows us to place phenomena such as drug addiction, drifting or gaming outside a moralising discourse and to analyse them simultaneously as movements towards liberation from the organism and new logics of capture. 'Find your body without organs.

Find out how to make it. It's a question of life and death, youth and old age, sadness and joy. It is where everything is played out' (Deleuze and Guattari 1987: 175).

The City as Organism and Its Critique

> Our first requirement will be an organ that is compact, rapid, lively and concentrated: this is the City with its well organized centre. Our second requirement will be another organ, supple, extensive and elastic; this is the Garden City on the periphery. (Le Corbusier 1929: 320)

The city as an organism has been a powerful image throughout the history of urban theory. Richard Sennett dates the notion of the city as a hierarchically organised body back to William Harvey's discovery of the circulation of the blood in 1628 (Sennett 1994: 255). Since then, urban planning has been obsessed with creating the city as a breathing, hygienic organism where blood (individuals) could circulate freely within its arteries – every blockage indicating illness – and where the waste products would be dealt with by specific organs and streams:

> The desire to put into practice the healthy virtues of respiration and circulation transformed the look of cities as well as the bodily practices in them. From the 1740s on, European cities began cleaning dirt off the streets, draining holes and swampy depressions filled with urine and faeces, pushing dirt into sewers below the street. (Sennett 1994: 263)

In the history of urban planning the functionalist logic of perfect circulation can be traced: from Haussmann's reconstruction of Paris in which the 'Attila of the straight line' laid his ruler over the old medieval streets and created a system of straight arteries and veins (Sennett 1994; Boyer 1994) to Ebenezer Howard's 'Garden Cities' which were based on a functional division of green residential areas and the central business district (Howard 1902) and to Le Corbusier's 'Contemporary City' in which green areas would be the 'lungs', the modern street 'a new type of organism' and centre and periphery specific types of organs (Le Corbusier 1929: 320).

The organic metaphor of the city implies that the organism is composed of specific organs, that it has a specific size and that it has clear boundaries that delimits it from other organisms or individuals. As such the city has been seen as a self-contained entity distinct from rural social formations. At the dawn of urban sociology, the city has been analysed as having a specific form of social organisation distinct from rural societies and with certain effects on solidarity, behaviour and the psychology of its citizens. Ferdinand Tönnies distinguished between the *Gemeinschaft* of the countryside and *Gesellschaft* in the city (Tönnies [1887] 1963) and Georg Simmel famously analysed the social psychology of the city and the blasé mentality of the *Großstädter* (Simmel 1903). In his major work *The Division of Labour in Society* ([1933] 1997) Émile Durkheim distinguished between mechanical and organic forms of solidarity that relate to the degree of division of labour and the growth of towns, among other things. The greater the division of labour in society, the greater the interdependence of its parts, resulting in the metaphor of organs that depend on each other.[2] In the 1920s the emerging Chicago School saw the city as a self-organising ecological unit with a specific spatial distribution of its functional parts, so called 'natural areas' that were culturally and functionally relatively homogeneous: 'Within the limits of any natural area of human habitation' there are forces at work which tend to 'bring about an orderly and typical grouping of its population and institutions' (Park and Burgess [1925] 1984: 1).

The image of the city as an organism is one that also results from the idea that there might be a totalising point of view on urban practices. The opening passage of Michel de Certeau's chapter on 'walking in the city' illustrates this well: from a vantage point on top of the former World Trade Center, the view 'transforms the bewitching world by which one was "possessed" into a text that lies before one's eyes. It allows one to read it, to be a solar Eye looking down like a god' (de Certeau 1984: 92). From this perspective 'everything that is not capable of being dealt with in this way [. . .] constitutes the "waste products" of a functionalist administration' (94).

Neo-organicist accounts and new materialism challenge these schools of thought. They aim to overcome the conception of entities as merely related *to* each other by emphasising the co-constitution of bodies and cities and a conceptualisation of the body and its environment not as closed ecologies. Within these frameworks, becoming does not mean a relation *between* something but, to use the words of Gilbert Simondon, it is the thinking about the relation of relations. Relations of interiority and exteriority are the constituting moment of individuation; becoming has to be thought of as complex interrelations instead of simple causalities between organised entities (Simondon 2005; Guchet 2010).

It is challenging but necessary, as Elizabeth Grosz recognises, to move beyond an understanding of the city as something coherent in which everything, the organs among them, has its place. Her analysis of the co-constitution of the body and the city entails a critique of the body-politic, in other words of the idea of the state as the state-body. Not only does it reinstate the opposition of nature and culture, but it implies that 'nature dictates the ideal form of culture' (Grosz 1992: 247). The same is to be held true when the city is considered as organism: it seems as though everything is by definition naturally given (e.g. bodies, objects). To overcome this thinking, the urbanist Matthew Gandy uses the image of the cyborg. He aims at describing a shift of emphasis 'away from an anatomical conception of space [. . .] towards a neurological reading of space as a diffuse and interconnected realm of human interaction' (Gandy 2005: 29). The cyborg metaphor, based on the manifesto of Donna Haraway, may serve as a way to conceptualise 'the corporeal experience of space' with virtuality embedded into materiality (Gandy 2005: 28).

The concept of the Body without Organs moves beyond this. Its strength is that 'it is not space, nor is it in space; it is matter that occupies space to a given degree – to the degree corresponding to the intensities produced' (Deleuze and Guattari 1987: 153). It comes neither before nor after the organism and thus allows a way out of such causal relations between entities, moments, events.[3] The BwO was introduced in reference to the French theatre writer Antonin Artaud in *The Logic of Sense* (Deleuze 1990). For Artaud the BwO goes beyond the limits of physical flesh and leaves the interiority behind. Referring to Artaud, Deleuze speaks about the 'duality of the body' and 'two types of nonsense, passive and active: the nonsense of the word devoid of sense, which is decomposed into phonetic elements; and the nonsense of tonic elements, which form a word incapable of being decomposed and no less devoid of sense. Here everything happens, acts and is acted upon, beneath sense and far from the surface' (Deleuze 1990: 90). Seemingly non-signifying practices in the urban context, such as in games, do not lack sense but, we would argue, free themselves from that which captures them.

Beyond the Organistic City: Desiring-production and the Urban

> Desiring-machines make us an organism; but at the very heart of this production, within the very production of this production, the body suffers from being organized in this way, from not having some other sort of organization, or no organization at all. (Deleuze and Guattari 1983: 8)

Gilles Deleuze and Félix Guattari provide their concept of the Body without Organs as an approach to desire that differs from Freudian and Lacanian psychoanalysis. Desire is not inherently produced by a lack and is not always trapped within a theatre of memories and fantasies as representations, projections or rejections. It is a productive force that makes connections but at the same time produces the organism, which makes it suffer.[4] This means that these desiring-productions, in order to free them from instinct and habitual patterns, are recorded on the BwO. Consequently, the body becomes stratified – as, for instance, the erogenous zones of the body become territorialised.[5] For Deleuze and Guattari bodies suffer from being organised in a certain way and from not having some other form of organisation or no organisation at all. The drive to destroy, to dis-organise – opposed to the libido as productive – is what Freud has called the death drive, *thanatos*:

> The body without organs is the unproductive, the sterile, the unengendered, the unconsumable. The death instinct: that is the name, and death is not without a model. For desire desired death also, because the full body of death is its motor, just as it desires life, because the organs of life are the working machine. (Deleuze and Guattari 1983: 8)

The BwO ceases to work for a functional structure, as it is a state that allows for new productive connections and desire to flow in new directions. It is a body that enters from an equilibrium state or comfort zone into a state of intensive crisis where new becomings are possible (Bonta and Protevi 2004: 62–3). Every substance, every body and every space is in a state of becoming. However, the actual, extensive state hides the intensive morphogenetic processes that lead to it and which have resulted in an equilibrium state under the guise of functional structures. The intensive is buried beneath the extensive; the virtual beneath the actual (20).

When Deleuze and Guattari ask how to discern each type of BwO, they ask for 'what will come to pass' and refer to 'surprises', the 'unexpected' and 'variants' (Deleuze and Guattari 1987: 152). Within cities, if understood in terms of practices, one of the first exercises with the aim to forge new relations between the self and the organisational structure of the city was carried out by Guy Debord and the 'Situationist International' movement. In the so-called *dérive* the Situationists would drift through the spaces of the city much as a rudderless ship would float across the ocean. Without a sense of direction or external coordinates these urban drifters opened up to a schizophrenic adventure in which they let their desire flow in multiple directions: towards strangers in bars, homeless in the streets and so on. They left their territory of fixed identities, normative subjectivity and habitual practices in order to uncover the virtual, intensive properties buried underneath the extensive, actualised systems of streets. By doing so they created a BwO where desiring-production could create new connections and where intensities could flow in new directions.

Probably the most poetic account of such practices has been given by de Certeau in his writings about everyday practices and walking in the city. He is interested in the everyday tactics of moving about in the city that transform the panoptic structure of the functionalist city into a network of so many unrecorded and unrecordable productions. For him, consuming – be it watching TV or walking in the streets – is always a production of something new: '[T]rajectories trace out the ruses of other interests and desires that are neither determined nor captured by the systems in which they develop' (de Certeau 1984: xviii). These movements cannot be represented with ordinary scientific procedures – statistics, maps – because those 'miss what was: the act itself of passing by' (97). Deleuze and Guattari speak about the map which is not restricted to geography, but rather 'something like a BwO intensity map, where the roadblocks designate thresholds and the gas, waves or flows' (Deleuze and Guattari 1987: 164).

With games that alter reality such as *Ingress*, modes of spatialisation are radically transformed in comparison to de Certeau's analogue walking practices. These new modes hold a potential to form connections that overcome the metrics of space – communication as immediate intensity rather than unfolding over extensive chunks of space: '[M]otionless voyaging in place of the full BwO: everything is flux, flow, becoming' (Doel 1995: 213). Augmentation of space unfolds or actualises a virtuality of socio-spatial practices – practices that appear to be 'idiotic' and non-sensical to the functionalist logic.

This augmentation, however, has to be considered as a new form of striating the seemingly non-signifying and liberating practices of walking as well. As Maurizio Lazzarato points out, based on Deleuze and Guattari's terminology, capitalism is not a mode of production but a series of devices for machinic enslavement operating on the molecular pre-individual level, and devices for social subjection operating on the molar level of roles, representations or social identities (Lazzarato 2006). The game *Ingress* follows the logic of another device for machinic enslavement, as the player becomes a cog in a data and capital extraction machine called Google. In his postscript to the disciplinary societies of Michel Foucault, Deleuze points out that the new form of 'control' works numerically (as modulations) compared to enclosed moulds in disciplinary societies. As he puts it: '[I]n a society of control, the corporation has replaced the factory, and the corporation is a spirit, a gas' (Deleuze 1997: 310). Individuals 'have become "dividuals", and masses, samples, data, markets, or "banks"' (311). He refers to how Félix Guattari pictured a city in which an electronic card would grant access or restrict access to certain areas: 'What counts is not the barrier but the computer that tracks each person's position – licit or illicit – and effects a universal modulation' (312). *Ingress* can be seen as a striking example of such a transformation. Combining an addictive gameplay that transgresses the everyday with such extensive data collection by a corporation such as Google works as if surveillance was a 'gift':

> [T]hey [urban pedestrians, MM and LB] trade the data of their living movements for the privilege of leaving their houses. Thus, as an increasing proportion of our lives is spent bouncing around the rooms of the digital enclosure we have witnessed the rise of a situation in which 'those who do not submit to surveillance become obsolete' [. . .]. The gift, in other words, is suspended obsolescence. Those who opt out get left behind. (Hulsey and Reeves 2014: 394–5)

While this describes the economy of games such as *Ingress*, it does not yet apprehend the experience, the thrill and the reasons why people engage with such intensity in this game. And as much as the movements of players become data, the game also hints at (and even visualises) possibilities for extracting oneself from social subjections and of actualising virtual subject positions. Following this line of thought we want to emphasise the liberatory potential of the game.

The Player Constructing His/Her BwO

> You never reach the Body without Organs, you can't reach it, you are forever attaining it, it is a limit. People ask, So what is this BwO? – But you're already on it, scurrying like a vermin, groping like a blind person, or running like a lunatic; desert traveler and nomad of the steppes. On it we sleep, live our waking lives, fight – fight and are fought – seek our place, experience untold happiness and fabulous defeats; on it we penetrate and are penetrated; on it we love. [. . .] The BwO: it is already under way the moment the body has had enough of organs and wants to slough them off, or loses them. (Deleuze and Guattari 1987: 150)

Playing seems to produce more intense affects than 'serious' activities ever could. Games do not lack the seriousness of 'reality'; indeed, they produce an ever more intense reality (Pfaller 2002: 93). This results from, among other things, the automatism granted in playing (202) which, similar to the program of the Masochist turning his body into a BwO, allows us to strip ourselves of representation, significance and subjectification – the three strata enslaving the BwO. The BwO emerges through the crack between these stratifications: 'The full BwO grows in this crack, not as an amorphous and undifferentiated mass, but as a swarm of virtual multiplicities, teeming singularities and experimental complications and inventions' (Doel 1995: 213). This point is crucial: the BwO is not the pre-Oedipal body of Freud or the Real of Lacan. It is a dissolution of organ–connections and the channelling of flows in service of the organism that allows a 'becoming other'.[6] The player, as in the case of *Ingress*, builds himself a role, he or she plays war where there is no war and mixes the virtual and the material as specific locations become digitally enhanced with meanings: 'It is by following this disintegration and decomposition of the human organism – with its striated flesh, envelope of skin and covering of face along the lines of absolute deterritorialisation that we are carried towards the full BwO' (Doel 1995: 220).

In *A Thousand Plateaus* Deleuze and Guattari differentiate between the full and the empty BwO. The empty BwO is one that results from a too violent smashing of strata – as, for instance, in the case of the drug addict (Deleuze and Guattari 1987: 150). According to Deleuze and Guattari one has to stay stratified enough to be able to communicate within the strata: 'If you free it with too violent an action, if you blow apart the strata without taking precautions, then instead of drawing the plane you will be killed' (161). A too violent transcendence is probably best illustrated by the phenomenon of gaming addiction (Cook 2010). In the case of *Ingress* there are examples of fatal accidents while playing, which show how one can lose oneself in these immersive practices. In Rio de Janeiro, Brazil, the first such case was reported in November 2014 after a player was fatally hit by a bus on the street while he was moving towards a targeted portal (Beltzung and Hoppenstedt 2014). In Darmstadt, Germany, also in November 2014, an agent of the resistance died on his way to a field operation in a car accident. Players from both parties decided to mourn by neutralising the 870 portals of their city – on this day the stats of the war within these regions were halted by Niantics. Players met and constructed a digital candle that flickered on the *Ingress* map. In the community 'In memoriam Aphilie' on *Google Plus*, a photo album from 17 November 2014 contains pictures showing people staring motionless at their mobile phones, which misses the intensity of their lived experience.

There is the danger of a too radical destratification, but also the possibility to overcome the limitations of the structure of signifier and signified, as shown in the example above. 'Becoming begins as a desire to escape bodily limitation' (Massumi 1992: 94). This involves, if not a

tearing down, a temporary dismantling of the three great strata: subjectification, signifiance and organisation. The use of an avatar and a new
name transcends subjectification, and the practices of moving about in
the city are non-signifying practices in relation to the actual organisation of the city. This is nicely illustrated in the numerous posts of *Ingress*
players on the network *reddit*, who report how they were arrested
for their 'suspicious' behaviour. The game not only requires targeting
specific points in the landscape, but also to repeatedly walk the same
route in order to acquire items such as weapons. This leads to groups of
players walking repeatedly around the same block of houses, stopping
every few metres to tap on the screen of their smartphones. This behaviour escapes the functional logic of the city, just like the pure sounds of
a word escape meaning. Within the functional logic of the city, going
from one point to the next is something that makes *sense*; it produces a
surplus. Playful practices, however, become detached from any surplus,
not because they lack something, but because they aim at constructing
a BwO. Deleuze and Guattari illustrate this point in relation to certain
erotic practices:

> The condition for this circulation and multiplication is that the man not
> ejaculate. It is not a question of experiencing desire as an internal lack, nor
> of delaying pleasure in order to produce a kind of externalizable surplus
> value, but instead of constituting an intensive body without organs, Tao,
> a field of immanence in which desire lacks nothing and therefore cannot
> be linked to any external or transcendent criterion. (Deleuze and Guattari
> 1987: 157)

The joy involved in the circulation of flows without surplus-production
is illustrated by the player Morka, who describes his experience of
playing twenty-four hours with other agents, riding bikes and 'greening
the city' of Paris systematically with others as one of the most beautiful
moments of *Ingress* (Beltzung 2015).

Conclusion

'Virtual worlds are simulations', argues Rob Shields, comparing them
with a map. Starting from depicting 'actual worlds, real bodies and
situations [. . .] they end up taking on a life of their own' (Shields 2003:
4). Somewhere in the process of departing from what they depict, they
become 'more real than real'. This, we argue, applies to games like
Ingress to the extent that they create a world with new zones of intensities. Portals – the so-called landmarks that have to be conquered in the
game – can range from a monument to an object, or a little graffiti on

an unnoticed wall. Much as the masochist redefines zones of intensities – not the leg of a woman but the boot becomes the attraction (Deleuze and Guattari 1983: 156) – the cities are recoded when players gather at these points to fight for conquering them, even if this is only displayed within a program.

To free the city from its organisation, if only temporarily by games, can be a practice of liberation. Constructing a BwO collectively can become a political practice – instead of encounters between subjects communicating on a plane of signifiance, the stripping down of subjectivity, of organisation and significance allows for the becoming of a new swarm of multiplicities, a new collectivity. It is not a 'me' or 'you' that is encountering but an indefinite 'a':

> Thus the BwO is never yours or mine. It is always a body. It is no more projective than it is regressive [. . .] 'A' stomach, 'an' eye, 'a' mouth: the indefinite article does not lack anything; it is not indeterminate or undifferentiated, but expresses the pure determination of intensity, intensive difference. (Deleuze and Guattari 1987: 164)

How can we then imagine a city without organs, or a non-organismic city? Deleuze and Guattari's example of a schizophrenic table offers an answer to this question. A table in its pure materiality consists of parts that only begin to be a table if they are organised in a specific way and if their function is subsumed under the function 'table'. The schizophrenic table is without organisation; the parts exist in their own right and are not working for the organism 'table', their value is not derived from the machinic output (Deleuze and Guattari 1983: 6). Thus we may imagine the city without organs exactly as a materiality and praxis that is not organised as an organism, that does not derive its meaning from the *socius* of the capitalist city. The game we have used as example does risk being subsumed by societies of control, but it shows also how we might strive to go beyond imposed structures: towards sidewalks and streets that are freed from their functional organisation in the city organism, freed from normative inscriptions (one walks from A to B on the sidewalk, one does not touch other bodies, one does not stop without reason on the sidewalk, etc.) and from symbolic representation in the cartography of the city.

Notes

1. The concept varies between *Anti-Oedipus* (AO) and *A Thousand Plateaus* (ATP) insofar as the BwO is conceptualised as an anti-productive recording surface of desiring-productions in AO whereas in ATP the BwO comes closer to a liberating

(political) practice; accordingly, the focus here will be on the BwO as laid out in ATP.

2. Solidarity comes from this interdependence, rather than from similarities among members of traditional and small-scale societies.

3. 'The BwO is not "before" the organism; it is adjacent to it and is continually in the process of constructing itself' (Deleuze and Guattari 1987: 164).

4. 'The error of psychoanalysis was to understand BwO phenomena as regressions, projections, phantasies, in terms of an image of the body' (Deleuze and Guattari 1987: 165).

5. The ways in which the body becomes stratified and in which productive connections are allowed or repressed depend on the social organisation (Holland 1999: 29). Deleuze and Guattari call the social organisation of anti-production the *socius*, which could be the earth, a tyrant or capital.

6. 'The so-called fragmentation exhibited by the "pre-Oedipal" body is in fact the fractality of part-objects [. . .] not the debilitating lack of an old unity but a real capacity for new connection [. . .] A return to the body without organs is actually a return of fractality, a resurfacing of the virtual. Not regression: invention' (Massumi 1992: 85).

References

Andersen, M. (2014) 'Google's Ingress takes mobile gaming to the streets', *Wired Magazine*, 1 February (http://www.wired.com/2014/01/a-year-of-google-ingress/).

Batty, M. (1997) 'The computable city', *International Planning Studies*, 2 (2): 155–73.

Beltzung, L. (2015) 'The king of augmented reality street fighting', *Motherboard VICE*, 8 January (http://motherboard.vice.com/read/the-king-of-augmented-street-fighting-the-worlds-best-ingress-player).

Beltzung, L. and Hoppenstedt, M. (2014) 'Ingress-Agent stirbt beim Spielen in Verkehrsunfall', *Motherboard VICE*, 17 February (http://www.vice.com/alps/read/ingress-agent-stirbt-beim-spielen-in-verkehrsunfall).

Bonta, M. and Protevi, J. (2004) *Deleuze and Geophilosophy: A Guide and Glossary*. Edinburgh: Edinburgh University Press.

Boyer, C. (1994) *The City of Collective Memory: Its Historical Imagery and Architectural Entertainments*. Cambridge, MA: MIT Press.

Buchanan, I. (2010) 'Deleuze and the Internet', in M. Poster and D. Savat (eds), *Deleuze and New Technology*. Edinburgh: Edinburgh University Press, pp. 143–60.

Cook, I. (2010) 'The body without organs and gaming addiction', in M. Poster and D. Savat (eds), *Deleuze and New Technology*. Edinburgh: Edinburgh University Press, pp. 185–205.

de Certeau, M. (1984) *The Practice of Everyday Life*. London: University of California Press.

de Certeau, M., Giard, L. and Mayol, P. (eds) (1998) *The Practice of Everyday Life: Living & Cooking*, 2 vols. Minneapolis: University of Minnesota Press.

Deleuze, G. (1990) *The Logic of Sense*. London: Athlone Press.

Deleuze, G. (1997) 'Postscript on the societies of control', in N. Leach (ed.), *Rethinking Architecture: A Reader in Cultural Theory*. London: Routledge, pp. 309–13.

Deleuze, G. and Guattari, F. (1983) *Anti-Oedipus: Capitalism and Schizophrenia*. Minneapolis: University of Minnesota Press.

Deleuze, G. and Guattari, F. (1987) *A Thousand Plateaus: Capitalism and Schizophrenia.* Minneapolis: University of Minnesota Press.

Doel, M. (1995) 'Bodies without organs: schizoanalysis and deconstruction', in S. Pile and N. Thrift (eds), *Mapping the Subject: Geographies of Cultural Transformation.* London: Routledge, pp. 208–21.

Durkheim, E. ([1933] 1997) *The Division of Labor in Society.* New York: Free Press.

Gandy, M. (2005) 'Cyborg urbanization: complexity and monstrosity in the contemporary city', *International Journal of Urban and Regional Research*, 29 (1): 26–49.

Graham, M., Zook, M. and Boulton, A. (2013) 'Augmented reality in urban places: contested content and the duplicity of code', *Transactions of the Institute of British Geographers*, 38 (3): 464–79.

Grosz, E. (1992) 'Bodies-cities', in B. Colomina (ed.), *Sexuality & Space.* New York: Princeton Architectural Press, pp. 241–54.

Guchet, X. (2010) *Pour un humanisme technologique: Culture, technique et société dans la philosophie de Gilbert Simondon.* Paris: Presses universitaires de France.

Holland, E. (1999) *Deleuze and Guattari's Anti-Oedipus: Introduction to Schizoanalysis.* London: Routledge.

Howard, E. (1902) *Garden Cities of Tomorrow.* London: S. Sonnenschein & Co.

Hulsey, N. and Reeves, J. (2014) 'The gift that keeps on giving: Google, Ingress, and the gift of surveillance', *Surveillance & Society*, 12 (3): 389–400.

Laporte, D. (2002) *History of Shit.* Cambridge, MA: MIT Press.

Lazzarato, M. (2006) *The Machine* (http://eipcp.net/transversal/1106/lazzarato/en).

Le Corbusier ([1929] 2003) 'The city of tomorrow and its planning', in R. T. LeGate and F. Stout (eds), *The City Reader*, 3rd edn. London: Routledge, pp. 317–24.

Massumi, B. (1992) *A User's Guide to Capitalism and Schizophrenia: Deviations from Deleuze and Guattari.* London: MIT Press.

Mitchell, W. J. (1996) *City of Bits: Space, Place, and the Infobahn.* Cambridge, MA: MIT Press.

Park, R. E. and Burgess, E. W. ([1925] 1984) *The City: Suggestions for Investigation of Human Behavior in the Urban Environment.* Chicago: University of Chicago Press.

Pfaller, R. (2002) *Die Illusion der anderen: Über das Lustprinzip in der Kultur.* Frankfurt: Suhrkamp.

Ruby, A. (2001) 'The time of the trajectory', in J. Armitage (ed.), *Virilio Live: Selected Interviews.* London: Sage, pp. 58–65.

Sennett, R. (1994) *Flesh and Stone: The Body and the City in Western Civilization.* New York: W. W. Norton.

Shields, R. (2003) *The Virtual.* New York: Routledge.

Simmel, G. (1903) 'The metropolis and mental life', in N. Leach (ed.) (1997) *Retinking Architecture: A Reader in Cultural Theory.* London: Routledge, pp. 69–79.

Simondon, G. (2005) *L'individuation à la lumière des notions de forme et d'information.* Grenoble: Éditions Jérôme Millon.

Tönnies, F. ([1887] 1963) *Gemeinschaft und Gesellschaft. Grundbegriffe der reinen Soziologie.* Darmstadt: Wissenschaftliche Buchgesellschaft.

Chapter 4

The Impredicative City, or What Can a Boston Square Do?

Marc Boumeester and Andrej Radman

[I]t is necessary first to see the machine at work before attempting to deduce the function from the structure.

Canguilhem (1992: 56)

The [. . .] City is sociology, happening.

Koolhaas (1995: 1255)

A system is simple if all its models are simulable. A system that is not simple, and that accordingly must have a nonsimulable model, is complex.

Rosen (2000: 292)

In his photographic series 'Selected People', the American photographer Pelle Cass displays a remarkable space-time axis reversal, the striking simplicity of which exemplifies the schizoanalysis of the city (Guattari 2013). The prefix 'schizo' is used to designate resistance to the paranoiac fixation on a *single* (and supreme) source of all signification (Deleuze and Guattari 2003: 194). The subject-matter of his experiments takes us to a square in Boston, USA. Yet, in terms of our investigation, the choice is purely contingent. Our ambition is to map the becoming of a specific place by way of non-correlationist hetero-poietic mattering, irremovable impredicative (auto-catalytic) looping and non-local causing (Turvey 2004: 57–70). In simple terms, it is the movement that determines the space, not the other way around. As Deleuze put it in his theses on movement, '[the] production of singularities (the qualitative leap) is achieved by the accumulation of banalities (quantitative process), so that the singular is taken from the any-whatever, and is itself an any-whatever which is simply non-ordinary and non-regular' (Deleuze 1986: 6). We will follow his call to renounce any order of preference, any teleology.

Our chapter will draw upon schizoanalytic cartography to concentrate on perception which occurs not on the level at which actions are decided but on the level at which the very capacity for action forms. If representation is a means to an end (tracing), cartography is a means to a means (intervention). The goal-oriented human action cannot be used as *the* design criterion because the freedom of action is never a de facto established condition, it is always a virtuality (Evans 2003: 16–17). This antecedent level of potentialisation is proto-epistemological and already ontological. It concerns change in the degree to which a life-form is enabled vis-à-vis its (built) environment (Massumi 2011). It is precisely the reciprocal determination of the life-form and its environment (mode of existence) that makes perception a pertinent area of study. After all, *living* has interests that do not (always) coincide with those of *thinking* and it is for this reason that one perceives invariants, not forms (Gibson 1986). To depict, one has to learn to perceive form. *To design* (built environment), *one has to unlearn to perceive form*, as we will attempt to demonstrate with the help of Cass.

The *life*-form never pre-exists an event, hence the prefix 'life' or, more to the point, the *city*-life-form. Simpler still, action, perception and environment are located on a continuum. Only recently have biologists conceded the effect that 'niche construction' has on the inheritance system, whereby a life-form does not *passively* submit to the pressures of a pre-existing environment, but *actively* constructs its existential niche – the city as a case in point (Odling-Smee 2007: 276–89). Baldwinian Evolution, or evolution by epigenetic means, is achieved through accumulation and improvement of cultural artefacts and practices. The quote 'we shape our cities; thereafter they shape us' is to be taken literally (Wexler 2013: 185–218). This is to say that, under the onto-topological commitment, experience is not an event 'in' the mind. Rather, the mind emerges from an interaction with the environment. The implications for the discipline of architecture and urbanism, considering its role in the 'evolution by other means', remain significant and binding. It is from this perspective that we will challenge the predominant homeostatic fixation on structure in architectural thinking in favour of the event-centred ontology of relations (Bains 2006). Moreover, we will insist that relations are irreducible to their terms (Deleuze and Parnet 1987: 55). The process – counterposed to the metaphysics of substance – seeks to grasp existence in the very act of its becoming (Guattari 2008: 19–45). Architects cannot take geometric ideologies as their starting point. Instead, as Guattari would have it, they need to think in terms of ecologies, that is 'transversally' cutting across the scales of the socius, the psyche and the environment.

Urban Schizoanalyses

The City as the 'noumenon closest to the phenomenon' has to be theorised by keeping both mechanistic reductionism and vitalist essentialism at bay (Deleuze 1994: 222). This is the lesson of Deleuzian 'machinism' which maintains a strict distinction between virtual singularities as irreducible emergent properties of systems (the problem) and the actual system itself (the solution). To put it bluntly, let scientists and engineers focus on problem-solving. No one does it better. However, a problem always gets the solution it deserves. What we want to claim for art and architecture is the domain of problem-making (counter-effectuation). Human beings might be excellent at passive *adaptation*, but in the Anthropocene they must become better at active existential *niche-construction*. Instead of changing habitats as migrants do, they are forced to change habits as nomads do (Braidotti 2010: 215). Paradoxically, nomads stay put. They take intensive travels, rather than extensive. In the first part of the chapter we will embark on one such intensive journey at the end of which four lessons will be drawn. In the second part we will change the speed of delivery and style of argumentation in order to speculate on a new image of thought. This image of thought reconstrued as 'thought without an image' is not restricted to the representation, correspondence or adequation of a self-identical object to a self-identical subject, but foregrounds the reciprocal determination of the knower and the known. As the feminist philosopher Claire Colebrook recently put it:

> Not only could there not be a subject as some fully self-present substance that subsisted and persisted before and beyond all relation, for the very self as identity must refer back to (and therefore be different from itself); but also, any supposed ground from which relations would unfold must itself be effected from relations. [. . .] the actualized world of constituted terms does not exhaust what can be said to be: actuality emerges from virtual tendencies, and those tendencies could always create new systems and new terms. (Colebrook 2014: 63)

First, a few caveats and one concrete example are in order. Architects are proverbially good at primary or predicative properties such as lengths, heights and depths. Take a ruler, take an object and juxtapose them. What the discipline needs to unlock are relational properties. An example of such an impredicative property is a walk-on-able surface where the conditions and the conditioned are determined at one and the same time. *Affordance* is expressed by one's relation with another object (like a primary property) and actualised in one's relation with another object (unlike a primary property). This neologism was coined by the founder of the ecological approach to perception, James Jerome Gibson:

> [A]n affordance is neither an objective nor a subjective property; or it is both if you like. An affordance cuts across the dichotomy of subjective-objective and helps us to understand its inadequacy. It is both physical and psychical, yet neither. An affordance points both ways, to the environment and to the observer. (Gibson 1986: 129)

This puzzle has eluded us across three centuries. Primary and relational properties are two different yet complementary concepts sustaining two different yet complementary causalities, related to the dynamic and static geneses respectively (Deleuze 1994: 89, 183). The impredicative loop is built by interacting (actual) parts that cause an incorporeal (virtual) effect, which in turn becomes a (non-dynamic) quasi-cause by determining the degrees of freedom for the very interacting parts.[1] Proscription: the a priori. Prescription: cartography.

Any Square Whatever

In this part we will address the issue of how the urban milieu defies analysis based on primary properties, description and intentionality or phenomenological surveillance. We propose to regard the municipal or metropolitan fabric solely as a conjunction of flow, as an actual, physical and virtual aggregate which stretches along several temporal and spatial axes. We will map this relational space by examining a single image by Pelle Cass. To that end, it will be imperative to switch recursively from the mode of analysis, to the analysis of image, to the image itself and back again. With the mode of analysis we indicate a static type of visual examination of a digital reproduction of the digital file, now located in the printed environment of a book, or even as an electronic book. The analysis of the image itself provides more difficulty, because we cannot speak of *the* image. It is not only the continuous change of milieu (field or plane) which modulates the experience of the image, but also the continuous change of the beholder which changes the image. The temporal consequences of recognition in re-seeing cause the image to become its own context. After all, the image can never be unseen. Even the very anticipation of the image creates a pretext for seeing the image for the first time – not to mention the cultural, gender, age and other backgrounds which have already charged each viewer with a completely different set of perceptual sensitivities. Then there is the image itself, which can never be understood as anything other than *what it does* with the viewer at the specific moment that it is viewed. An image is immanent, it is not a representation of something else, just as every depiction is already a selection of all there is to a certain situation.

In his photo series 'Selected People', Cass exemplifies a 'fitness landscape' which itself resists reification. In the image called 'Shoppers 2, Quincy Market, Boston' (see Fig. 4.1) we can see a pedestrian surface which appears to be a square filled with a blend of North American people walking in a multitude of directions. Although the image reveals no information about the connecting streets or places, all present on the image seem to have a vague sense of bearing and seem to strive to stay on a specific track, albeit in a very casual way. There seems to be a balanced selection of persons in terms of gender, race and age, and there is no hint of violence, threat or misbehaviour. The picture was taken on a warm day, most of the 'inhabitants' of the image wear summery outfits, yet there are no distinct shadows, suggesting that the square was overcast during the time the photograph was taken. At first glance the image appears to be a 'natural' depiction of a mild afternoon in a leisurely environment – presumably an area near the Quincy Market in Boston, as the title suggests. The photo was not taken from an exceptional angle, but perhaps out of the window of an adjacent building. The artistic style does not seem to have an urge to draw much attention to itself, nor is there any trace of complicated procedure in terms of production or any specific technical requirements in order to make this image. The only anomaly that is at first detected is a seemingly predominant penchant for orangey-yellow colours in this city. Then there is the crowdedness of the place, which does not seem to bother any of the actors in the frame. Yet this first impression is deceptive.

On second inspection, the number of 'inhabitants' of the image is much smaller than at first appears to be the case. We observe that most of them are duplicated, triplicated or multiplied many times over. This immediately explains the previously detected anomalies. The colour dominancy is caused by the multiplication of a handful of people wearing outfits in the same hue. Secondly, it is clear that the deceptive mutual unawareness is caused by the fact that they were never in a crowd to begin with. They simply could not see each other at the *moment* they were there. Note that for many it is possible to see the other(s) from their position, but not at that particular moment, procuring a first step in what we have called space-time axis conversion. The method used here must consist of layering several images taken from the exact same angle and position, in which only a few of all the possible postures are actually used in the final product. This tells us that what we see is already a

Fig. 4.1 'Shoppers 2, Quincy Market, Boston' by Pelle Cass (2013)

selection of possibilities and cannot be mistaken for a non-constructed depiction. Even the colour scheme comes into question again. It could well be that the author of the post-production of the photograph only chose those with a certain tint of yellow for the image.

The author must also have made a second choice, to do with the 'credibility' of the image. If any of the people were superimposed, creating multiplications of themselves, or blending with others, that would immediately alarm us. Despite the fact that the image is already highly manipulated and heavily hyperrealistic, having people blend into each other would make it worse, which is a nice indication of the elasticity of our imagination. The author must have invested much care in 'giving everyone their own niche', and thus limiting all potential options dramatically. Once the woman with the trolley was featured more or less in the middle of the image, most subsequent options were already rendered impossible. As soon as all the photographer's 'free gifts' were placed (such as the girl with the ponytail facing herself or the woman with the sarong), the rest had to follow automatically. Note that we have not even begun to address the 'content' of the image itself, or its 'meaning' and connotations, and we will not do this either, as it is completely gratuitous. It does not matter if it was winter, or if the people were Polish, or if the woman with the trolley was placed first in the image. The image is 'industrially' produced, only following the drift of its inhabitants based on very pragmatic rules and principles. The image is not an image about subjects. Rather, it goes straight to the heart of the matter: the urban flow. And this is what makes this image so strong.

The (photo-)camera has often been seen as an extension of the eye, an artificial medium in the way McLuhan would describe an 'extension of man' (McLuhan 1964). The tool is used as a hylomorphic instrument to carve a soul out of the optical sensation. It enables us to witness the vivre and style of the artist in charge of the production. Cass, however, uses the instrument in a different and, we would claim, 'constructionist' way. The obvious quality of photography is to instantly freeze time and the quality of cinema is to bring us the movement image. Bodies are not described in movement, but instead the continuity of movement describes the object. In fact we could not even describe Cass as a photographer, not only because he manipulates his products in the way an editor of a film would do, but because he photographs literally everything. Yet it is the *selection* he makes and the intervals he chooses to put in between each section that defines what he does. We could call him the *intervalist*. The strength of this mix lies in the fact that Cass specifically uses some weaknesses of both photography and film. Photography does not excel in sequencing (at least not in one picture) and film does not shine in arresting time or in creating time out of space (but it does excel in the creation of space out of time). Thus Cass draws upon the weakest points of both these media to create this new world, the existing-yet-never-directly-visible momentum 'no longer recomposed from formal transcendental elements (poses), but from immanent material elements (sections)' (Deleuze 1986: 4).

Lesson One: Haptic Space

There are four good reasons for this lengthy exposure of the image. Firstly, the image shows us all the basic principles that drive and create the city in all its appearances. And the abstraction imposed upon it helps us to see different patterns and grids, attractors and repellers, drives and affects. We see the futurity, which holds the potential of multiple actualisations. Of all the physical, mental, economic, affective and physiologic flows, we see only a few highlighted. The selection is already made, that is why we are in no need of a narrative, for it does not matter why someone is moving from this spot to the next, or why some paths are more often chosen than others. What matters is the mere fact that it occurs and that we can witness it, following a single basic rule: no person can create the same space at the same time as someone else. Paths can be slightly diverted or temporally disrupted, affective encounters may cause slowing-downs or speeding-ups or path changes, but on a *metamodelling* level all will remain the same (Watson 2009).[2] We are witnessing a meta-stable system in progress, spatially compressed to enable temporal expansion. It is the description of space being produced by time. Time is the third dimension, not the fourth. Any shape of *chronos* stands to *kairos* as a Euclidean *optical* space stands to a *haptic* topological space. This means that the first movement creates a space that is forever occupied. This first space will set the agenda for the emergence of the next and so on. And even long after the first space has been vacated it will never be non-space again, it will always be charged by its own quasi-causality. It has dictated the next step and the next. *The square has never been empty.* And that shows itself most clearly in the editing of Pelle's image; once the first person is placed the whole grid snaps into place, a mild grid, but a grid nevertheless. The established relations are only ever *contingently obligatory*. Unlike those that are *logically necessary*, these relations are not conceptual but immanently causal (DeLanda 2006: 31).

Lesson Two: Absolute Survey

Secondly, there is the most pragmatic level. It is about the place itself: the square, which allows for a multitude of engagements. In our case this place is used primarily for transit, and a variety of destinations of the inhabitants of the image suggest that there are several options to connect different points. We can also see that there is a tendency towards the vertical crossing of the square but because of heavy manipulation we cannot be sure of that. Or can we? The applied abstraction serves as a filter, a stroboscopic filter. It only illuminates the situation with a certain interval, rendering deeper layers and patterns of flow visible by way of 'absolute survey' or the capacity to surpass the given (Massumi 2014: 36, 77). This Spinozian 'third kind of knowledge' precedes the emergence of the phenomenological 'aboutness' and its finite movement from one discrete part to another. The survey is absolute by virtue of its 'infinite speed' that reveals a consistency of the heterogeneous whole without reducing it to the parts (Deleuze 1984: 148). It shows the chatoyancy of the city.[3] In the image we can see two market stalls at the edge of the compass card. They were probably not allowed to be located in the middle of the place, as that would excessively disrupt flows. This type of intervention by municipal regulations is often mistakenly thought to be contributing to city making, while we all know that laws are always constructed ex post facto. A beautiful example of (a comment on) phallic thinking is the short film by John Smith *The Girl Chewing Gum* from 1976. As with our Boston image, it takes a while to realise that the 'instructions' given in the film are in fact descriptions of the scene that immediately follows. The film is edited in such a way that the sound precedes the image and the tone of the voice is set in an instructive mode, rather than a descriptive one.

Lesson Three: Energetics

Thirdly, the image addresses flows as a two-step sling. Let us assume for a moment that life-forms are driven by two forces and not dispute or discuss the nature or origin of these forces. The first layer could be called desire (aka aspiration, aka agency) and the second one affect. To be clear, this is not an attempt to classify affect as a secondary force, or to mimic Sylvan Tomkins' classification of putting affect into nine categories (Tomkins 1995). But could we regard 'autonomous' drives (as the need for food, sex, shelter, warmth, etc.) as being the deep attractors in Waddington's epigenetic landscape (Chreod) and name them *desires*, and could we take 'connected' drives (as interactions, stimuli, preferences) as specified forms of drives and call them *affects*?[4] In that case – in relation to Waddington – affects can be seen as accelerators, the differences that make a difference, and the desires can be seen as the strength of the attractions (Kwinter 2008: 40–5). The depth of attractor is desire, the angle of elevation or decline is affect. In this image we can see that some inhabitants have clear goals, they walk with a pragmatic purpose, coming from one place to go to another. Yet the exact path is never completely predictable; along the way there can be diversions, obstacles, interactions (positive or negative), attractions, collisions (or the avoidance thereof) and so forth. In other cases we can see people being driven by the need for interaction; they meander around the place in search for interaction (shopping, inspiration, 'das mittendrin sein', flirtation, perversion and so on). The need for interaction can be seen as a meta-drive as it provides us with the potential to resolve the myriad of specific drives (molecular perspectivism of drives, not of molar egos). Perhaps it is more precise to refer to it as an intra-action. In contrast to inter-action which presupposes molar individuals that *precede* their interaction, Karen Barad's neologism signifies the mutual constitution of 'entangled agencies' that remain *antecedent* and exterior to the *relata* (Barad 2007: 33).

Lesson Four: Posthumanism

We come to the fourth and final lesson that we can learn from the image: debunking a system of vanity and the megalomania of correlationism, or how to break through the anthropocentric frame of reference. The market had been there before the marketplace as such existed. This square is just an expression of the infra-action which resonates transindividually (Massumi 2015: 14). The wound was always here, we just lived to embody it (Deleuze 1990: 148).[5] The flow dictates its causes; roadside-restaurant as the ultimate new city, completely attuned to modern flows, converters, hubs, the parking lot. Post-surveillance, auto-surveillance, engendering, emplacement. Meta-narrative, sub-narrative. Religiosity, despairing, clairvoyance, abiogenesis. The voyeur, the *flâneur*. They all belong to *this* world. In his *Difference and Repetition* Deleuze gives due credit to his nemesis' achievement: 'Kant is the one who discovers the prodigious domain of the transcendental. He is the analogue of a great explorer – not of another world, but of the upper or lower reaches of this one' (Deleuze 1994: 135).[6] The transcenden*tal*, it must be underscored, is not transcendent but always a product of immanence or 'thisworldlyness' (Deleuze 2001: 25–33). For our purposes, it is worth remembering that Deleuze and Guattari tether transcendence to the State while making a strong connection between immanence and the City: '[Cities] develop a particular mode of deterritorialization that proceeds by immanence; they form a *milieu of immanence*' (Deleuze and Guattari 1994: 87). The irony of Pelle's image about flows is that it shows so clearly that the days of pilgrimage are over. The image comes to you, you don't need to go to the image.

Grades of Sense

There is arguably no greater influence upon architectural thinking than René Descartes and his metaphor of the ghost in the machine. The ecological psychologist Michael Turvey provides an updated version of this metaphor (Turvey 2004: 57). Nowadays, to establish a link to the outside world, the ghost has all the digital media at his disposal. Let us briefly revisit the three Cartesian 'grades of sense' as spelled out by Turvey. The first one is strictly physical and accessible through science in general and mechanics in particular. The second grade of sense is more challenging as it concerns *qualia*, or secondary qualities. It is hybrid, physical *and* mental. How do agitated molecules of carbon and oxygen become the experience of redness and warmth of colour? The answer to this (hard) question lies in probably the most influential scientific metaphor of all times, namely that the relationships between the two grades follow from the mere arrangement of the machine's organs every bit as naturally as the movements of a *clock* follow from the arrangements of its counterweights and wheels (Whitehead 1957: 32; Descartes 1985: 99–108). The third, mental grade of sense concerns the notions of formal systems and goes beyond the mechanistic conception just described. It took a few centuries for this quasi-rational symbol-manipulating process to catch on.

Before listing the influential assumptions originating in the seventeenth century, let us note that the current discourse around Speculative Realism is divided on the very issue of primacy of the first two grades of sense, derivative of the 'bifurcation of nature' that Alfred North Whitehead denounced as the most serious error of modern western thought (Whitehead 1957: 26–48). The editors of the recent *Speculations* issue on twenty-first-century aesthetics offer a helpful broad-brush picture of a new struggle between rationalism and empiricism within contemporary speculative philosophy in general and its take on aesthetics in particular:

> [F]or the contemporary rationalists, mathematics (Meillassoux) and science (Brassier) dictate the discourse on and the place of aesthetics within the larger framework of epistemology with the concomitant intent to hunt down any manifestation of the, in their view, illusory 'immediacy thesis'. The empiricists (Harman and Grant, but also Shaviro and Morton) in turn insist upon 'immediacy' and a theory of taste in disguise holding that we immediately taste something before we conceptually know it. (Askin et al. 2014: 29–30)

The authors concede that the dichotomy is too neat. Yet, it is symptomatic enough of the contrast between, on the one hand, the resilient seventeenth-century assumptions of inertness, context-independent parts and local (contiguous) cause and, on the other, the twenty-first-century hypotheses of self-organising matter, systems with irremovable impredicative loops and non-locality. Drawing upon Turvey, we will demonstrate that it is high time we dismantled the ghost-in-the-machine model so that neither the ghost nor the machine survives (Turvey 2004). For this we need to update our inadequate all-too-representational toolbox. There is no better testing (groundless) ground for the task than the City. As Guattari put it, 'the aesthetic rupture of discursivity is never passively experienced. It leads to heterogeneous levels which must be related to a heterogenesis' (Guattari 1987: 82–5).[7]

The Clock as the Image of Thought

Let us list the essential seventeenth-century mechanistic assumptions. First, *locality* dictates that all causes are local by contact. From the angle of aesthetics, the question is: what might be taken as the proximal, contiguous cause of some particular experience? Aesthetics is defined here in the most general sense of sensory or, *per negativum*, the opposite of anaesthetic.

Second, *matter* is passive and inert, lacking any morphogenetic capacity. If a thing itself moves, then one part of it must be the mover and another part that which is moved. It is in this way that the absence of self-cause or self-motion gets resolved. Here the ghost-in-the-machine becomes the unmoved mover.

Third is the *entailment* assumption, the legacy of Newton, who proposed the *single* entailment mode whereby the present entails the immediate future. In contrast to Aristotelian categories of causation, Newton holds that only an efficient cause is properly causal. Causal chains flow from parts to whole and never the other way around. This is the *predicative* direction, the way one writes computer programs. The lack of reflexivity effectively eliminates the possibility of *auto-catalysis* with interdependent parts. It eliminates a quasi-formal cause related to Deleuze and Guattari's 'exteriority of relations', or the relation that is exterior to its terms and as such presents 'a vital protest against principles' (Deleuze and Parnet 1987: 55).[8] There are two more (reductionist) assumptions that follow from the entailment assumption: the *component* and *superposition* assumptions. The former posits that parts are context-independent while the latter states that the whole is the sum of its parts. In spite of the inadequacy that the 'interiority of relations' suffers in the realm of biology and psychology, had it not been for these mechanistic hypotheses the whole enterprise of modern science would have been unimaginable. In the Deleuzian parlance the 'image of thought' expressive of this paradigm is the *clock*. In the context of this chapter, we would have to imagine the City as the Clock. If we take the clockwork city and break it into its constitutive parts, they retain their particular functions. In other words, synthesis becomes analysis in reverse. According to Turvey, the pure reversibility of putting together and taking apart prescribes both the ghost and the machine:

> The two assumptions of local contiguous cause and inert matter give us a prescribed ghost. Entailment is recursion in which the present, and only present, entails the immediate future. And, with context-independent components, analysis and synthesis are reciprocal and components entail

function. These give us the machine, they prescribe the machine [. . .] (Turvey 2004: 59)

What would be the 'thought without image' which rejects identity as the governing principle and instead embraces multiplicity, singularity and pure (non-dialectical) difference (Deleuze 1994: 132, 147)? Perhaps the hypotheses of *non*-locality and *active* matter taken together will suffice to proscribe the ghost, while *multiple* entailment modes and reflexivity with context-dependency will proscribe the machine (Turvey 2004). Of the two, the machine might turn out to be the tougher nut to crack. In the case of the city, the material, formal, efficient and final causes are not only indiscernible but also constantly mutating. The interacting parts produce the emergent distributed whole, which in turn constrains the parts. 'The parts compose the whole, which comprises the parts. The definition of what the parts are is dictated by the emergent distributed whole' (Turvey 2004: 64). Following the distinction which Deleuze appropriates from Henri Bergson, one ought to distinguish between the *actual* traits of a physical system and the *virtual* – real but abstract – thresholds at which it either adopts or changes those traits.

Cracks in the Street

It should be obvious by now that not all causes are by contact. Already in the mid-1950s Gibson challenged psychological orthodoxies by claiming that perception did not require a simultaneous composite in the brain, a representation (Gibson 1986). Moreover, amodal and ambulant perception (of the indiscernible) is not an exception but the 'rule'.[9] In other words, we do perceive the imperceptible (prehension). Life-forms perceive potentials (for action) directly and never re-emerge as self-identical in becoming. They respond to perceptual *signs*, not to causal impulses (Bains 2006: 63). As far as Gibson is concerned, the real problem is not the presupposed poverty of stimulation but the poverty of entailment, given that *not* all potentiality is (already) an accrued value. Georges Canguilhem cautions against facile analogies:

Clearly, an organism has a greater range of activity than a machine. It is less bound by purposiveness and more open to potentialities. Every aspect and every movement of the machine is calculated; and the working of the machine confirms how each calculation holds up to certain norms, measures or estimates; whereas the living body functions according to experience. Life is experience, meaning improvisation, acting as circumstances permit; life is tentative in every respect. (Canguilhem 1992: 58)

It is worth pointing out that non-local causation extends beyond the psychological register or existential grasp. It is coextensive with the lived experience but not reducible to it. It is a feature of all *open* hetero-poietic matter/energy systems as opposed to closed deterministic ones which exist only under laboratory conditions and in digital simulations. It is the feature of the impersonal non-organic life.

Vibrant matter as the second 'ghostbuster' is equally pertinent for its ability to wake architects from their correlationist slumber (Bennett 2010). By endowing matter with agency of its own, the unbearable narcissism of the anthropos and the bad habit of hylomorphism start to evaporate. Self-organising matter does not need the imposition of a transcendent form to organise its putative chaos. The way Rem Koolhaas contrasted two paradigmatic cities is telling in this respect:

> Paris can only become more Parisian – it is already on its way to becoming hyper-Paris, a polished caricature. There are exceptions: London – its only identity a lack of clear identity – is perpetually becoming even less London, more open, less static. (Koolhaas 1995: 1248)

Finally we turn to the *machinism* of impredicativities, which is not to be confused with either organicism or mechanicism, agency or structure. We ought not to separate the doer from the deed, as the Nietzschean maxim goes. Complex systems, such as cities, contain impredicativities that cannot be removed. The term was introduced by the founder of non-linear dynamics, Henri Poincaré. Put simply, you cannot offer an understanding of actual parts in the absence of a virtual whole. Simpler still, *what is defined participates in its own definition* (Wolfendale 2014: 246). Yet the abduction problem seems to have gone unnoticed in Parametricist quarters, judging by their synoptic ambition to be achieved through simulation. In the words of the architect Ingebor Rocker, '[t]he formal exuberance characteristic of parametricism's architecture and urban planning scenarios pretends to cope with socie-ties' and life's complexities, while in fact they are at best expressions thereof, empty gestures of a form-obsessed and strangely under-complex approach to architecture and urbanity' (Rocker 2011: 97). Newtonian syntactic formalism is simply not abstract enough when it comes to complex systems. As we have argued, simple systems can be captured predicatively, complex systems cannot.[10] The most important logician of our times, Kurt Gödel, proved conclusively that one can never convert impredicative into predicative. It is not the result of the alleged limit of our minds, Turvey cautions. It is the limit of predicative perspectives on entailment: 'Predication without impredication is not powerful enough;

syntax without semantics is too feeble for understanding explanation and entailment' (Turvey 2004: 61). To put it laconically, the digital can be generalised (logically formalised) while the analogue is always singular, i.e. eco-logical. In the words of the semiologist Paul Bains:

> [U]nivocal, semiotic reality – the reality of experience – is not reducible to the mind's own workings (e.g., as in the Kantian synthesis) nor is it to that of a prejacent external physical world in which the mind has no part. It is a limitless interface where the line between what is and what is not, independent of interpretative activity, is a constantly shifting [asignifying] semiotic process. (Bains 2006: 68)

No wonder Deleuze insisted that the smallest unit of reality is the assemblage, *agencement* (Deleuze and Parnet 1987: 51). 'Thinking with AND [. . .] instead of thinking for IS: empiricism has never had another secret' (Deleuze and Parnet 1987: 57). The assemblage preserves certain symmetries and breaks others. Meta-stability rests on both difference *and* repetition in the relation of mutual determination. This is not an epistemological principle, but an ontological one. If the seventeenth-century concepts have given us remarkable discoveries, the next revolution based upon impredicativity will be nothing like what we have seen before (Rosen 2000). It is key to most phenomena of the universe, not the few we have tackled thus far. The extension and comprehension of a concept are inversely proportional. The more specified the concept, the fewer the objects subsumed by it. By contrast to the vertical (transcendentally organised) State, we will never know conclusively what the horizontal city can do (Deleuze and Guattari 1994: 89). It is not about bringing all sorts of things under a single concept of the city, but about relating each city to the variables that determine its mutation, its becoming (Deleuze 1995: 31). After the proscription of the a priori, the prescription of cartography becomes unavoidable. The non-mimetic mapping of affective capacities and virtual tendencies renders visible a condition 'that is no wider than what it conditions, that changes itself with the conditioned and determines itself in each case along with what it determines' (Deleuze 2006: 50). Deleuze has never had another formula except for the $N - 1$. It is an ecological formula that spells out 'subtract the meta-signifier'. Bring into existence. Do not judge (Deleuze 1997: 135). That is *the* injunction of immanence.

Notes

1. A dynamic genesis moves from an encounter with intensity in sensation to the thinking of virtual Ideas, while a static genesis moves from the virtual Idea through an intensive individuation process to an actual entity.
2. By contrast to a scientific paradigm, Guattari characterised his metamodelling activity as an 'ethico-aesthetic paradigm'.
3. Cat's eye effect.
4. This neologism of Conrad Waddington's denotes the necessary path of any becoming. It is a 'figure of time'. As Sanford Kwinter explains, a Chreod refers to an invisible but not imaginary feature in an invisible but not imaginary landscape on which a developing form gathers the information and influence necessary for it to make itself what it is.
5. Deleuze's reference to Bousquet's poem whereby the wound becomes not an effect but precisely a quasi-cause.
6. Deleuze referred to his book on Kant as 'a book on an enemy'.
7. On the issue of asignifying rupture, see Hauptmann and Radman (2014).
8. Autocatalytic process produces more of what is there. Autocatalysis drives pattern formation by making components interdependent. It is thus causal in the formal, not efficient, sense.
9. Amodal perception is a term which describes the full perception of a physical structure when it is only partially perceived; for example, a table will be perceived as a complete volumetric structure even if only part of it is visible. See Noë (2002).
10. In abductive reasoning, unlike in deductive reasoning, the premises do not guarantee the conclusion.

References

Askin, R., Hägler, A. and Schweighauser, P. (2014) 'Introduction: aesthetics after the speculative turn', in R. Askin, P. Ennis, A. Hägler and P. Schweighauser (eds), *Speculations V: Aesthetics in the 21st Century*. New York: Punctum Books, pp. 6–38.

Bains, P. (2006) *The Primacy of Semiosis: An Ontology of Relations*. Toronto: University of Toronto Press.

Barad, K. (2007) *Meeting the Universe Halfway: Quantum Physics and the Entanglement of Matter and Meaning*. Durham, NC: Duke University Press.

Bennett, J. (2010) *Vibrant Matter: A Political Ecology of Things*. Durham, NC: Duke University Press.

Braidotti, R. (2010) 'Elemental complexity and relational vitality: the relevance of nomadic thought for contemporary science', in P. Gaffney (ed.), *The Force of the Virtual: Deleuze, Science, and Philosophy*. Minneapolis: University of Minnesota Press.

Canguilhem, G. (1992) 'Machine and organism', in J. Crary and S. Kwinter (eds), *Incorporations*, trans. M. Cohen and R. Cherry. New York: Zone Books, pp. 45–69.

Colebrook, C. (2014) *Sex After Life: Essays on Extinction Vol.2*, at http://openhu manitiespress.org/essays-on-extinction-vol2.html (accessed 7 June 2015).

DeLanda, M. (2006) *A New Philosophy of Society: Assemblage Theory and Social Complexity*. New York: Continuum.

Deleuze, G. (1984) *Kant's Critical Philosophy: The Doctrine of the Faculties*, trans. H. Tomlinson and B. Habberjam. Minneapolis: University of Minnesota Press.

Deleuze, G. (1986) *Cinema 1: The Movement-Image*, trans. H. Tomlinson and B. Habberjam. London: Athlone.

Deleuze, G. (1990) *The Logic of Sense*, trans. M. Lester. London: Athlone.

Deleuze, G. (1994) *Difference and Repetition*, trans. P. Patton. New York: Columbia University Press.

Deleuze, G. (1995) *Negotiations, 1972–1990*, trans. M. Joughin. New York: Columbia University Press.

Deleuze, G. (1997) *Essays Critical and Clinical*, trans. D. W. Smith and M. Greco. Minneapolis: University of Minnesota Press.

Deleuze, G. (2001) *Pure Immanence: Essays on A Life*, trans. A. Boyman. New York: Zone Books.

Deleuze, G. (2006) *Nietzsche and Philosophy*, trans. H. Tomlinson. New York: Columbia University Press.

Deleuze, G. and Guattari, F. (1994) *What Is Philosophy?*, trans. H. Tomlinson and G. Burchell. New York: Columbia University Press.

Deleuze, G. and Guattari, F. (2003) *Anti-Oedipus: Capitalism and Schizophrenia*, trans. R. Hurley, M. Seem and H. R. Lane. Minneapolis: University of Minnesota Press.

Deleuze, G. and Parnet, C. (1987) *Dialogues*, trans. H. Tomlinson and B. Habberjam. New York: Columbia University Press.

Descartes, R. (1985) 'Treatise on Man', in *The Philosophical Writings of Descartes, Vol. 1*, trans. J. Cottingham, et al. Cambridge: Cambridge University Press, pp. 99–108.

Evans, R. (2003) 'Towards architecture', in *Translation from Drawing to Buildings*. London: AA Documents 2, pp. 11–33.

Gibson, J. J. (1986) *The Ecological Approach to Visual Perception*. Hillsdale, NJ: Lawrence Erlbaum Associates.

Guattari, F. (1987) 'Cracks in the street', trans. A. Gibault and J. Johnson, in *Flash Art*, No. 135, pp. 82–5.

Guattari, F. (2008) *The Three Ecologies*, trans. I. Pindar and P. Sutton. London: Continuum.

Guattari, F. (2013) *Schizoanalytic Cartographies*, trans. A. Goffey. London: Bloomsbury.

Hauptmann, D. and Radman, A. (eds) (2014) 'Asignifying semiotics: or how to paint pink on pink', *Footprint*, 14, at http://www.footprintjournal.org/issues/show/asignifying-semiotics-or-how-to-paint-pink-on-pink (accessed 7 June 2015).

Koolhaas, R. (1995) 'Generic city', in OMA and B. Mau (eds), *S, M, L, XL*. New York: Monicelli Press, pp. 1238–64.

Kwinter, S. (2008) 'A discourse on method (for the proper conduct of reason and the search for efficacity in design)', in R. Geiser (ed.), *Explorations in Architecture: Teaching, Design, Research*. Basel: Birkhäuser.

McLuhan, M. (1964) *Understanding Media: The Extensions of Man*. New York: McGraw-Hill.

Massumi, B. (2011) 'Perception attack: the force to own time', in J. Elliott and D. Attridge (eds), *Theory After Theory*. New York: Routledge, pp. 75–89.

Massumi, B. (2014) *What Animals Teach Us about Politics*. Durham, NC: Duke University Press.

Massumi, B. (2015) *The Power at the End of the Economy*. Durham, NC: Duke University Press.

Noë, A. (2002) *Is the Visual World a Grand Illusion?* Thorverton: Imprint Academic.

Odling-Smee, J. (2007) 'Niche inheritance: a possible basis for classifying multiple inheritance systems in evolution', *Biological Theory*, 2 (3): 276–89.

Rocker, I. M. (2011) 'Apropos parametricism: if, in what style should we build?', *Log*, 21: 89–101.

Rosen, R. (2000) *Essays on Life Itself*. New York: Columbia University Press.

Tomkins, S. (1995) *Exploring Affect: The Selected Writings of Sylvan Tomkins*, ed. E. V. Demos. Cambridge: Cambridge University Press.

Turvey, M. T. (2004) 'Theory of brain and behaviour in the 21st century: no ghost, no machine', in *Language and Cognition 2003–2004*, University Seminar #681, New York: Columbia University.

Watson, J. (2009) *Guattari's Diagramatic Thought: Writing Between Lacan and Deleuze*. New York: Continuum.

Wexler, B. (2013) 'Neuroplasticity, culture and society', in A. De Boever and W. Neidich (eds), *The Psychopathologies of Cognitive Capitalism: Part One*. Berlin: Archive Books.

Whitehead, A. N. (1957) *The Concept of Nature*. Ann Arbor: Ann Arbor Books.

Wolfendale, P. (2014) *Object-Oriented Philosophy: The Noumenon's New Clothes*. Falmouth: Urbanomic.

Chapter 5

Laboratory Urbanism in Schladming

Magnus Eriksson and Karl Palmås

On a ski slope in the Austrian Alps, tourists and semi-professional skiers are making their way down the slope. Seven of the skiers are, however, on a special mission. The only thing that sets them apart from rest of the crowd is the ski goggles they are wearing; they are donning a new generation of goggles, recently released by a leading brand. These so-called smart goggles feature a built-in screen in the bottom right of the visual area, and are currently directing the seven skiers along a navigational route.

At the bottom of the slope, a team of engineers are fiddling with the wifi connection of their server, monitoring a stream of real-time data coming from the seven skiers. There are many factors that the engineers are trying to keep track of – the wifi and 3G connections, the GPS reception and the logging of the backend server. At the end of the run, the skiers are given a questionnaire by the team. They are also invited to do a short interview. The experiment conducted by the engineering team is investigating the user needs and requirements for the development of new smart goggle apps – a product that has only recently become a potential commercial reality.

The experiment is one of several at various venues, part of an EU-funded initiative. The project aims to spur innovation in culture and tourism-related services, using new media and Internet technology. Apart from this test run, the experiment also consists of co-creation workshops with a focus group of potential users and a broader online survey to investigate business models and pricing, as well as meetings with local business stakeholders. The objective is to search for desirable uses for the goggles, be it weather information, ski-lift queuing times, special offers from retailers and restaurants in the area and a live twitter feed. As it turns out, the navigation feature mentioned above is the one that seems to strike a chord among the test subjects (see Fig. 5.1).

What is at stake in a contemporary politics of the urban? From a classical politico-economic perspective, urbanisation may be viewed as that

Fig. 5.1 From a would-be consumer's point of view: navigation app in ski goggles (photograph by Evolaris)

which currently absorbs the surplus product of capitalists (Harvey 2008: 25). Here, a number of related problematics come into view: the vested interests that emerge from the inflated valuations of urban property; the physical displacement of the underprivileged and marginalised; the fact that 'quality of urban life has become a commodity' (31). Such a line of inquiry also sheds light on the urban governance arrangements that make these processes possible – be it the rise of post-political 'choreographies of participation' (Swyngedouw 2005) or the shift from managerialism to entrepreneurialism (Harvey 1989). This chapter will to some extent continue this investigation into how urban space is engineered in ways that facilitate 'public-private partnerships', rendering the cityscape a space of speculation rather than of rational planning (7). However, using a Deleuze-inspired 'spatial politics of affect' (Thrift 2004) as the point of departure, the chapter will explore a tendency towards a *laboratory urbanism*, and thus proposes an alternative framing of the speculative element in contemporary urban centres.

In this argument, the Austrian city of Schladming – and its participation in 'Experimedia', the EU-funded research project introduced above – serve as a 'vanguard' or 'best practice' case that signals the direction of general tendencies within urban planning as well as within management thought. As the chapter will show, these tendencies are present in the wider discourse on 'Smart Cities', on urban test-beds, on so-called 'design thinking' and within recent experimental approaches to innovation and entrepreneurship. In the most advanced cases, these developments are expressed in Smart Cities such as Songdo, Korea – a city built from scratch using such experimental principles. In such cases, techno-scientific knowledge production is not about generating knowledge 'about' the city, but is part of the city's very performativity. Drawing upon Nigel Thrift's (2004) work on the spatial politics of affect, the chapter will depict Schladming as a tourism space in which the main challenge is to manage the affects of visitors – before, during, and after the visit to the city. Tourism is thus presented as not primarily related to mobility but to a special way of relating to materialities where matter and space are experienced as charged with affective potential. Following this point, Schladming will also be presented as a place that utilises the infrastructure for such affect management for laboratory purposes. The chapter seeks to show how the experiment outlined above chimes with trends within the scholarship on design, entrepreneurship and innovation, and will adopt Deleuze's reading of Simondon to re-articulate the stakes of the laboratory urbanism currently emerging in the context of what Thrift (2008) has characterised as a 'vitalist capitalism'.

The Affective Register of Schladming

Why have city officials in Schladming decided to turn their city into an experimental space? Arguably, the concept of 'affect' may take us some way towards an answer. The past decade has seen a surge of interest in the uses of the term within social theory, and this term acts as a productive starting point in an exploration of what is at stake on the slopes of Schladming. The rationale for participating in Experimedia is that innovations in information technology may shape and capture the affects of visitors. These technologies can also cut the costs of maintaining these affects. What, then, do we mean by affect? In an attempt to rectify the scholarly neglect of the affective register of cities, Thrift (2004) proposes that cities can be construed as 'roiling maelstroms of affect' (57). The reference to Deleuze in his argument is explicit. For Thrift, Deleuze – more specifically, his 'ethological spin on Spinoza's assertion that things are never separable from their relations to the world' (62) – constitutes one out of four possible translations of affect. Quoting Deleuze's (1988: 127–8) discussion on how a body can be mapped – as longitudes of relations of momentum and rest, and as latitudes of affect (see also Deleuze and Guattari 1988: 260–1) – Thrift thus subscribes to the idea of affect as a capacity for interaction between bodies; the idea that emerged in Deleuze's project of 'retrieving affect from Spinoza's *Ethics*', correcting the 'mutilating' misreadings of his text (Seigworth 2005: 160). This understanding of affect is closely linked with Deleuze's treatment of becoming. Paul Patton states:

> Defining bodies in terms of the affects of which they are capable is equivalent to defining them in terms of the relations into which they can enter with other bodies, or in terms of their capacities for engagements with the powers of other bodies. In *A Thousand Plateaus*, what Deleuze and Guattari call processes of 'becoming' are precisely such engagements with the powers of other bodies. This is the reason for their assertion that 'affects are becomings'. (Patton 2000: 78)

In other words, to speak of the affective register of cities is also to speak of bodies as becomings in an urban setting. What new political stakes are raised by placing focus on such becomings? Thrift points to changes in the form of politics – contemporary political mobilisation tends to be more ad hoc and contextual – and to *mediatisation* in the form of an increasing pervasiveness of screens (Thrift 2004: 65). He also points to the advent of new technologies, which render the 'small spaces and times' in which affect thrives visible and enlarged. In the course of this process, these spaces of affect have become subject to manipulation and experimentation (66). Much of his interest lies in an 'undiscovered country' which 'has gradually hoved into view', namely 'the country of the "half-second delay"' (67). He thus points to the political issues that emerge when we consider the fact that body anticipation precedes cognition – and the concomitant tendency for this half-second delay to be exploited by various agencies. Following Thrift, this chapter will explore the work that goes into designing corporeal experiences, as well as the instrumentalist modes of charting the capacities that emerge when composing new relations between bodies. It will, however, steer clear of the more specific neuroscientific or psychobiological disputes that have rendered the 'turn to affect' subject to recent criticisms (Leys 2011; Wetherell 2015).

An attentiveness to the affective register and an understanding of experience; a pervasiveness of screens and a conscious engineering of small spaces and times – these themes are all represented in the Schladming case. The Experimedia project's involvement in Schladming aims to supply the city with a technical platform that provides computing power and experimental data logging, as well as organisational structures and access to test subjects (see Fig. 5.2). This generates an ability to test new technologies and evaluate how they are taken up by Schladming visitors.

The documentation of the Experimedia project (Binder 2014: 41)

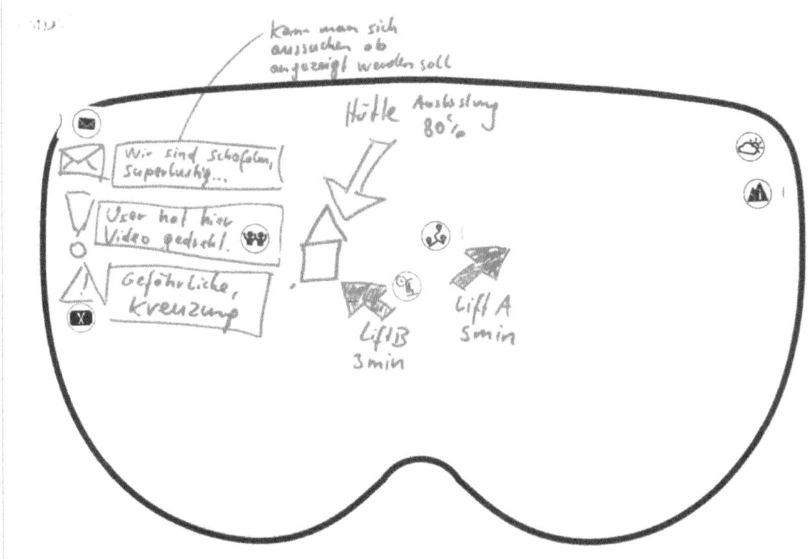

The figure sketch contains handwritten notes (in German):

> Kann man sich aussuchen ob angezeigt werden soll
>
> Hütte · Auslastung 80%
>
> Wir sind Schofeln, Superlustig...
>
> User hat hier Video gedreht!
>
> Gefährliche Kreuzung
>
> Lift A 5 min
>
> Lift B 3 min

```
05-02-2014;11-01-32;47.369858;13.717761;1767;gps
05-02-2014;11-01-37;47.369858;13.718019;1775;gps
05-02-2014;11-01-38;47.369858;13.718019;1775;Navigation-Duration;240109
05-02-2014;11-01-38;47.369858;13.718019;1775;Weather-Start;1391594498135
05-02-2014;11-01-38;47.369858;13.718061;1776;Weather-Duration;384
05-02-2014;11-01-38;47.369858;13.718061;1776;Community-Start;1391594498520
05-02-2014;11-01-38;47.369858;13.718061;1776;Community-Duration;191
05-02-2014;11-01-38;47.369858;13.718061;1776;Hospitality-Start;1391594498712
05-02-2014;11-01-39;47.369858;13.718125;1776;Hospitality-Duration;614
05-02-2014;11-01-39;47.369858;13.718125;1776;LiftInfo-Start;1391594499328
05-02-2014;11-01-39;47.369858;13.718125;1776;LiftInfo-Duration;566
05-02-2014;11-01-39;47.369858;13.718125;1776;Individual-Start;1391594499897
05-02-2014;11-01-42;47.369827;13.718276;1778;gps
05-02-2014;11-01-47;47.369797;13.718554;1781;speed;14
05-02-2014;11-01-47;47.369797;13.718554;1781;gps
```

Fig. 5.2 Getting close to users: workshop sketches and log files (photograph by Evolaris)

suggests that this set-up may solve a particular kind of chicken-and-egg situation: how does one make sure that there is a market for smart ski goggles, as well as desirable applications for these goggles? The EU funding enables small companies to engage with an ecosystem of public and private stakeholders in Schladming. Thus firms within resort management, retail, tourism and marketing can explore the potential benefits of different future consumer propositions. The experiment described in the vignette led this ecosystem of commercial actors to conclude that the optimum solution is to offer smart ski goggles as a rental service. By experimenting promptly, Schladming will be the first movers in this market, ahead of the competing resorts. This, city officials believe, is crucial when alternative tourist destinations are only a few mouse-clicks away. Using the urban space as a laboratory has enabled Schladming to enhance the experience of tourists, and to brand itself as a ski resort at the forefront of innovation. This, in turn, facilitates the emergence of an entrepreneurial ecosystem around the city.

Aside from our own (*etic*) use of the term affect (briefly sketched above), the Schladming case is also to be understood in relation to how 'affect' and 'affective' are used as *emic* terms – how they are mobilised within Experimedia. In the documentation of the project, the term is used in relation to testing methodology, more specifically so-called 'Quality of Experience' reporting. The tests conducted are thus meant to explore 'the subjective perception of an individual within a specific usage context considering cognitional, affective and emotional dimensions' (Gabriel et al. 2012: 9). This interest, in turn, reflects a wider discussion on how tourism management is to engage with information technology.

A simple view of the relation between information technology and affect within tourism would state that lack of information produces frustrated tourists who are missing out on opportunities to experience various tourist offers. However, since the consumption of tourism takes place after the purchase which is transacted without the ability of the consumer to inspect the offer, tourism is a special form of industry that has a particular relation to information technologies (Buhalis 1998). Meta-information about the experience is crucial for the decision to consume, as tourists-to-be browse websites and social media before making the decision where to go. They seek out information, imagine possible experiences and watch other people's affective responses to a destination. The affective experience of being tourists has already begun then and there, well before they have even left their home.

Furthermore, the quality of the tourist experience is defined by the interaction between the supplier and the consumer. This interaction *is* the tourist experience itself, not something external to it (Morella 2006). ICTs (information and communication technologies) are not operating as mere informers about the tourist experience; they form an integral part of the experience itself. If a certain, ICT-mediated element of the tourist experience is perceived as troublesome and disturbing, the whole experience is perceived as such. On the contrary, if the experience of getting the information is perceived as meaningful in itself – such as asking a local for the best restaurant in newly acquired German instead of looking it up online – this provides value to the experience. The act of seeking information and unlocking a destination by learning more about it as one goes along, discovering things through experience – this forms a part of the construction of a narrative that makes the tourist experience meaningful and valuable (Leontidou 2006). The problem is, however, that the technologies meant to facilitate this – from booking systems to navigation and recommendation tools – are often the source of negative affects. Tourism is thus always a risky business. The same activity can be both enjoyed and despised based on a body's disposition. Real-time response and ability to match a suitable experience with the affective register is thus crucial. A tourist can quickly change their mind and try out another experience – one which may suit their current mood better – and the experienced supplier needs to register this change and have other offers ready. Thus, in a sense, the tourist city cannot, strictly speaking, engineer affects. The tourist city can only provide a space in which affect evolves and prevent disruptions to this process.

This complex relation between tourism and technology, where the supplier can never know when technology enhances or disturbs the tourist experience, is the motivation for Schladming to engage in projects that allow quick iterations of experiments, trying out different technology-based enhancements of the tourist experience. The technical platform and the living lab approach of Experimedia allow prototype technologies to be tested by 'real' users in an early stage of development that would otherwise require large infrastructural investments. Experimedia allows experiments to fail and adapt at an early stage of the development by letting the affective responses of visitors to Schladming determine their success or failure.

One key aspect of the Schladming experiment is that it is not a simple evaluation of an existing design. Rather, it seeks to come up with the optimal design for a near-future implementation of a technology – one that would respond to user needs and desires. Great efforts are made to ensure that the potential users involved in the focus group and test runs understand that they have to see beyond the current implementation of the technology. They must, in the language of design professionals, see the technology in the context of a 'design space' that includes a great number of potential uses and implementations. Tests can backfire when users have preconceived expectations of a technology, often gained from tech journalism or sci-fi. In the case of the Schladming experiment, a focus group aiming to brainstorm potential user interface designs had to be re-thought, since the users assumed that the smart ski goggles contained a fighter cockpit-style Heads-Up Display seamlessly projected across the surface of the glasses. In reality, the technology was far less glamorous and the screen was just a small display seen by a user when glancing down to the bottom right.

In fact, the navigational feature mentioned above was deemed a success precisely because the users were able to see beyond the current implementation of the feature. Though the tested application was quite limited and often failed to work due to bad connection, the test subjects saw the potential use of this feature, should it be properly implemented. This suggests that there are many factors that can affect the evaluation from a user – their mood at the time of the evaluation, if they are tired from the day before, if they would rather be sightseeing that day instead of skiing the slope. Since the tourist experience is based on dynamic consumer needs governed by affect in the moment of consumption (Morella 2006), it can be very hard to formulate any kind of objective measure of the potential success of a product or service. Nevertheless, the evolving user testing practices increasingly strive to control for such factors.

So where does this attentiveness to the affective register lead urban planning? It is clear here that the role of the curator or the designer is a better metaphor than the modernist notion of engineering (of affect). The designer must play 'the cautious Prometheus' (Latour 2008) who cannot simply dictate what affects are produced in a functional way; the designer has to provide for the self-actualisation of affects by the tourist/customer, although at the same time steering this process towards valoralisable activities. The notion of care as a socio-technical construct is also actualised in the tourist situation. Care involves a constant monitoring of the state of some entity, and the constant adaption and modulation of it and its environment. Nevertheless, it also involves a recognition of this entity as an active and autonomous being with its own ability to act in the world based on sensing the environment. All of these factors underscore the point of referring to the politics of affect as a form of microbiopolitics (Thrift 2004): in order not to 'disrupt' the life of the governed object, the process of governing must be subtle and self-limiting (Foucault 2008: 16). Given that this is a new art of government, Thrift (2004: 71) calls for an investigation of such microbiopolitics – one 'which understands the kind of biological-cum-cultural gymnastics that takes place in this realm'. Heeding this call, the next section will explore a special form of such microbiopolitics. This does not operate on the half-second delay that Thrift mentions, but in a different space – the space of non-actualised products and services alluded to above.

Laboratory Urbanism and Virtualisation

We have already seen how Schladming hopes to become more attractive to visitors, seeking to use ICTs for affective rather than informational purposes. However, the argument has also shown that the city is fashioning itself as a place for experimentation and innovation. As a part of this effort, Schladming enters partnerships with external partners who are attracted by a technology platform that allows entrepreneurs to speculatively test the projected profitability of new business concepts. In other words, Schladming is not solely engaged in the engineering of affect; it is simultaneously engaged in the cultivation of commercial inventiveness. This chimes with a wider development in the contemporary economy. Nigel Thrift (2006) sketches this tendency in relation to new ways of managing corporate R&D (research and development) processes. Judging by the recent trends within innovation management, a 're-invention of invention' seems to be underway. A new set of corporate innovation practices are being institutionalised by 'an increasingly sophisticated corporate vanguard' (280) that spearheads the development of a vitalist capitalism. This, he states, should be seen in the context of 'a long-term profits squeeze', leaving corporations scrambling to increase 'the rate of innovation and invention through the acceleration of connective mutation' (281). In line with this development, they are moving away from the corporate R&D laboratories established during the twentieth century and focus instead on 'open innovation' outside the confines of the corporate hierarchy. By trying to 'get close' to users and communities of practitioners, corporations may find ways of turning this proximity into new commodities. Hence the orchestration of experimental situations in the everyday lives of users. Given the efforts to mobilise the affective register of cities, urban spaces are well suited for conducting such experiments.

The idea of turning physical sites into test-beds has also made it onto the EU research agenda. Indeed, it forms a part of its Future Internet research, which aims to make Europe a leader in the next-generation, media-intense Internet. This research agenda features programs like FIRE – Future Internet Research and Experimentation – which allows researchers to do large-scale 'virtual' testing of new technologies, such as cloud computing and high-bandwidth services. It also features ENoLL – the European Network of Living Labs – which coordinates a number of small-scale, real-life test and experimentation environments, allowing users and producers to co-create innovations. Here, user inputs come in the form of co-design workshops, focus groups, user experience studies and other methods to try out prototypes together with users. Schladming, as designed by Experimedia, combines the 'test-bed' approach of FIRE with an approach inspired by living labs, inasmuch as it constitutes *both* a large-scale *and* a real-life environment.

As highlighted in the previous section, tests like the one carried out on the Schladming slope are not an evaluation of an actual, existing design. It is *concepts*, not particular *actualisations* of such concepts, that are explored. Again, the Experimedia approach encapsulates a general tendency in the contemporary economy. The heuristics of testing would-be products is in line with the 'rapid prototyping' imperative of 'design thinking' – a concept that has become exceptionally influential within contemporary business thought (Brown 2008). Similarly, such speculative testing is standard procedure within the 'lean startup' movement (Ries 2011). Closely aligned with Thrift's arguments regarding the rationales for the 're-invention of invention', today's entrepreneurs seek to minimise development costs by testing business ideas before they become actual products. Tests are conducted by 'dummy' products that simulate a potential product, thus allowing the entrepreneur to explore the preferences and desires of would-be customers. Such experimentation is conducted in a speedy and iterative fashion; the results from the monitored tests are used to construct the next, slightly mutated, version of the product-to-be. This development implies that a start-up is no longer construed as a company, in the traditional sense of the term. Rather, it is seen as – in the words of entrepreneurship guru Steve Blank – a 'search for a repeatable and scalable business model'.

There is thus a gravitation towards a 'virtualisation' in how entrepreneurship is imagined and practised. Entrepreneurs no longer conceive of competition as something that primarily concerns actual products. Instead, competition is thought to be played out in a space of non-actualised commodities. This tendency within contemporary business – and in the urban governance that facilitates such enterprising endeavours – represents something different from the entrepreneurialism described by Harvey (1989: 7). First, in the case of Schladming, PPPs (public-private partnerships) have morphed into PPPPs – the European Commission description of living labs as 'public-private-*people* partnerships' that facilitate 'user-driven open innovation'. Secondly, Harvey's 'speculative construction of place' (1989: 8) is no longer solely related to financial risks and rewards – it also concerns the speculative orchestration of urban experiments, causing cityscapes to be populated by dummy products that probe the potential desires of would-be consumers.

A Deleuze-inspired take on the political economy of this laboratory urbanism may start from an assessment of how this form of capitalism intervenes in the universal history of desiring-production. In the laboratory urbanism of Schladming, the 'production of productions' and the 'production of recording processes' (Deleuze and Guattari 1983: 4) are re-engineered. The connecting and breaking of flows, as well as the registering of 'hot spots' of intensity that are subject to reactivation (Bonta and Protevi 2004: 77), are sped up. While there are previous accounts of how 'virtualism' relates to political economy (cf. Carrier and Miller 1998), it is tempting to describe the Schladming case by invoking the Deleuzian virtual: the frantic activity of capitalism – the ever increasing flow of differenciated products and services – now seems to be boosted by the invention of techniques that serve to harness the creativity of virtual differentiation (Deleuze 1994: 206–7). The next section will interrogate that proposition in further detail.

Why, then, is the term 'vitalist capitalism' warranted as a description of these business practices? For one, design thinking and the lean start-up movement have introduced a certain amount of bio-mimicry in how entrepreneurs and managers think about design, innovation and creativity. For instance, the notion of 'design space' – a design thinking term, mentioned above – is inspired by Dennett's (1995) use of the term. Thus user tests are seen as the equivalent of the evolutionary algorithm by which 'design space' is probed (Korhonen and Hassi 2009). Similarly, Deleuze's adoption of Simondon's biophilosophy can be a powerful tool when outlining the stakes of Schladming's laboratory urbanism. The city is re-engineered as a device for the exploration of the 'pre-individual' realm (Simondon 1989), whose affective potentials are charted by iterative testing of pre-product concepts. In many ways, the modus operandi of this reinvented product development seems to mirror Simondon's account of individuation through transduction: a germinal idea is allowed to progressively propagate itself, gradually yielding a structured product. Such a structure, however, is only actualised as a commodity if it manages to connect virtualities in the pre-individual level – if it manages to connect entities in a manner that releases new 'assembling, assembled, desire' (Deleuze and Guattari 1988: 399) This transduction is ultimately a matter of information transfer, and Schladming's ICT infrastructure constitutes the material medium that facilitates this transfer.

In keeping with this conception of a vitalist capitalism, the practices enabled in Schladming can be compared with how contemporary agribusiness is, in the words of *The Economist* magazine (2009), 'turbo-charging Mendel' when breeding new products. Agricultural corporations are now capable of predicting the likely properties of a plant that would grow from a seed by analysing its DNA in laboratories. This allows them to plant only the most promising seeds, and the process is repeated with the seeds that those plants go on to produce. This practice, however, reflects the type of 'hylomorphism' famously criticised by Simondon. For one, the agribusiness practice implies that the plant is completely 'preformed' by DNA. Moreover, the agribusiness corporation searches for a pre-determined set of properties in the product. As we shall see in the next and final section, this instrumentalism is indicative of how contemporary vitalist capitalism is turbo-charging the evolution of commodities. While living labs and real-life testing are portrayed as practices that will yield unpredictable outcomes – designs that would be unimaginable for designers – the current implementation of these approaches leaves little room for radical outcomes.

Politics and Organisation

In concluding this chapter, three interrelated issues of political concern will be discussed. First, given the charge that Deleuze appears to be 'the ideologist of late capitalism' (Žižek 2004: 163), to what extent are the Deleuze-inspired conceptions of creativity emerging within *emic* accounts of laboratory urbanism? Secondly, what does this mean for social scholars involved in the 'research and development' aimed at the expansion of 'the envelope of the political' (Thrift 2004: 75)? Thirdly, given recent debates on the political resonances of Simondon's work (Toscano 2009: 391–3), how can radical politics position itself in relation to the tendencies sketched in this chapter?

When surveying the actors' accounts of the tendency instantiated in Schladming, one can detect more or less explicit references to the notion of affect. This is not the case when it comes to Simondon's account of transduction; the actors themselves are not using such terminology. These concepts are, however, slowly making their way into the bodies of knowledge deployed in this particular mode of entrepreneurialism within urban governance. For instance, Deleuze- and Simondon-inspired attempts to transcend the hylomorphism of traditional design processes have emerged within management (Styhre 2008), as well as within anthropological approaches to design (Ingold 2010). That said, these experimental practices tend not to be put to open-ended uses. Rather, design thinking and lean startup techniques are implemented for purely instrumental, product development purposes, with profit maximisation acting as the main constraint on creativity. For this very reason, it would be misleading to state that contemporary capitalism feeds on the type of creativity that signifies Deleuze's account of the virtual. Indeed, as we have already seen, the dominant evolutionary metaphor is that of Dennett's account of an algorithm that searches for local optima in a fixed 'design space'.

Thrift (2008: 90) has pointed to a similar kind of instrumentalism in relation to a 'capitalist meteorology' that seems to chime with contemporary social theory. For Thrift, the challenge for social scholars is to 'produce formats of inquiry that counter the brutally instrumentalist view that underlies' (92) these developments within contemporary business. Here, a Deleuze-inspired approach may prove productive, since it allows us to distinguish Schladming's entrepreneurialism from that discussed by Harvey (1989), and thus to re-articulate the stakes of urban politics. Again, this is Thrift's point in relation to a spatial politics of affect: a critically informed research and development may allow us to expand the envelope of the political, bringing new forms of politics into being. 'If we don't do it, others most surely will' (Thrift 2004: 75).

In a similar vein, one may imagine a social scientific research and development programme in relation to the politics of laboratory urbanism. Granted, the type of experimental practices discussed above are connected to issues of transparency, personal integrity, informed consent and the tendency for corporations to exploit the free labour of consumers. It would, in other words, be easy to denounce laboratory urbanism altogether. Nevertheless, one may imagine inquiries that facilitate the emergence of lines of flight. Could the practices of this laboratory urbanism be deployed as 'new weapons' (Deleuze 1995: 178)? What would happen if urban experiments were run without the capitalist constraints introduced by corporate actors? What if Deleuze's account of a creative virtual space, rather than Dennett's fixed 'design space', becomes the dominant trope for experimenters?

This, however, raises issues of a politico-ontological nature. From reading Hardt and Negri (2000) or Lazzarato (2004), one might infer that the political problem of the laboratory urbanism described in this chapter emerges during re-territorialisation – at the point where the creations of the pre-individual realm are *captured*. The challenge seems to be one of disengaging the apparatus of capture, thus releasing the immanent productive force or vitality of the multitude. However, our survey of this vanguard of vitalist capitalism suggests that this immanent force is not, as it were, readily available. After all, one thing that the Schladming case points to is the sheer amount of work and organisation that goes into the systematic search for new designs.

Here, we may follow Alberto Toscano, who discusses this issue in relation to Deleuze's (1994) treatment of Simondon. Rather than a 'reserve
of creativity that could *express itself* in a given political occasion', the
pre-individual is 'a transcendental field populated by disparate singularities and series' (Toscano 2009: 392). He therefore questions Negri's
description of the pre-individual as common, and instead suggests:

> Following the indications provided by Deleuze in *Difference and Repetition*,
> we could thus extrapolate from Simondon a conception of politics as the
> invention of a communication between initially incompossible series; the
> invention of a common that is not given in advance . . . (Toscano 2009:
> 393)

Toscano's remark suggests that the invention of a common involves a
minimum requirement of organised experimentation. Indeed, there is
'a certain irony' (Buchanan 2011: 7) in the fact that Deleuze does not
discuss the organisational difficulties of social change – yet proclaims
that the 'question of a revolution [. . .] has always been organisational, not at all ideological' (Deleuze 1987: 145). Thus, rather than
denouncing laboratory urbanism, we may be better off learning from
the capitalist avant-garde: how can we devise truly open-ended urban
experiments?

References

Binder, G. (2014) 'Smart ski goggles experiment results and evaluation', Experimedia
consortium, at http://www.experimedia.eu/deliverables/.
Bonta, M. and Protevi, J. (2004) *Deleuze and Geophilosophy: A Guide and a
Glossary*. Edinburgh: Edinburgh University Press.
Brown, T. (2008) 'Design thinking', *Harvard Business Review*, June, pp. 84–92.
Buchanan, I. (2011) 'Desire and ethics', *Deleuze Studies*, 5, 'Deleuzian futures' sup-
plement, pp. 7–20.
Buhalis, D. (1998) 'Strategic use of information technologies in the tourism indus-
try', *Tourism Management*, 19 (5): 409–21.
Carrier, J. and Miller, D. (1998) *Virtualism: A New Political Economy*. Oxford:
Berg.
Deleuze, G. (1987) *Dialogues*. London: Athlone.
Deleuze, G. (1988) *Spinoza: Practical Philosophy*. San Francisco: City Lights.
Deleuze, G. (1994) *Difference and Repetition*. New York: Columbia University
Press.
Deleuze, G. (1995) *Negotiations*. New York: Columbia University Press.
Deleuze, G. and Guattari, F. (1983) *Anti-Oedipus: Capitalism and Schizophrenia*.
London: Athlone.
Deleuze, G. and Guattari, F. (1988) *A Thousand Plateaus: Capitalism and
Schizophrenia*. London: Athlone.
Dennett, D. (1995) *Darwin's Dangerous Idea: Evolution and the Meanings of Life*.
New York: Simon & Schuster.

Economist, The (2009) 'Monsanto: The parable of the sower', 19 November, at http://www.economist.com/node/14904184.

Foucault, M. (2008) *The Birth of Biopolitics: Lectures at Collège de France, 1978–79*. London: Palgrave Macmillan.

Gabriel, M.-H., Ljungstrand, P., Vandezande, N., Kosta, E. and Boniface, M. (2012) 'First EXPERIMEDIA Methodology', Experimedia consortium, http://www.experimedia.eu/deliverables/.

Hardt, M. and Negri, A. (2000) *Empire*. Cambridge, MA: Harvard University Press.

Harvey, D. (1989) 'From managerialism to entrepreneurialism: the transformation of urban governance in late capitalism', *Geografiska Annaler. Series B: Human Geography*, 71 (1): 3–17.

Harvey, D. (2008) 'The right to the city', *New Left Review*, 53: 23–40.

Ingold, T. (2010) 'The textility of making', *Cambridge Journal of Economics*, 34 (1): 91–102.

Korhonen, J. and Hassi, L. (2009) *Design Thinking Unpacked: An Evolutionary Algorithm*. Paper presented at the 8th European Academy of Design Conference.

Latour, B. (2008) *A Cautious Prometheus? A Few Steps Toward a Philosophy of Design (with Special Attention to Peter Sloterdijk)*. Keynote lecture, 'Networks of Design' meeting of the Design History Society, Falmouth.

Lazzarato, M. (2004) 'From capital-labour to capital-life', *Ephemera*, 4 (3): 187–208.

Leontidou, L. (2006) 'European informational cultures and the urbanization of the Mediterranean coasts', in M. Giaoutzi and P. Nijkamp (eds), *Tourism and Regional Development: New Pathways*. Aldershot: Ashgate, pp. 99–111.

Leys, R. (2011) 'The turn to affect: a critique', *Critical Inquiry*, 37 (3): 434–72.

Massumi, B. (2002) *Parables for the Virtual: Movement, Affect, Sensation*. Durham, NC: Duke University Press.

Morella, E. (2006) 'Information technologies and tourism development in developing markets', in M. Giaoutzi and P. Nijkamp (eds), *Tourism and Regional Development: New Pathways*. Aldershot: Ashgate, pp. 15–28.

Patton, P. (2000) *Deleuze and the Political*. London: Routledge.

Ries, E. (2011) *The Lean Startup: How Today's Entrepreneurs Use Continuous Innovation to Create Radically Successful Businesses*. New York: Crown Business.

Seigworth, G. (2005) 'From affection to soul', in C. J. Stivale (ed.), *Deleuze: Key Concepts*. Chesham: Acumen, pp. 159–69.

Simondon, G. (1989) *L'individuation psychique et collective*. Paris: Aubier.

Styhre, A. (2008) 'Transduction and entrepreneurship: a biophilosophical image of the entrepreneur', *Scandinavian Journal of Management*, 24 (2): 103–12.

Swyngedouw, E. (2005) 'Governance innovation and the citizen: the Janus face of governance-beyond-the-state', *Urban Studies*, 42 (11): 1991–2006.

Thrift, N. (2004) 'Intensities of feeling: towards a spatial politics of affect', *Geografiska Annaler. Series B: Human Geography*, 86 (1): 57–78.

Thrift, N. (2006) 'Re-inventing invention: new tendencies in capitalist commodification', *Economy and Society*, 35 (2): 279–306.

Thrift, N. (2008) 'Pass it on: towards a political economy of propensity', *Emotion, Space and Society*, 1 (2): 83–96.

Toscano, A. (2009) 'Gilbert Simondon', in G. Jones and J. Roffe (eds), *Deleuze's Philosophical Lineage*. Edinburgh: Edinburgh University Press, pp. 380–98.

Wetherell, M. (2015) 'Trends in the turn to affect: a social psychological critique', *Body and Society*, 21 (2): 139–66.

Žižek, S. (2004) *Organs without Bodies: On Deleuze and Consequences*. London: Routledge.

Chapter 6

Never Believe That the City Will Suffice to Save Us! Stockholm Gentri-Fictions

Hélène Frichot and Jonathan Metzger

> ... thinking means something else than what you believe. We live with a particular image of thought, that is to say, before we begin to think, we have a vague idea of what it means to think, its means and ends.
>
> Deleuze (2004: 139)

Urban Noopolitics: What Is at Stake?

As an architect and a planner we might seek vain comfort in claiming some disciplinary expertise on the subject of the city, but as we will argue in this chapter, this makes us no better at understanding what a city can do, because our grasp is by necessity fragmentary and partial, and usually only achieved by way of a preconceived *image of the city* that is constrained by a hegemonic *Image of Thought*.[1] We only have a vague idea of a city, or what a city can do, its means and its ends. As Gilles Deleuze explains in *Francis Bacon: The Logic of Sensation*, the painter never arrives at an empty canvas when she begins to paint, but encounters a canvas that is overcrowded with habit, opinion and cliché, or by dominant modes of representational thinking (2003: 81). We always commence from a disciplinary milieu that is crowded with preconceived ideas, unconscious schemata, and the challenge is to avoid having our thinking over-determined by a dominant Image of Thought. Things become immediately more complicated, because an Image of Thought must be distinguished from images per se, and yet images of various kinds contribute to how an Image of Thought is established and stabilised. At the same time as doing battle with a prevailing Image of Thought that circumscribes how we think about a city, we want to acknowledge the role that images of a city play. We stress that images and how they work tend to be connected to histories and local problems and operate so as to secure an immediate relation with matter – and with what immanently matters. But such images also tend to become detached or transcendent when they turn into repeated and recognisable representations and significations or branded postcard images of a city. To destabilise such ingrained images and enable new practices of critical thinking we must vigilantly scrutinise any representative image of the city and critically examine how easily and seductively such images pre-scribe realities, foreclosing how future peoples, places, things and their admixtures might express themselves.

It is very important to understand that images do not stand in isola-tion, there is no such thing as a glossy architectural or urban planning image that can be taken as a thing in itself, because images operate within animated networks or arrangements involving all manner and matters of relations. As Deleuze asserts, 'The image is not an object but a "process"' (Deleuze 1998: 159); Claire Colebrook insists that life and image are embroiled in each and every emergent event of life, as '"Image" is the power of something to be perceived' (Colebrook 2005: 53). To ask what is at stake in a contemporary urban noopolitics – which determines the way a population *thinks* together – we must commence by going in search of architecture and planning's very own dogmatic Image of Thought, which, as it turns out, is populated by innumerable images. In this chapter we want to address two important tendencies that we believe contribute to the Image of Thought that cir-cumscribes how well-to-do Western urbanites currently think about the city: the desire-organising aspects of processes of gentrification and the affiliated role that sustainability discourse plays, which we will discuss with the help of the concept of *sustainability gentri-fiction*.

In Deleuze's philosophy of the image, as Miguel de Beistegui explains, 'thought cannot operate without a certain image, an image that, fur-thermore, it cannot quite turn into a concept' (Beistegui 2010: 10). The image stands for what is sensed prior to conscious conceptualisation and organised thought, and furthermore that which institutes thought is something like the unthought, something 'like a background, an *arrière-plan*' from which 'the foreground of a picture becomes visible' (11). At the same time the image suggests something that is *ahead* or directive, 'orienting and shaping whatever it is the *plan* of' (11, emphasis in origi-nal). The image is both a backdrop and plan of thought, both 'behind' and 'ahead', signifying that 'thought, as creation of concepts, unfolds on a stage that it does not quite create' (12). To interrogate our images of the city is therefore to scrutinise the unthought presuppositions that support all our conceptualisations of the city – the unthought that stands outside and before thought, but nevertheless conditions how it unfolds.

We agree with Beistegui that it is important to recognise that 'our ideas are not innate, and so are precisely not ours [. . .], that the conditions of thought are not within thought itself, that thought is not its own ground, and so certainly not that of the intelligibility of the real' (13). This does not mean that thinking about the city, or the images that underpin it, can be reduced to 'mere ideology', which somehow obscures the pristine reality above and/or beyond; on the contrary, the universe becomes graspable only as a *universe of images*, which we can never dream of exhausting. Instead, we must evaluate how singular images operate, and inquire which plan/e they draw, and whether we choose to 'adopt it ourselves, or draw a different one' (Beistegui 2010: 9). What Beistegui is describing here is effectively the operation of what Deleuze calls the Image of Thought, and while at first it might seem that the Image of Thought is a problem for philosophers alone with their privileged relation to thinking, we argue that the Image of Thought is the sullied canvas crammed with opinions, habits and clichés – or else something like a dust-obscured battlefield (Deleuze 1990: 100) – with which every discipline necessarily contends.

To get at the Image of Thought that constrains our thinking about a city, we also need to understand how images work. We will commence with a survey of the dominant and colonising images of a city, from which we can proceed into a discussion concerning how these collectively come to actualise a deeply problematic Image of Thought. We propose to draw out a crucial distinction between what images of the city can do and how Deleuze's concept of the Image of Thought operates, and while it is crucial not to muddle the two formulations, we will argue that it is important to articulate their inextricable relation. We will see how an image, or plural images, of a city might contribute to an Image of Thought of the city established as *doxa* and how, at the scale of an urban population, habits, clichés and opinions associated with thinking about a city are apt to follow well established paths, in what can be called a *noopolitics*. This has an impact on how affective relations (and non-relations) in a city continue to unfold heterogeneously as so many problematic fields requiring constant tending and care.

Current developments in urban theory and spatial geography complicate things, because to speak of 'a city', understood as a partially stable relationship between *urbs* and *civitas* conceptualised as some kind of unit, is already to speak of a past form that has since been superseded by the extraterritoriality of special economic zones in the midst of becoming urban conglomerates themselves (Easterling 2014), or else by megalopolises that territorialise great swathes of the earth. Theorists such as

Brenner and Schmid (2014) and Merrifield (2013) argue that we should not conceptualise the advent of the 'Urban Age' as a quantitative shift measured by a stark percentage, but rather as a *qualitative* shift toward a new era of urbanisation in which the supply lines of cities interconnect with and transform, both virtually and actually, every inch of the surface of the earth, making any precise distinction between 'urban' and 'rural' quite irrelevant.

We acknowledge that to speak of 'a city' is today to speak of something that has become anachronistic in terms of the sheer scale and complexity of global urban development. The city as thought-image is, by now, something quaint, deceptively self-contained, something that still holds to a brand controlled identity, appearing as an almost ubiquitous stage set: Paris, Rome, New York, Rio de Janeiro, Sydney and Stockholm. These are 'world cities' of the past, cities-in-the-world rather than world-in-urbanisation, that can no longer be used to stand in for what has become of urbanity (Brenner and Schmid 2014). A dangerous tendency to intensify the celebration of these neatly curated representational images of the city persists, as though to obfuscate the looming events that gather toward an era of 'planetary urbanization' (Merrifield 2013). Existing images of a city must be challenged, destabilised and deterritorialised in all their specificity, or as Brenner and Schmidt aptly put it, '[g]iven the sweeping heterogeneity of settlement configurations and transformative processes that are subsumed under the notion of an urban age, it is highly questionable whether any meaningful theoretical content can be ascribed to it' – implying that since 'urbanization processes produce a wide range of sociospatial conditions across the world', these 'require contextually specific analysis and theoretization' (2014: 748, 751).

We agree that the challenge is to achieve a certain level of contextually specific analysis and theorisation, and so we will highlight images of a city produced in the unholy marriage of consumerist gentri-fiction and imaginaries of 'quick-fix sustainability', the bastard offspring of which we call *sustainability gentri-fiction*. These consensually shared urban imaginaries frame urban consumerist lifestyles that are both ethically and politically problematic, and which become particularly dangerous and toxic when coupled with sustainability discourse. The challenge is to look at a specific city, and as we believe it is best to start where we are, we welcome you to *Stockholm, 2015* – a city with a well-oiled marketing apparatus that has managed to 'tap into' the most sought-after urban 'brand position' of all, the central 'image' that trumps all the rest in an age of ecological crisis: the reassuring gentri-fiction that we live in a sustainable city, *sustainable Stockholm*! We now pay a visit to this small, polite and neatly constrained collection of people and their houses and civic institutions, so as to explore some approaches by which we might turn all these exhausted images of the sustainable city upon their precious roofs.

The New Urban Hyperbole and Stockholm Sustainability Gentri-Fiction

Welcome to Stockholm, and now that you are with us here in our purportedly sustainable and green northern city, we must also introduce you to the (pseudo-) scholarly producers of totalising, celebratory ideals of a city such as the one we inhabit, expressed in the new urban hyperbole of academic prophets of urbanity such as Edward Glaeser and Richard Florida who argue that the answer to global matters of concern can be found in the City (capital 'C'; cf. Metzger 2015), and particularly in 'amenity-rich', 'vibrant' cities such as Stockholm, Melbourne or Toronto, which can also be branded 'sustainable'. Ananya Roy has noted that iconic former mayors such as Enrique Peñalosa of Bogotá and Rudolph Giuliani of New York are becoming today's new 'planning gurus, disseminating their ideas and interventions to worldwide audiences' (Roy 2015: 295) from the scale and point of view of the city. One of the most high-profile recent additions to this crowd is Michael Bloomberg who in 2013 set up his 'global mayoralty' as Bloomberg Associates, an organisation described as a 'high-powered consulting group to help him reshape cities around the world long after he leaves office' (Barbaro 2013). The rationale behind the consultancy is to showcase how 'urgent human problems from public health to environmental sustainability' can be best tackled at the scale of the city (Roy 2015). Bloomberg Associates have been described as an 'urban SWAT-team' that can confront global challenges on the urban scale, a claim that implicitly establishes the urban as the proper vantage from which such challenges should be addressed. This focus on the city, as though it will suffice to save us, is our central concern. We want to echo the lament Deleuze and Guattari make in *What Is Philosophy?* (1994: 10) that the 'ideas men' have taken hold of the concept (of 'the city'), and we further argue that one of the things they have artfully done with it is to apply it to the branding of urban agglomerations such as the one called Stockholm, making many of us believe its compelling *sustainability gentri-fiction*, the bedtime story its well-to-do inhabitants lull themselves to sleep with, shutting out the horrible churning existential anxiety expanding in the shadow of a rapidly growing mountain of personal and collective debts and doubts (Lazzarato 2012), and the abyss of ecological destruction that is opening up beneath us all.

A gentri-fiction is a reassuring story we tell ourselves about 'life in the city' that quickly becomes an insistent refrain, a civic song of the city stuck in the head (Frichot 2014). Gentri-fictional images of the city operate in the half-second delay before pre-personal affect becomes an identifiable feeling so famously described by Nigel Thrift (2008: 70, 186). They generate instincts and format affect. Not the infinite speeds of survey associated with a liberation of thought (Deleuze and Guattari 1994), but a relative speeding up or slowing down that instead conditions an anti-thinking. Where the slowing down of thought risks producing explanatory practices that simplify the complexity of cities, the speeding up of thought leads to an exhaustion of concepts resulting in default mechanisms that return us to cliché and opinion. The speeding up of the consumption of concepts, we argue, is assisted through the image-making practices of branding. Deleuze and Guattari explain, 'we constantly lose our ideas. That is why we want to hang onto fixed opinions so much. We ask only that our ideas are linked according to a minimum of constant rules' (1994: 201). Once it becomes a sedimented refrain or a habit of thought, a recalcitrant noological knot, a gentri-fiction can over-determine habits of living, and how the well-to-do denizens of urban space live out their over-curated lives, following the full programme, rarely countering it or reinventing it. Further, the 'gentri-' of gentri-fiction is meant to act as a reminder of the position of relative privilege of those who generally participate, either as characters, narrators or perhaps even omnipotent voices in the spinning of the tales of the city. As Ruth Glass, who coined the term gentrification in the 1960s explains, it is a privileged 'gentry', those we now call a comfortable middle-class, who enjoys such stories (Glass 1964).

We propose to map *sustainability gentri-fiction* as a sub-species of gentri-fiction which marries representations of urban consumerist lifestyles with a promise of the 'sustainability' of such practices. A prime example is the branding efforts relating to Hammarby Sjöstad, Stockholm's flagship 'eco-neighbourhood'. A so-called 'brownfield development' of a very centrally located former industrial area, the neighbourhood was first planned as an Olympic village using a 'sustainability' marketing ploy that was part of Stockholm's bid for the Summer Olympics of 2004. On the advice of marketing consultants and partially with a view to appease NGOs that were strongly opposed to the bid, Stockholm developed a prominent eco-profile in their candidacy – also building upon inspiration from Sydney's successful branding of the summer games of 2000 as a 'green Olympics'. Stockholm's Olympic bid eventually failed, but construction of Hammarby Sjöstad still went ahead. The high sustainability ambitions of the now world-renowned neighbourhood neatly aligned with the governing Social Democrats' 'Green welfare state' (*gröna folkhemmet*) policy doctrine (or literally: 'Green People's Home') from the mid-1990s. The City council thus received substantial financial support from central government to further develop and implement the eco-profile of the area – which was seen as a flagship project for the national policy. Since then, and particularly after the sweeping national and local electoral victories of Conservative-led coalitions in 2006, the Hammarby Sjöstad area was also utilised and developed as a showcase for Swedish clean-tech and eco-technology – positioning it as a key node in the national export strategy for such products, which has been in place for roughly a decade now (Metzger and Rader Olsson 2013: 4).

Rewarding the official branding ambitions of the City of Stockholm and the Swedish government, Hammarby Sjöstad has become internationally renowned as a 'sustainable neighbourhood' exemplar, drawing daily swarms of international professional visitors who come for inspiration and guidance, amounting to 7,000 foreign visitors per year to the local information centre (Högström et al. 2013: 165). The presentation of the neighbourhood on the official website of the city focuses exclusively on the innovative technical solutions implemented, for instance highlighting that 'when Hammarby Sjöstad is fully completed, the residents of the area will produce half of the energy they need. This is done by way of harvesting heat from purified waste water and energy from the combustible waste.'[2] The message conveyed is that just by living in one of the dwellings in this area, a resident will become more 'sustainable' in their way of life – the technology takes care of that for you. Yet as it happens, the iconic status of Hammarby Sjöstad as a showcase for sustainable urban development is rapidly being overtaken by the Stockholm eco-neighbourhood 2.0, the Royal Seaport, some five kilometres to the north. Here, technological solutions are even more advanced and the bold plans for the area state that it should be a completely 'fossil-fuel free' neighbourhood by 2030 and that the carbon footprint of the average resident there should be below 1.5 tonnes/CO_2-equivalents per year.[3]

Of course – as always – the devil is in the detail. The problem with Hammarby Sjöstad from a sustainability point of view hasn't primarily been the ineffectiveness of its technological solutions (although this too has been a serious issue), but rather how the whole equation regarding what constitutes emissions or not has been construed. This particularly relates to the contentious urban lifestyle aspect of these areas and the indirect message that the imagery employed for Hammarby Sjöstad, and more recently the Royal Seaport, communicates a seemingly unproblematic consumption-based urban lifestyle that is being staged in the image-saturated promotion materials for these areas. One of the issues is that the carbon-emission accounting methods utilised by the City of Stockholm to substantiate their dramatic environmental progress, as well as the means by which they set their ambitious goals, in no way take into account the emissions generated by and through these very urban lifestyles. By using a production-based accounting method that only takes into account local emissions, and not the emissions generated by the offshoring of goods production and the resulting 'export of environmental "bads"' (Rader Olsson and Metzger 2013: 203), emissions and pollutions are conveniently displaced 'out of sight, out of mind', even though they are actually generated because of local consumption demands in Stockholm. While Stockholm with its service-based economy performs well in terms of production-based measurements of carbon footprint, what tend to be overlooked are the avidly pursued consumption practices of Stockholmers. As Karin Bradley and her colleagues point out, 'compared to other large Swedish cities, Stockholmers in fact have the largest carbon footprint, because of larger emissions from food, consumer goods, furniture, and renovation compared to the other cities', resulting from a consumerist lifestyle in which imported consumer goods and (not-so-)durables are purchased and disposed of at a breakneck pace (Bradley et al. 2013: 178).

   These are exactly the goods that relate to the consumption habits promoted by the image of the city generated in and through gentri-fiction – the goods that produce stylish home interiors, a vibrant cafe lifestyle and elegant sartorial statements. Given the correlation between income and emissions in Stockholm demonstrated by Bradley et al. (2013) and geodemographic analyses of lifestyles in Hammarby Sjöstad (Metzger 2008), and also taking into consideration the even more skewed socio-economic profile of the emerging population of Royal Seaport, together this suggests that such neighbourhoods will have some way to go before they can reach the 2020 target of 1.5 tonnes CO_2 equivalents per resident and year – considering that this would imply a decrease in emissions of more than 90 per cent in less than five years for the inhabitants of these areas (see Bradley et al. 2013).

   Far from providing us with any form of transcendent, final or universal truth, consumption-based accounting of CO_2 emissions, such as that alluded to above, does offer a sobering counter-image to Stockholm sustainability gentri-fiction. It also provides a means for us to further specify the concrete effect of this image of the city, the conveying of a message that the well-to-do urbanite consumer can be careless and thoughtless in relation to their lifestyle habits and take comfort in that under-interrogated assumption that the 'sustainability' of her life is being ensured by someone else, somewhere else. Much like other currently dominant and colonising images of the city, such as 'urbanisation is necessary for economic growth and well-being', sustainability gentri-fiction thereby further fortifies a dogmatic Image of Thought that functions to discourage and prevent an immanent engagement of thought on current processes of (planetary) urbanisation. This function of sustainability gentri-fiction is quite perfectly captured in the website of the municipality of Stockholm, where proclamations tacked to attractive pictures of lifestyle residences in Hammarby Sjöstad boldly proclaim that the main challenge for the city is not about change, but rather how to '*remain* [*sic*!] Sustainable'.[4] It is toward this integral relation between the functioning of specific, prevalent images of the city and actualised Images of Thought that we now wish to turn.

The Image of the City and the Image of Thought

An interest in images of the city has in recent times been refined and politicised by thinkers on 'urban imaginaries' such as Kaïka (2010), who prefers to conceptualise images as collective or ideological representations. Wachsmuth (2014) and Brenner and Schmid (2014) go even further, arguing not only that particular 'imaginaries' of cities have an ideological content, but that the idea of 'the city' per se is an ideologically saturated construct. Although we are sympathetic with Wachsmuth's pathos, we baulk at his critical-realist conceptualisation that situates images of the city as ideologically distorted representations of supposedly objectively existing urban realities, where the city is to be comprehended as a 'thought object' (i.e. not-so-real) in contrast to any kind of 'real object' (Wachsmuth 2014: 77–8). Along classic realist lines sporting a genealogy that stretches all the way back to Plato's philosopher kings, he subsequently positions the social scientist (presumably one of his own ideological bent and flavour) as a superior epistemological subject in relation to these ideological 'thought objects', a know-it-all and know-it-better who can sift out the true from the false, or erroneous aspects of the distorted 'ideological representations' of urban life produced and enacted by mere 'social actors in everyday life', clarifying 'to what extent "the city" faithfully represents these processes and to what extent it distorts them as ideology' (Wachsmuth 2014: 79). To begin with, regarding 'to what extent "the city" faithfully represents' urbanisation processes, we feel obliged to rehearse William James' famous, and still all too relevant, rebuttal to any correspondence theory of truth: if 'no bell in us tolls to let us know for certain when truth is in our grasp, then it seems a piece of idle fantasticality to preach so solemnly our duty of waiting for the bell' (James 1896). Even if there were a 'right' or 'wrong' way to grasp things, how would we ever know when we got it 'right'?

The purpose of this operation is of course to 'call into question the attributive logical schema which privileges questions of essence while prejudging the identity of the interrogated object, and which always asks: what is it?' (Zourabichvili 2012: 48). How can we move beyond this dead end of construing thinking as the activity of correctly recognising pre-given objects, to go from asking the question of what the city 'is' and how well our images of it 'correctly' correspond, to asking instead: 'what happened?' (Zourabichvili 2012: 54). Here we are actually helped by extending some sympathy to the task that Wachsmuth sets before himself but fails to articulate as it is blocked by his realist Image of Thought – that is, by paying more careful attention to the *concrete effects* of a particular way of articulating images of the city. This gets us closer to where we want to go, returning us to our preferred pragmatist plane of consistency, by avoiding asking the 'useless' question of whether something is right or wrong and instead delineating the specific plane of a particular image based on *what it does* (Beistegui 2010: 9), immanently evaluating what relational effects it produces through its articulations and deciding whether we see grounds for concretely challenging the production of these effects or not.

To highlight the problematic presupposition of what thought is and what it does, which in differentiated ways underpins both celebratory accounts of 'the City', such as those of the new urban prophets and the role played by sustainability gentri-fiction as well as critical accounts such as those of Wachsmuth, we find critical power in the Deleuzian concept of the Image of Thought and its relation to noology and noopolitics (Hauptman and Neidich 2010). *Noology* is the study of what Deleuze calls the 'Image of Thought', which is an ambivalent concept that can enable either affirmative socio-political relations or else oppressive ones, depending on how we engage with it (Zourabichvili 2012). Deleuze and Guattari further stress that 'Noology is the study of images of thought and their historicity' (1987: 376). This in turn suggests powerful political implications pertaining to the way we construct cities, from both the material effects of imaginaries, and the signifying capacities of concrete occasions, together producing a material semiotics. *Noopolitics* is the logic of how minds think together (Hauptman and Neidich 2010), producing, for instance, imaginaries of place that procure real material relations and spatial outcomes that express themselves through both convivial as well as conflictual encounters, through both agreement and agonistic struggle. Deleuze offers eight postulates (1994: 167) in addition to three theses (1983: 130) that pertain to the 'dogmatic' Image of Thought, or that which in Western culture is given and received or taken-for-granted, becoming too often debilitating. The eight postulates and three theses reiterate many key points pertaining to assumptions concerning the inherent 'goodness' of good sense, the assumed universality of common sense and the way we presume the best intentions of the thinker who is supposedly always in search of 'truth' and that in the search for truth finds the means to ward off error by securing an adequate method.

The whole problem here is based in the assumption that thinking in terms of 'right' or 'wrong', or in terms of the good sense of the thinker naturally inclined toward a pursuit of what is true, is even relevant (Deleuze 1994, 2000). It is presumed, as Zourabichvili writes, that 'we think naturally' (2012: 45–6) and that in thinking we express a goodwill, as though this were an inevitable orientation of thought, placing us squarely on the path of the good – and if not on track, then it is only because some ill-willed external force has led thought astray: hence the 'morality' and moral judgement of good sense. In their full choreography, these presuppositions enact the muddle of a *representational Image of Thought*, setting thought the task of 'getting the picture right' as a more or less clear 'mirror of nature' (Rorty 1980).

What is of interest to us is that the potential is expressed across several of Deleuze's texts (1983, 2000, 2004) for cascades of new Images of Thought to counter dogmatic ones (Zourabichvili 2012). With Deleuze and Guattari as our guides, we therefore want to imagine the workings of thought, specifically thought about 'the city', in other ways. This might be to ask of the image of the city not whether it is more or less correct, but rather how it might follow the fault lines of another, more pragmatic Image of Thought, which demands that we ask at each moment, again and again, 'what does it do?' Such a mood of curiosity requires not a dogmatic but a rhizomatic Image of Thought, allowing us to avail ourselves of Deleuze and Guattari's assistance when we ask:

'What can we make an image of the city do?' This question can only be answered in exploratory and experimental terms, including speculative 'adventures in thought'. It is obvious in the works of Deleuze and Guattari that they see such noopolitical struggles as a vital battleground for humanity's future. Therefore it is crucial to consider the effects of modes of thinking and what types of Images of Thought specific images of the city actualise or enact. Do they engender a slowing down of thought on 'the city', or do they short-circuit it? When do they bypass thinking on a city altogether, producing vacuoles of non-critically or, in Deleuzian terms, constituting devices for non-thinking and stupidity?

If we do not take thought seriously, Deleuze and Guattari warn us, thought will begin to think for us, thereby empowering 'new functionaries', civil servants, planners, policy-makers, to make decisions for us in terms of how we live inside cities: 'Because the less people take thought seriously, the more they think in conformity with what the State wants' (Deleuze and Guattari 1987: 376). But these words were written at a specific time and place – when the state apparatus was still dominating civic life in Western liberal states – and today it does beg the question of what has become of the State, especially in an era of the retreat of the welfare state. Problems shift and philosophical concepts should likewise be adapted to suit their immanent, localised problems. We have made some attempts above to outline an argument concerning how far problems have shifted with regard to the City, by addressing a specific city, Stockholm. We acknowledge that as much as there was a dire need to generate mechanisms of creative resistance to ward off the influence of the State in the 1970s, perhaps what is needed today are mechanisms to ward off unchecked and feral urban capitalism (cf. Steele 2015) – the unfettered expansion of the *ville*, and the colonising Image of Thought upon which it rests, supported by the memes of *sustainability gentri-fiction*, the refrains we murmur to ourselves to reassure ourselves that now we are at home and chaos has been left outside, that everything is OK and taken care of, so we can go ahead and continue consuming. The functional effects of the image of the city produced by *sustainability gentri-fiction* thus appear to alleviate any guilt, angst or even thought relating to the possible problematic effects of current western well-to-do urbanite consumption practices, instead pre-emptively framing these as the *solution* to urgent global ecological challenges. All the while contemporary strands of urban capitalism aim at staging life (and perhaps particularly well-to-do life in the city) as a Disney theme park attraction, or as so aptly put by Nigel Thrift, 'Lifeworld Inc.': no need to worry, just come along for the ride – we have it all sorted out for you (Thrift 2011).

But alas, no – upon closer scrutiny, it becomes obvious that no matter what the urban hyperbole of the 'global mayoralties' proclaims, the City will not suffice to save us. Our aim with stating this here in our conclusion is not to pass judgement on 'the City', nor on the phenomenon of urbanity, but rather to engender thinking on the conditions of possibility of the City, on current planetary urbanisation and related colonising Images of Thought. We thus argue for the need for continuous immanent evaluation (cf. Hillier 2015) of the current situation, (haec)c(e)ities and processes of urbanisation.

Finally, we wish to note that, while in itself important, the contestation of colonising images of the city that actualise a dogmatic Image of Thought must also be thought of here in relation to its *milieu* as a minor skirmish in the presently ongoing 'battle for intelligence' (Stiegler 2010). A mapping of the problematic effects of these images of the city thus entails an attempt at a concrete interference, a call for the friction-generating slowing down of thought in opposition to a constantly increasingly refined cognitive-capitalist apparatus for anti-thought, which to a large extent functions through curating affect, bypassing reflection and thus conditioning responses. With this in mind, perhaps the most important 'urban developer' of this time might be those 'idiots' who in the face of currently dominant trends of western urban consumption instead proclaim 'I would prefer not to' (Melville 1985; Stengers 2005). We don't have to emulate them, but it may be important to listen to what they are trying to say.

Postscript

Immediately after being ousted from office at the general election, one of the foremost champions of Stockholm sustainability gentri-fiction, the former municipal commissioner for urban environment in Stockholm, Per Ankersjö, announced in January 2015 that he had founded the new PR agency 'A Beautiful Soup'. Apparently loosely modelled on the Bloomberg Associates set-up, and thus a recent addition to the 'global mayoralty' bandwagon, Ankersjö boldly proclaimed that 'PR consultants can actually save the world'. In addition to rendering services such as 'lobbying' and 'media training', the company also offers inspiring accounts of 'the Stockholm Example'. Explaining the choice of name for his company, Ankersjö makes (a badly misconstrued) reference to the joke about the Mock Turtle in Alice in Wonderland, making the point that 'mock turtle soup is a soup that doesn't contain turtle'. We are left pondering whether this may indeed be a suitable grounding narrative for 'ideas men' offering up a concoction of 'sustainable urban development' that doesn't contain any 'sustainability' whatsoever.

Notes

1. The concept of the Image of Thought is central to much of Deleuze's thinking (Deleuze 1983, 1994, 2000; Deleuze and Guattari 1994; see also Beistegui 2003; Zourabichvili 2012).
2. http://bygg.stockholm.se/Hallbar-stad/Miljoprofilomraden/Hammarby-sjostad/ (accessed 24 March 2015).
3. http://bygg.stockholm.se/Alla-projekt/norra-djurgardsstaden/ (accessed 24 March 2015).
4. http://international.stockholm.se/city-development/sustainable-efforts/ (accessed on the 2 June 2015).

References

Barbaro, M. (2013) 'Bloomberg focuses on rest (as in rest of the world)', *New York Times*, 14 December, online at: http://www.nytimes.com/2013/12/15/nyregion/bloomberg-focuses-on-rest-as-in-rest-of-world.html?_r=0 (accessed 4 April 2015).
Beistegui, M. de (2010) *Immanence: Deleuze and Philosophy*. Edinburgh: Edinburgh University Press.
Bradley, K., Hult, A. and Cars, G. (2013) 'From eco-modernizing to political ecologizing: future challenges for the green capital', in J. Metzger and A. R. Olsson (eds), *Sustainable Stockholm: Exploring Urban Sustainability in Europe's Greenest Capital*. London: Routledge, pp. 168–94.
Brenner, N. and Schmid, C. (2014) 'The "urban age" in question', *International Journal of Urban and Regional Research*, 38: (3): 731–55.
Colebrook, C. (2005) 'Noology', in Adrian Parr (ed.) *The Deleuze Dictionary*. Edinburgh: Edinburgh University Press, pp. 193–4.
Deleuze, G. (1983) *Nietzsche and Philosophy*, trans. Hugh Tomlinson. London: Athlone Press.
Deleuze, G. (1986) *Cinema 1: The Movement Image*, trans. Hugh Tomlinson. London: Athlone Press.
Deleuze, G. (1989) *Cinema 2: The Time Image*, trans. Hugh Tomlinson. London: Athlone Press.
Deleuze, G. (1990) *The Logic of Sense*, trans. Mark Lester with Charles Stivale. New York: Columbia University Press.
Deleuze, G. (1994) *Difference and Repetition*, trans. Paul Patton. New York: Columbia University Press.
Deleuze, G. (1995a) 'Control and becoming', in *Negotiations*, trans. Martin Joughin. New York: Columbia University Press, pp. 169–76.
Deleuze, G. (1995b) 'Postscript on societies of control', in *Negotiations*, trans. Martin Joughin. New York: Columbia University Press, pp. 177–82.
Deleuze, G. (1998) 'The exhausted', in *Essays Critical and Clinical*, trans. Daniel W. Smith and Michael L. Greco. London: Verso.
Deleuze, G. (2000) 'The image of thought', in *Proust and Signs: The Complete Text*, trans. Richard Howard. Minneapolis: University of Minnesota Press, pp. 94–104.
Deleuze, G. (2003) *Francis Bacon: The Logic of Sensation*, trans. D. W. Smith. Minneapolis: University of Minnesota Press.

Deleuze, G. (2004) 'On Nietzsche and the Image of Thought', in *Desert Islands and Other Texts 1953–1974*. Los Angeles: Semiotext(e), pp. 135–42.

Deleuze, G. and Guattari, F. (1987) *A Thousand Plateaus: Capitalism and Schizophrenia*, trans. Brian Massumi. Minneapolis: University of Minnesota Press.

Deleuze, G. and Guattari, F. (1994) *What Is Philosophy?*, trans. Graham Burchell and Hugh Tomlinson. London: Verso.

Easterling, K. (2014) *Extrastatecraft: The Power of Infrastructure Space*. London: Verso.

Frichot, H. (2014) 'Gentri-fiction and our (e)states of reality: on the exhaustion of the image of thought and the fatigued image of architecture', in N. Lahiji (ed.), *The Missed Encounter of Radical Philosophy with Architecture*. London: Bloomsbury, pp. 113–32.

Glass, R. (1964) 'Introduction: aspects of change', in University College London, Centre for Urban Studies (ed.), *London: Aspects of Change*. London: MacKibbon & Kee, pp. xiii–xlii.

Hauptman, D. and Neidich, W. (eds) (2010) *Cognitive Architecture: From Biopolitics to Noopolitics; Architecture & Mind in the Age of Communication and Information*. Rotterdam: 010 Publishers.

Hillier, J. (2015) 'Throwing dice: between contingency and necessity in spatial planning', in J. Hillier and J. Metzger (eds), *Connections: Exploring Contemporary Planning Theory and Practice with Patsy Healey*. London: Ashgate, pp. 95–112.

Högström, E., Wangel, J. and Henriksson, G. (2013) 'Performing sustainability: institutions, inertia, and the practices of everyday life', in J. Metzger and A. R. Olsson (eds), *Sustainable Stockholm: Exploring Urban Sustainability in Europe's Greenest Capital*. London: Routledge, pp. 147–67.

James, W. (1897) 'The will to believe', in *The Will to Believe and other Essays in Popular Philosophy*, New York: Longmans, Green, & Co., pp. 1–31.

Kaïka, M. (2010) 'Architecture and crisis: re-inventing the icon, re-imag (in) ing London and re-branding the City', *Transactions of the Institute of British Geographers*, 35 (4): 453–74.

Lazzarato, M. (2012) *The Making of the Indebted Man*. Los Angeles: Semiotext(e).

Melville, H. (1985) 'Bartleby', in *Billy Bud Sailor and Other Stories*. Harmondsworth: Penguin, pp. 57–100.

Merrifield, A. (2013) 'The urban question under planetary urbanization', *International Journal of Urban and Regional Research*, 37 (3): 909–22.

Metzger, J. (ed.) (2008) *Livsstilar och konsumtionsmönster i Stockholmsregionen: ett regionalt utvecklingsperspektiv*. Stockholm: Regionplane- och trafikkontoret.

Metzger, J. (2015) 'The City is not a Menschenpark: conceptualizing the urban commons across the human/non-human divide', in C. Borch and M. Kornberger (eds), *Urban Commons: Rethinking the City*. London: Routledge, pp. 22–46.

Metzger, J. and Rader Olsson, A. (2013) 'Introduction: the greenest city?', in J. Metzger and A. Rader Olsson (eds), *Sustainable Stockholm: Exploring Urban Sustainable Development in Europe's Greenest City*. New York: Routledge, pp. 1–9.

Rader Olsson, A. and Metzger, J. (2013). 'Urban sustainable development the Stockholm way', in J. Metzger and A. Rader Olsson (eds), *Sustainable Stockholm: Exploring Urban Sustainable Development in Europe's Greenest City*. New York: Routledge, pp. 195–211.

Rorty, R. (1980) *Philosophy and the Mirror of Nature*. Oxford: Blackwell.

Roy, A. (2015) 'The universal and its others: reflections on twenty-first-century planning', in J. Hillier and J. Metzger (eds), *Connections: Exploring Contemporary Planning Theory and Practice with Patsy Healey*. London: Ashgate, pp. 295–304.

Steele, W. (2015) 'Planning wild cities', in J. Hillier and J. Metzger (eds), *Connections: Exploring Contemporary Planning Theory and Practice with Patsy Healey*. London: Ashgate, pp. 179–88.

Stengers, I. (2005) 'The cosmopolitical proposal', in B. Latour and P. Weibel (eds), *Making Things Public: Atmospheres of Democracy*. Cambridge, MA: MIT Press, pp. 994–1003.

Stiegler, B. (2010) *Taking Care of Youth and the Generations*. Stanford: Stanford University Press.

Thrift, N. (2008) *Non-Representational Theory: Space, Politics, Affect*. London: Routledge.

Thrift, N. (2011) 'Lifeworld, Inc. – and what to do about it', *Environment and Planning D. Society and Space*, 29 (1): 5–26.

Wachsmuth, D. (2014) 'City as ideology: reconciling the explosion of the city form with the tenacity of the city concept', *Environment and Planning D: Society and Space*, 31: 75–90.

Zourabichvili, F. (2012) *Deleuze: A Philosophy of the Event – The Vocabulary of Deleuze*, trans. K. Aarons. Edinburgh: University of Edinburgh Press.

Chapter 7

Urban Democracy Beyond Deleuze and Guattari

Mark Purcell

In 2011, masses of people in city after city across the world gathered together in central squares to denounce the current systems of power and to discuss what kind of world they wanted to create instead. They occupied those squares not so much as a military act to challenge the State, but more as a way to appropriate a space in the heart of the city where they could encounter each other, engage with each other, and decide together both what was wrong and how it could be made right. Citizens who had been absent from the *agora* for so long decided, spontaneously and en masse, to return to it, and to take up again the work of governing themselves. In Greece, for example, the first declaration issued by the citizens gathered in Syntagma Square read:

> For a long time decisions have been made for us, without consulting us. We ... have come to Syntagma Square ... because we know that the solutions to our problems can only be provided by us. We call all residents of Athens ... and all of society to fill the public squares and to take their lives into their own hands. In these public squares we will shape our claims and our demands together ... DIRECT DEMOCRACY NOW! (People's Assembly of Syntagma Square, 2011)

The movements of 2011 (and beyond, e.g. Montreal and Mexico City in 2012, Rio de Janeiro, São Paulo and Istanbul in 2013) were extremely diverse in terms of the local context, the desires people expressed, the way they interacted, the way the authorities responded. I only want to highlight, from among those varied strands, a clear desire, expressed by many, many people, to gather together in the square and to take responsibility for the decisions that matter to their community. Among the many desires that were present in those squares, in other words, there was an urgent desire for democracy.

In their collaborative work (1977, 1987, 1994), Deleuze and Guattari rarely write about the city, and that is surprising because their con- temporaries did. Many among those who inspired, participated in and were influenced by struggles in France and Italy in the late 1960s and throughout the 1970s concluded that the city and urban space had become a vital – if not the primary – site and stake of struggle. The goal of the present volume is to explore how we might use Deleuze's (and Deleuze and Guattari's) work to think about the city. My argument in this chapter is that in order to do so well, we must bring Deleuze and Guattari into conversation with other thinkers who explored the city and urban space much more carefully and explicitly.

Within the book's broader topic of Deleuze and the city, I focus atten- tion here on a more specific question: how might we use Deleuze and Guattari's work to think about the theory and practice of urban democ- racy? I begin the chapter by discussing democracy, and I construct an idea of it that I think is appropriate to and useful in the current moment. I do so in partnership with Deleuze and Guattari's political concepts and imagination. Or rather, more accurately, as I construct my idea of democracy I try to connect up its components and values with those in Deleuze and Guattari's work, intending that each will grow stronger for having been connected. As the chapter unfolds, I keep my concept of democracy engaged with Deleuze and Guattari's thought as long as I can, connecting as many concepts as possible, but at the point at which I try to conceptualise a properly *urban* democracy, Deleuze and Guattari become much less useful and it becomes necessary to engage with both Henri Lefebvre (and the experience of Paris 1968) and Hardt and Negri (and the experience of Italy in the 1970s) in order to achieve a full con- ceptualisation. Whereas the city is mostly absent from the dramatis per- sonae of Deleuze and Guattari's thought, in Lefebvre the city and urban space play a leading role, as they do also in the thought of the Italians.

What Is Democracy?

When people use the word democracy, what they usually mean is the liberal-democratic State, with its enshrined constitution, system for electing representatives, established parties and legitimated laws. That is not democracy. It is an oligarchical structure whose purpose is to organ- ise a vast effort to *prevent* democracy from emerging. So at the outset, it is important to acknowledge that the way I understand democracy is dif- ferent from that usual meaning. What is more, my conception is actively opposed to that meaning. When I use the word, I mean something most might call radical democracy. I mean a community in which people actively manage their own affairs for themselves. Democracy is a way of living in which people continuously and actively use their own power to decide the future of their community.

To dig a little deeper into that general statement, I think it is productive to creatively explore democracy's etymology. Democracy is made up of *demos* and *kratia* (see, among others, Weekley 1952; Soanes and Stevenson 2008; Harper 2014). The second term, *kratia*, is typically thought to mean something like rule, government or authority. It even holds traces of the idea of domination. And indeed the root of the word does in fact have those connotations, both in the way it was used in ancient Greece,[1] and in the meaning of our own words that bear its imprint (e.g. aristocracy, bureaucracy, meritocracy, etc.). *Kratia* in this sense refers to a power that controls, that limits, that dominates. It is a 'power over', a power of one entity to control or rule others, a power that Deleuze and Guattari often call *pouvoir*. And in fact this word, *kratia*, is the most direct point of contact with Greek for our word 'democracy': the ending '-cracy' is most closely connected to *kratia*. But *kratia*'s own etymology can be traced to another word, *kratos*, which means something more general: strength or power or might.[2] If we read this more general term, *kratos*, in the mode of Spinoza or Nietzsche, it comes to mean something like the power that humans have to act into the world, their capacity to affect the world around them in some tangible way. In this sense, *kratos* takes on a meaning more like 'power to', which is to say our power to create, to invent something new, to produce. This meaning is quite close to what Deleuze and Guattari call *puissance*.[3] And so if we go back to the first Greek word, *kratia*, we can reappropriate its meaning, insisting that while it does bear the meaning of 'power over' or *pouvoir*, it also evokes, from down deep in its roots, the idea of 'power to', *puissance*, or our human capacity to act into and change the world.[4]

The other root of democracy, *demos*, is similarly complex. Certainly we think we know very well what it means, especially in the context of the word democracy: it means 'the people'. And by this term, we think we mean *all* people, everyone. However, for the Greeks, and in particular in Aristotle's conception of democracy, *demos* did not mean all people. It meant instead the many poor, or, to be more precise, it meant those who worked for a living and so lacked the leisure time necessary to devote themselves to political participation as citizens. Aristotle (1997) calls this class *banausos technitēs*, rendered as 'vulgar craftsmen' by Reeve. They are 'vulgar' because they spend their time working, doing the tasks necessary for the city's survival, and so they do not have the leisure time (*schole*) to participate fully in politics and develop their civic excellence.⁵ For Aristotle, 'democracy' means government or rule by the *demos*, and he understands *demos* to mean this class of labourers who lack civic excellence. As a result, he is quite critical of the idea.

However, in the modern era this classical, limited idea of the *demos* was expanded to include everyone. Hardt and Negri (2004: 240) trace this expansion to Spinoza's *Political Treatise* and to his concept of democracy as the absolute political form, the form in which all people rule. But the idea is already there in Hobbes (1996: chapters 17–18), for whom political society is established when each person contracts with every other person, so that they all leave the state of nature and enter together into the commonwealth. Even though almost every actual political community in the modern era restricted participation in political affairs greatly – restrictions based on property ownership, gender, race, religion, age and the like – those restrictions are not there in Hobbes. In his text, *all persons*, undistinguished by any social categories, are party to the contracts that establish the polity. And so in the modern era, at least since Hobbes, the word *demos* is absolute. It means *all* people.

If we put the parts of this not-so-simple etymology back together, we get a concept of 'democracy' that joins the modern idea of *demos* – all people – to a *kratia* that has been returned to its roots in *kratos*, *puissance* or the capacity of people to act in the world to create something new. And so, if we choose to interpret democracy this way, it is not at all a system for organising formal political power; it is instead a form of life in which all people are joined to their *kratos* and use it together to directly produce and manage their lives in common.

This condition of remaining joined to their *kratos* is important, because the principal operation of the modern State, the State as it is imagined in Hobbes, Locke, and Rousseau and right up to the present day, is to *separate* people from their *kratos*. This separation is most palpable in Hobbes, where in the contract⁶ that creates the State all persons agree explicitly to surrender the *kratos* they have in the state of nature to a power outside themselves, a power that is separate from and other than the people: the State or Leviathan. The State's purpose is to use everyone's aggregated power to control them, 'to keep them all in awe', as Hobbes puts it in Chapter 13, and thereby achieve peace. This separation is baked into the design of almost all such foundational political contracts: people are separated from their *kratos* and that *kratos* is transformed into a *kratia*, or *pouvoir*, that is used to rule them.⁷

This same operation that separates people from their *kratos* also turns democracy into oligarchy. That is because people no longer retain their *kratos* to produce and manage their lives in common. Instead they surrender their *kratos* to a subset of society, to a governing few who have been set aside to rule the rest. This is, in fact, precisely the meaning of the word 'oligarchy', a community in which the few (*oligos*) rule the rest.

So democracy means that people refuse to surrender their *kratos* to Leviathan and use it themselves to decide their lives in common. But if we choose to think of democracy this way, we must be alert to the challenges. Perhaps the most apparent one is that to realise this democracy, to *be* democratic in this way, would require us to fully retain and use our *kratos*. But this state of being, it seems clear, would be exhausting. It is not something we could sustain for long. It would require too much activation, too much effort.[8] It would overwhelm us and leave us spent. And so it is necessary to think of democracy not as a state of *being*, but as a process of *becoming*. Democracy is better thought of as a constant struggle to become democratic. A struggle by everyone, all of us, to increasingly refuse to surrender our *kratos* to Leviathan, to practise producing the world together with others, and to learn to more effectively manage our affairs in common.

Deleuze and Guattari

As I have already been suggesting, this way to think about democracy has multiple points of contact with Deleuze and Guattari's ethical and political project. One of the central features of that project is to emphasise, discover and nurture the productive force that creates the world, what Deleuze and Guattari call 'desiring-production'. Throughout *Anti-Oedipus* a pitched battle is being waged: desiring-production struggles to produce according to its will, but it is captured, controlled and ruled by Oedipus and by the apparatuses of capture more generally. But desiring-production does not capitulate; it is always working away inside the structures that contain it, looking for ways out, trying to produce according to its own drives rather than the drives Oedipus assigns to it. The mission of schizoanalysis – Deleuze and Guattari's central project in the book, at once psychoanalytical and political – is for each of us to break free of Oedipus and (re-)discover our own desiring-machines, the agents or relays of desiring-production that are always working away within each of us. Schizoanalysis helps us know more about how these desiring-machines work, and how we might help them produce on their own terms (e.g. 1977: 338).

Deleuze and Guattari insist that desiring-production is primary – it is the source of all production. The apparatuses that capture desiring-production are themselves unproductive, a negative force that can only contain desiring-production's positive, productive force. Deleuze and Guattari's argument here is modelled on some very old ideas. They are taking strength from Hobbes, who insisted that people are necessarily the source of all power, and that the power of the State, awe-inspiring though it may be, can only ever be the aggregated power that people have chosen to give to it. They are also drawing from David Ricardo's (1817) argument that the act of Labour is the source of all economic value, as well as Marx's follow-on point that Capital must suck, like a vampire, on the economic value that Labour produces (1993: Chapter 10, Section 1). Throughout the first part of *Anti-Oedipus*, for example, where the despotic State is codifying and capturing flows of desire and capital is falsely claiming to have produced economic value, we see the influence of these classic thinkers.

Given that desiring-production is captured in this way, Deleuze and Guattari argue (most fully in *A Thousand Plateaus*), our positive political project must be to help desiring-production escape the apparatuses that contain it, to help it create lines of flight. Even if this act of escape comes naturally to desiring-production, lines of flight are extremely difficult to create and to sustain. Most commonly, when their energy wanes, they are recaptured by the apparatuses. Or sometimes their energy can be too strong and take on a negative quality. They go too far and career off into self-destruction. And so it is crucial, Deleuze and Guattari say, for escaped elements of desire to discover how to sustain their flight, how to avoid the two pitfalls of recapture and self-destruction. They argue (1987: esp. chapter 9) that the key to sustaining lines of flight is for each line to *connect* with other lines. They must connect to form rhizomes, living blocs of fleeing elements. This act of connection, if done correctly, will augment the speed of both elements, it will increase their energy in flight. Deleuze and Guattari envision a connected mass or mesh of lines of flight that comes together for the collective project of avoiding both recapture and suicide, the project of remaining free from the apparatuses by sustaining flight for as long as possible.

In part, the goal of this activity of fleeing-and-connecting is destruction. As it flees, each element of desiring-production can carry with it a piece of the apparatus (or stratum or socius). As more and more flights are launched, more and more parts of the apparatus will have been carried away, and it will begin to lose its integrity, erode and crumble. However, for Deleuze and Guattari the goal of fleeing-and-connecting is primarily *production* rather than destruction. The elements in flight, as they connect up into rhizomes, are engaged in producing a positive alternative to the apparatuses. If they are successful in forming thriving rhizomes and in maintaining their flight, they will begin to trace out, with their continual movement, what Deleuze and Guattari variously call a new plane, a new earth or a new land (1977: Part 4, especially p. 318). They can create another world, a new land that is pervaded by the dense traces left by schizoid, molecular elements of desiring-production in flight.

To be clear, for Deleuze and Guattari the new land is not simply a new regime, an alternative political order with a structure similar to the old one but led by a different social group. Rather, the new land is the absence of such order. It is a condition that is made up of flight, of the condition of being in flight from social order. Still less is the new land an ideal society at the end of history. It is in no sense a utopia. Even if elements of desiring-production are able to break through the limits of the apparatuses and begin tracing out a new land, the apparatuses will always re-emerge: the capitalist axiomatic, the molar aggregate, the subjected-group and the sovereign State will attempt to reassert control. Escape is never achieved once and for all. Flight must always be a perpetual struggle. The apparatuses must be continually warded off. There is no stable condition of freedom in Deleuze and Guattari, no *being* free. There is only a perpetual flight, a continual process of *becoming* free. It is precisely the same as democracy. As we saw, there is no way, really, to *be* democratic. We must instead perpetually struggle to *become* democratic. Democracy and flight must both be a perpetual struggle of becoming.

As this resonance between their new land and democracy suggests, it is possible to imagine Deleuze and Guattari's very abstract idea of desiring-production more concretely. They themselves, in fact, explore how we might imagine desire, capture and flight to operate in concrete and recognisable political struggles. In *Anti-Oedipus*, they urge people to engage in schizoanalysis precisely in order to refuse the imposition of the Oedipal triangle by Freudian psychoanalysis. They want people to come to know their own desiring-machines (1977: 45). In *A Thousand Plateaus* (especially chapter 13), they urge people who are currently ruled by the State to flee and begin to govern themselves. Or they hope workers, the producers of economic value, can flee the capitalist axiomatic[9] and manage production for themselves.[10] In the abstract, Deleuze and Guattari present the concept of a new land pervaded by desiring-production and beyond any socius. But they also talk concretely of new lands pervaded by communities of people becoming free beyond the

State, and new lands pervaded by the free activity of producers beyond capitalism. In such new lands, people refuse to surrender power to the State and use it in common to manage their affairs for themselves. They struggle to prevent the emergence of transcendent authorities (the State being the archetypical example), and to generate instead immanent modes of coordinating and organising their lives together. They struggle to ward off the apparatuses and to produce the world on their own terms. They reappropriate *puissance*, the power to act into the world.

It is not hard, I hope, to see the connection with democracy here: the new land is populated by people who are reappropriating their *kratos*, using it to escape the apparatuses of capture, to connect with others and to struggle to decide for themselves. In the new land people must continually ward off the reimposition of *pouvoir*. The new land is free from any transcendent authority, though that authority can always re-emerge. The new land is pervaded by immanent organisation, by self-management, by people fleeing oligarchy and using their *kratos* to govern themselves in common. It is, in so many ways, democracy.

The City, the Urban and Space

I have argued that Deleuze and Guattari do not discuss the city or the urban much, if at all. But they do offer lots of ideas on the question of space.[11] For example, their account of desiring-production fleeing the apparatuses and tracing out a new land parallels their discussion of the nomad, a free element who moves across smooth space and remains beyond the reach of the striated space of the State. The State and its striated space is a central concern for Deleuze and Guattari, especially in *A Thousand Plateaus*. They even theorise a whole concept, the war machine, designed to work in and through smooth space and in opposition to the striated space of the State. The war machine is a complex concept, but in this context Deleuze and Guattari are working directly against Hobbes. For Hobbes, we agree to submit to the authority of the State in order to bring ourselves out of the state of nature, which for Hobbes is necessarily a state of war because anyone, at any time, can kill anyone else. Hobbes calls our condition in the state of nature *bellum omnium contra omnes*, the war of each person against every other person. So for Hobbes our life in the state of nature – that is, life outside of State authority – is necessarily a state of *war*, a miserable state of constant dread that is 'solitary, poor, nasty, brutish, and short' (1996 [1651]: chapter 13). For Hobbes we enter into a state of peace, of civil society, of commonwealth, only when we agree to surrender our own power to the State. Hobbes' argument here is what forms the glowing core of Deleuze and Guattari's idea of the war machine – it is a machine whose purpose is to generate war in this Hobbesian sense: war as a condition outside the State, a life in which we have not surrendered our power to the State. Of course, Deleuze and Guattari do not accept Hobbes' argument that such a life would necessarily be a *bellum omnium contra omnes*. Rather 'war', or life outside the State, is instead a radically open proposition.[12] In our life outside the State, for Deleuze and Guattari, we can choose relations of peace or war; we can choose to thrive or destroy ourselves. Hobbes thought we were naturally inclined to war. Locke thought we were naturally inclined to reason and peace.[13] Deleuze and Guattari, much more plausibly, suggest that in our life beyond the State we are capable of the full range of human relations. And so the question is, for Deleuze and Guattari, what kind of human community the war machine will build, what kind of life the nomads will trace out for themselves in smooth space. The only thing we know for sure is that they will be operating beyond the State and its oligarchical structure, and they will be actively warding off its reimposition. They will refuse Hobbes' contract, refuse to surrender power to the State, refuse to be contained by striated space. Instead, they will use that power to move through smooth space and manage their affairs for themselves.

Whereas space is a regular theme in Deleuze and Guattari, references to the city and the urban are much more fleeting (see the meagre offering in 1987: 432, 481–2 and 500; and also 1994: 4). Where they do mention the urban, they typically portray it as a problem rather than a source of potential. In *A Thousand Plateaus*, they write that 'the city is the striated space par excellence [. . .] the force of striation'. They say that, in ancient times, the town invents agriculture, and then 'it is through the actions of the town that the farmers and their striated space are superimposed upon the cultivators operating in a still smooth space' (1987: 481). They do recognise that smooth spaces and nomadism can arise in the city, and they point to the 'shantytowns of nomads' as an example. But for Deleuze and Guattari, when such nomadic forces arise in the city, it is as a kind of 'counterattack', a way of 'turning back against the city' (481–2), which, again, is conceived of primarily as a force of striation or capture.

There is, however, one moment in *A Thousand Plateaus* when it is possible to see, if we want to, an opening for democracy in Deleuze and Guattari's meagre conception of the city. In the concluding paragraph of the plateau on smooth and striated space, there is this sentence: 'Even the most striated city *gives rise to* smooth spaces: to live in the city as a nomad, or as a cave dweller' (500, emphasis added). Here we can infer the argument that the city is not only a striated location par excellence where nevertheless agents of smoothing are able to operate heroically, but that the city *itself* has the potential to *give rise to* smooth spaces. Deleuze and Guattari are intimating that there might be something about the urban that *engenders* smooth space, something that encourages elements of desiring-production to escape the apparatuses and trace out a new land beyond the State.

Lefebvre

But this idea is latent in Deleuze and Guattari, embedded deep in their second volume, and really only there if we squint while reading. I think that the work of Henri Lefebvre is a much better ground for exploring the possibility of a specifically *urban* democracy, of what it would mean to become democratic in, and by means of, our life in the city. Like Deleuze and Guattari, Lefebvre proposes a struggle for something very similar to what I have been calling democracy, a struggle by people to use their own power to manage their affairs for themselves. But especially after 1968, and in particular in *La révolution urbaine* (1970), written a few years before Deleuze and Guattari wrote *Anti-Oedipus*, Lefebvre imagines this struggle for democracy to be intimately bound up with a struggle for space, and particularly for urban space.

In broad outline, Lefebvre argues, our society is dominated by the joint forces of capitalist corporations and the State, a force he calls the 'State Mode of Production' (SMP) (2009: 106ff.). In order to maintain its domination, he insists, the SMP must necessarily control the production of space. The SMP imposes on people what Lefebvre calls *abstract space*, a space that reduces the complexity of space as a whole to a homogenised and standardised grid on which the regime of private property can define equivalent entities that can be measured, recorded and exchanged in the market (1991: especially chapter 4). Or, rather, the SMP *aspires* to impose abstract space: it maintains its control by actively homogenising and standardising space in this way, by *abstracting* space, even if it cannot actually achieve the complete abstraction of space it would like.

Because the SMP dominates us by producing space in this way, Lefebvre argues, the struggle against it must necessarily be a struggle against the SMP's homogenisation of space. 'Revolution was long defined', he writes:

in terms of a political change at the level of the state [and] the collective or state ownership of the means of production [. . .]Today such limited definitions will no longer suffice. The transformation of society presupposes a *collective ownership and management of space* founded on the permanent participation of 'the interested parties' [the inhabitants or users of space]. (1991: 422, emphasis added)

He argues that revolution must struggle against abstract space and for what he calls *differential space* (1991: especially chapters 5 and 6), a space that is other than the abstract space the SMP is trying to create. Differential space arises when the inhabitants or users of space reappropriate the production of space, and they produce and manage space themselves, together and in common.

In *The Urban Revolution*, Lefebvre addresses the more particular case of the city and urban space. The city produced by the SMP is what he calls the 'industrial city'. In the industrial city, private property and exchange value are the dominant ways to organise space, people are segregated from each other and from their work, and they are warehoused in sterile living spaces Lefebvre calls 'habitat'. This separation is designed to make people politically passive so that they will be reduced to workers and consumers and they will not participate actively in a lively urban political community. The primary purpose of the industrial city is to facilitate accumulation and exchange, to be an engine of capitalist economic growth. The industrial city is not at all democracy. Rather it is an oligarchy: a community that is managed *for* its inhabitants by the SMP's elite few state experts and corporate executives.

Lefebvre contrasts the industrial city with what he calls 'urban society'. In urban society, space is not managed *for* inhabitants; rather they appropriate it, make it their own again, and use it to meet their needs. As they produce space in urban society, inhabitants overcome the segregation of the industrial city, and they draw themselves together into central spaces where they encounter each other and engage in collective and meaningful interactions about what kind of city they desire. These encounters are *political* in the ancient sense: they are collective discussions about how the community should best live together, about what the good city is like.[14] They build a shared sense of a common project, a sense among inhabitants that they live together in a coherent community. But at the same time, these encounters also help inhabitants understand that there are substantive differences among them, that urban society is never homogeneous, never free of conflict. Instead, in urban society conflict and struggle are constitutive of the political community, and inhabitants must both manage and mobilise these differences in the project of deciding their urban future together. And so in urban society inhabitants are politically active. They take up the project of *l'habiter* (a term Lefebvre contrasts with 'habitat'), which means that they participate fully in all aspects of urban life. In urban society, the primary purpose of the city is not capitalist economic accumulation; it is the free development of each person's human potential. Urban society is, in short, a city in which urban inhabitants appropriate the production of space and manage that space for themselves. And they do so without the state and without capital. It is spatial self-management[15] of the city. It is a particularly *urban* understanding of democracy.

Italy

For Lefebvre in his context, space and the urban were, in part, a way to think beyond the class-reductionism of the French Left, and the French Communist Party in particular, in the middle-to-late 1960s. He was searching for a way to think politics as more than just class politics. And so the figure of 'inhabitants' can be seen as a way for him to conceive of a more complete political subject than the limiting figure of the industrial proletariat. Similarly, for him 'urban space' was a way to imagine a broader and richer site (and stake) of political struggle beyond the factory floor alone.

This attempt by Lefebvre to think and act beyond class and the factory was also very much part of the thought and action among those on the Italian Left in the late 1960s and 1970s. Throughout that period in Italy, activists engaged in a series of vibrant struggles over urban space and urban life, primarily in northern cities. They fought for affordable and decent shelter, improved public services and in general for a more liveable and dignified urban life (Lotta Continua 1973). A host of theoretical work that emphasised the importance of the city – e.g. Cherki and Wieviorka (1980), Del Re (1996), Illuminati (1996), Negri (2008), Hardt and Negri (2009) – grew out of (and contributed to) this history of struggle. During that period it became clear to many activists in the north of the country that it was not enough to just organise and mobilise workers in the factory, that the factory was not the only place where politics took place and that workers were not the only agents of political struggle. These activists turned their attention also to organising neighbourhoods – to the places where people lived. This shift was partly due to a feminist critique of the economic reductionism of prevailing Marxist theory at the time, but it was also due to the actual experience of women (and men) who were struggling to secure a decent life in the neighbourhoods of Italian cities (Del Re 1996).

This habit of thought, that the spaces of the neighbourhood and the city were key sites and stakes of struggle, never really died out in the Italian tradition, even after the reactionary 'Years of Lead' in the early 1980s. For example, Augusto Illuminati (1996: 175–6) argues that in our search for new political subjectivities we should explore the notion of citizenship conceived of as 'living in a city', rather than in terms of membership in a nation-state. Antonio Negri retains an emphasis throughout his recent work on the importance of 'the metropolis'. In *Goodbye Mr. Socialism* (2008 [2006]: 221) he expresses the gist of the idea when he couples his central political subject, the multitude, with the metropolis: 'I am convinced that the multitude is at the metropolis like the working class was at the factory' – a sentence that could easily have been written by Lefebvre. In *Commonwealth* (2009), Negri and Michael Hardt argue that the multitude can only become conscious and act for itself in and through the metropolis. For them the metropolis is the key reservoir of common wealth that the multitude must reappropriate. The metropolis is 'the skeleton and spinal cord' of the multitude, the multitude's 'body without organs' (249). Here the connection with Deleuze and Guattari is apparent: the multitude must become a (political) body without (party) organs. Unlike in Deleuze and Guattari, however, and in common with Lefebvre and the movements in Italy in the 1970s, Hardt and Negri say explicitly that the metropolis is absolutely vital to the multitude's flourishing. That flourishing would mean that the multitude comes to understand itself as a political subject, reclaims its common wealth in the metropolis, and manages that common wealth itself, without transcendent authorities. Thus for Hardt and Negri, as for Lefebvre, the reappropriation and democratic self-management of urban space is a vital element of their political vision for the future.

Conclusion

When we conceive of urban democracy in this way, it is always tempting to think in terms of utopia, in terms of a community at the end of history in which democracy has been won and division and conflict have been overcome. But Lefebvre, for one, is clear that this is not the way we should think about urban democracy at all. For him urban democracy, or what he calls urban society, should be thought of as a 'virtual object' (2003: especially chapters 1 and 3), as a possible world that is currently incipient, that is in the process of emerging inside the body of the (more fully actualised) industrial city. Urban society, for Lefebvre, is not 'out there', a fully formed Kallipolis beyond our current city. It is not a destination toward which we must move. It is, instead, already here, struggling to emerge, grow and flourish. For Lefebvre, the question is not how we get from here to there, from oligarchy to democracy. The question is, rather, how we better know urban society when we see it, here in the city we already inhabit. To help urban society flourish, we must become better at perceiving it in the city here and now. We must become more attuned to the way inhabitants are struggling, already, to reappropriate their own *kratos* and to manage the production of urban space for themselves. Sometimes, as in Egypt or Spain or Greece in 2011, urban society appears more spectacularly, involves many more people and endures for weeks or months at a time. At other times, and more typically, its appearance is more fleeting, harder to see and lasts for a briefer period. The struggle to become democratic, in the context of the urban, would therefore mean a struggle to perceive urban society when and where it is emerging, and to help it grow and flourish on its own terms.

I have argued that in order to think urban democracy well we cannot rely on Deleuze and Guattari alone and must turn also to Lefebvre, to the Italians and toward others who more explicitly conceptualise the significance of the urban. Maybe the best way to think of it is that we should use Lefebvre to *augment the valence* of Deleuze and Guattari.[16] Lefebvre's urban society, struggling to emerge inside the industrial city, can be read as one instance of Deleuze and Guattari's new land made palpable, alive, real. The struggle of urban inhabitants for urban democracy, their struggle to increasingly retain their own power and use it to manage the production of urban space for themselves, is one aspect perhaps – one bloom – of the project of creating a new land. In this sense, urban society can be understood as urban inhabitants fleeing-in-place from the industrial city as an apparatus of capture, and coming together to appropriate space and manage it in common, to engage each other in substantive discussions and debates about the future of the city, to discover their desiring-machines, their *kratos*, to learn how to use their power together, to produce and manage urban space for them-selves. A becoming democratic, but one that is always, necessarily, both urban and spatial.

Notes

1. Here I mean, primarily, the way it is understood in Plato's and Aristotle's political philosophy.
2. Douglas Harper (2014) writes that this Greek word has even deeper roots, in the proto-Indo European *kre-tes*, also meaning power or strength.
3. Spinoza, by whom Deleuze and Guattari are greatly influenced, expresses similar ideas to *puissance* and *pouvoir* in his work, using the terms *potentia* and *potestas*, on which see Holland (1998), who refers the reader to Gueroult (1968/1974). Hardt and Negri (2000, 2004), also inspired by Spinoza, conceive of something very similar; their terms are 'constituent power' and 'constituted power'.
4. I am not arguing that my etymology of *kratia* reveals that its true meaning is 'power to' or *puissance* rather than 'power over' or *pouvoir*. Rather I am saying that the word contains both ideas, that each is very much present in the word's origins. And so we can choose to emphasise *kratia*'s meaning of *puissance* rather than its meaning of *pouvoir*. We are already doing the opposite now, favouring the *pouvoir* meaning over the *puissance* one. So I am suggesting merely that we have the option to see a different meaning in the word, one that emphasises *kratia*'s potential to evoke the meaning of *puissance*.
5. This idea of *banausos technitēs* faded from our culture only very slowly. In *A Midsummer Night's Dream* (late sixteenth century), Puck calls the workingmen who are staging a play for the nobles 'rude mechanicals'.
6. It is really *contracts*, millions of them. This fact is important, but it is beyond the scope of the chapter.
7. Marx names and brilliantly critiques this separation in both 'On the Jewish Question' (1994) and 'Critique of Hegel's Doctrine of the State' (1975).
8. 'It would take too many evenings', as Oscar Wilde was supposedly fond of saying (about both democracy and socialism).
9. Or rather, in this case, to push it on further ahead, so that it breaks through its own absolute limit (see Deleuze and Guattari 1977: 239).
10. It is important to note here that they do not discuss concrete struggles in or for the city.
11. Although I would argue that when they write about space they are rarely talking about concrete space, and the discussion almost always takes on the feel of a metaphor, even if Deleuze and Guattari would deny they are being metaphorical.
12. This openness is reflected in the fact that the war machine has many different aspects, or ways it can manifest itself (see Deleuze and Guattari 1987: chapter 12).
13. And private property, his overriding obsession.
14. The influence here is a particularly Aristotelian one, of course, but Lefebvre is also inspired by his close relationship with the writings of the young Marx, especially 'On the Jewish Question'.
15. What he terms *autogestion* (Lefebvre 2009: especially chapter 5).
16. See Deleuze and Guattari (1987: 229).

References

Abensour, M. (2011) *Democracy Against the State*. Cambridge: Polity.
Aristotle (1997) *Politics*, trans. C. Reeve. Indianapolis: Hackett.
Cherki, E. and Wieviorka, M. (1980) 'Autoreduction movements in Turin', in

S. Lotringer and C. Marazzi (eds), *Autonomia: Post-Political Politics*. New York: Semiotext(e).

Del Re, A. (1996) 'Women and welfare: where is Jocasta?', in P. Virno and M. Hardt (eds), *Radical Thought in Italy*. Minneapolis: University of Minnesota Press, pp. 99–114.

Deleuze, G. and Guattari, F. (1977 [1972]) *Anti-Oedipus: Capitalism and Schizophrenia*, trans. R. Hurley, M. Seem and H. Lane. New York: Penguin.

Deleuze, G. and Guattari, F. (1987 [1980]) *A Thousand Plateaus*, trans. B. Massumi. Minneapolis: University of Minnesota Press.

Deleuze, G. and Guattari, F. (1994 [1992]) *What Is Philosophy?*, trans. H. Tomlinson and G. Burchell. New York: Columbia University Press.

Gueroult, M. (1968 and 1974) *Spinoza*, 2 vols. Hildesheim: Georg Olms Verlag.

Hardt, M. and Negri, A. (2000) *Empire*. Cambridge, MA: Harvard University Press.

Hardt, M. and Negri, A. (2004) *Multitude: War and Democracy in the Age of Empire*. New York: Penguin.

Hardt, M. and Negri, A. (2009) *Commonwealth*. Cambridge, MA: Belknap Press.

Harper, D. (2014) 'Democracy', in *The Online Etymology Dictionary*, at: http://www.etymonline.com/index.php?term=democracy (accessed 31 July 2014).

Hobbes, T. (1996 [1651]) *Leviathan*. New York: Cambridge University Press.

Holland, E. (1998) 'Spinoza and Marx', *Cultural Logic*, 2: 1.

Illuminati, A. (1996) 'Unrepresentable citizenship', in P. Virno and M. Hardt (eds), *Radical Thought in Italy*. Minneapolis: University of Minnesota Press, pp. 167–87.

Lefebvre, H. (1991 [1974]) *The Production of Space*, trans. D. Nicholson-Smith. Oxford: Blackwell.

Lefebvre, H. (1996) *Writings on Cities*, trans. E. Kofman and E. Lebas. Cambridge, MA: Blackwell.

Lefebvre, H. (2003 [1970]) *The Urban Revolution*, trans. R. Bononno. Minneapolis: University of Minnesota Press.

Lefebvre, H. (2009) *State, Space, World: Selected Essays*, ed. N. Brenner, S. Elden and G. Moore. Minneapolis: University of Minnesota Press.

Lotta Continua (1973) 'Take over the city: community struggle in Italy', *Radical America*, 7 (2): 79–112.

Marx, K. (1975 [1843]) *Karl Marx: Early Writings*, trans. R. Livingstone and G. Benton. New York: Vintage Books.

Marx, K. (1993 [1867]) *Capital, Volume 1*. New York: Penguin.

Marx, K. (1994 [1844]) *Karl Marx: Selected Writings*, ed. L. Simon. Indianapolis: Hackett.

Negri, A. (2008 [2006]) *Goodbye Mr. Socialism*. New York: Seven Stories Press.

People's Assembly of Syntagma Square (2011) Vote of the People's Assembly of Syntagma Square, Athens, 27 May, at: http://en.wikipedia.org/wiki/File:Vote_of_the_People's_Assembly_of_Syntagma_Square.svg (accessed 2 January 2015).

Ricardo, D. (1817) *On The Principles of Political Economy and Taxation*, at: http://www.marxists.org (accessed 30 August 2014).

Soanes, C. and Stevenson, A. (eds) (2008) *Concise Oxford English Dictionary*, 11th edition. Oxford: Oxford University Press.

Weekley, E. (1952) *A Concise Etymological Dictionary of Modern English*. London: Secker & Warburg.

Chapter 8

Genealogy of Capital and the City: CERFI, Deleuze and Guattari

Sven-Olov Wallenstein

Desire and the Social

From the mid-1960s to the early 1970s a new way of conceiving the urban form emerges and 'modernism' suddenly finds itself questioned in a wide variety of perspectives, which all tend to give the term a different meaning. The city becomes a text, a phenomenological space, a historical palimpsest, a collage, a metabolic structure and a form marked by complex power relations, a 'machine', overcoding materials and semiotic flows and organising desire in all of its forms. In the following I will look at one such debate, buried among historical documents and up to now very little studied, but whose repercussions extend into the present and the future, and where political, psychoanalytical and philosophical themes intersect: the discussions undertaken by the French research group CERFI (Centre d'études, de recherches et de formation institutionelles). Long before the recent interest in Deleuze among architects – which, typically, also tends to sidestep the role of Guattari, whose presence no doubt was instrumental in bringing Deleuze's earlier work, largely devoted to the history of philosophy, closer to politics – this was the first place where many of his ideas were tested for the first time in relation to urban space, in a way very different from the formalist and largely non-political agenda that has dominated the appropriation of his ideas since the mid-1990s. Cross-reading Deleuze and Guattari with Foucault, whose own work at the time was undergoing a shift away from the analysis of discursive formation to an analytic of power that brought a new attention to spatial and material forms, as well as locating them in a complex exchange with Marx, CERFI can in hindsight be seen as a laboratory of sorts.

Until its disbandment in the early 1980s, CERFI was a fluid network of independent researchers and political activists. The group provided the platform for an extra-academic encounter between psychoanalysis and the social and political movements of the period, and during its most active phase its president was Félix Guattari, whose experience as the director of the experimental psychiatric clinic La Borde was decisive for much of CERFI's work. The earlier development, starting from the mid-1960s – which included its break with the French Communist Party – cannot be explored here, and its various ramifications and inner conflicts will remain in the background.[1] The developmental line I will attempt to follow starts in the middle period with the research commissioned from the group by the Ministère de l'Equipement in 1971: to consider how the social demand for 'public facilities' (*équipements collectifs*) should be assessed, what the demand signifies, where it is coming from and how it can be met.

CERFI proceeded from a central distinction in Jacques Lacan between 'demand' (*demande*, a verbalised expression determined by supply), and 'desire' (*désir*, a phantasmatic projection),[2] and quickly conferred on the questions a more general and, to the commissioners presumably unexpected, dimension: What is the desire that circulates in our institutions, how is it connected to the 'axioms' of capitalism, to the city as metaphor and to a concept such as territory? While the concept of desire is introduced with reference to Lacan, the main source is Deleuze and Guattari's *L'Anti-Œdipe: Capitalisme et schizophrénie* (1972) which, against a dominant philosophical tradition from the Platonic *eros* to Hegel, Freud and Lacan, suggests that we should cease to understand desire in terms of lack, negativity and castration, and instead conceive of it as production, even as a founding ontological order that need not be explained by anything else. Desire, so Deleuze and Guattari argue, functions in terms of the 'desiring machines' that are operative at all levels of the socius, from the molecular level at which the body is an assemblage of partial objects all the way up to the molar level at which the social machine organises the socius by overcoding a territory and creating conduits for all its flows, enabling a kind of homeostasis between the forces of reterritorialisation and deterritorialisation. As we will see, this is where the concept of the city should be located: it overcodes a given territory while still being susceptible to all kinds of forces from the outside, as a kind of metastable relay; it is a concept that CERFI's analysis will eventually try to dissolve, even though it will remain enigmatic and opaque in the end, and refuse to go away.

In the case of collective facilities in relation to demand, this means that the question soon expands and must be addressed at a more general level that navigates between several conflicted theoretical models, drawing not only on the productivist conception of desire developed by Deleuze and Guattari, but also on the Nietzschean idea of genealogy inflected through Foucault, and finally engaging a critical reading of Marx. 'We are fabricating a strange machine, made up of bits and pieces borrowed from the genealogist Foucault, stolen from the bicephalous savant Deleuze-Guattari and his construction site, or quite simply picked up from local artisans',[3] the editors state in the introduction to their journal *Recherches*, where the first results in response to the Ministère de l'Equipement's commission were presented and which will be my main source in the following.

On another level, the question of desire, of how it works in capitalism to both disrupt and uphold the latter's axioms and principles, signals one of the many crises that Marxist thinking was undergoing at the time. The synthesis of Marx and Freud, of political and libidinal economy, was no doubt always a tenuous one, but at this historical juncture it reaches a critical stage. By drawing desire as an ontological category into the theoretical work, not just as an object but also as a formative moment in theory itself, this type of question emphasises the co-implication of the question's subject and object – all of which was emphatically already there since Marx's eleventh thesis on Feuerbach and the claim that the aim of philosophy is not to interpret the world but to change it – and begins to imply the need for an interrogation of the particular will to knowledge that is at the basis of every thinking that aspires to be 'critical', for a self-reflexive questioning of the will to power implied in theory and of the imbrication of power and truth. This was visible in the problem of desire that seemed to explode everywhere in French thought in the early 1970s, above all in Deleuze and Guattari and the early writings of Jean-François Lyotard, but which also, from a certain distance, informs Foucault's analytic of power and knowledge.[4]

In this context, it is significant that one of the definitions of the desiring machine used by Deleuze and Guattari is drawn from the urban historian Lewis Mumford's concept of the 'megamachine': 'A combination of solid elements, each with its specialised function, at work under human control in order to transmit a movement and carry out a task.'[5] For Deleuze and Guattari, and even more so for CERFI, this implies a decisive shift in the concept of the machine that is concomitant with the shift away from the subject assumed to be the sole consumer of the city and its facilities, in a double desubstantialisation. This implies at least two steps. First, we move from the iconography of the first machine age and its fascination with the outward look of the machine, its physical form and capacity to project a sense of modernity (which in architecture had been analysed a decade before by Reyner Banham (1960)) toward a definition based on information, a machine that deals with connectivity, flows and transmissions of any kind and makes Mumford's 'solid elements' into a relic of the past. Second, we also move from a subject assumed to be already there to a machinic subject located as a temporary intersection of flows. When CERFI speak of the city, their imagery tends to draw on the most advanced informatics of the time, and 'elements' should no longer be seen as analogous with substances, but as relations and relations between relations that give rise to temporary convergences, intersections and captures: 'the city is a computer which fabricates its own program, an informational machine that produces new information by way of a constant mixing, by controlling heterogeneous series that without this machine would pursue their homogeneous development separately' (Recherches 1973: 18–19). This is why even the term 'imagery' is misleading, since the machine, just as in Deleuze and Guattari, is not at all a metaphor, but the most precise concept that can be construed in order to grasp a series of relations that traverse the social field in its entirety.[6]

The Context: Debates on Urbanism

CERFI's work on the city and on the genealogy of collective facilities also takes place, however, in the more specifically theoretical landscape of urban studies, whose main features we should now delineate, at least insofar as they concern the immediate French intellectual context.

One of CERFI's most important precursors in urban sociology was Henri Lefebvre, who, immediately after the war, initiated a new form of spatial analysis, beginning with the first volume of *Critique de la vie quotidienne* (1947). (The title recurs in two later volumes, in 1962 and 1981, and could serve as a guiding thread through his labyrinthine authorship; for an in-depth study of Lefebvre, see Stanek (2011).) Lefebvre's claim is that Marxist theory, if it is not to remain at the level of abstract truth, must be grounded in an analysis of those structures of everyday life that mediate between individuality and history. As a consequence, this intermediary level, where alienation and reification occur and become possible to experience, begins to displace work as an analytic category. This in turn signifies a shift from the economic to the socio-cultural level, and develops into a critical reflection on the ideological role of 'planning' (or *l'aménagement du territoire*, to cite the more broad French term) as the way in which modern state-governed capitalism annexes the life-world. Lefebvre's critique of everyday life attempts to show how our experience is colonised by the state and by capital functioning together as a levelling force, against which he sets the constant potential for reversal and transgression inherent in the everyday. This analysis signals a step away from the essentially systemic analysis of Marxism, which at the time – above all because of the role played by Althusser and structural theory – seemed to be moving in the opposite direction, away from concrete subjectivity toward the construction of strictly theoretical models within which individual experience is constituted as caught up in the imaginary.

Lefebvre's path would, at approximately the same time as CERFI's dissidence within Marxism took shape, eventually culminate in a series of works focusing on the city and the urban question: *Le droit à la ville* (1968), *La révolution urbaine* (1970), *La pensée marxiste et la ville* (1972) and *La production de l'espace* (1974). The city, urban space and modernity are the themes that connect the different elements of the analysis of the everyday and give it a marked spatial dimension similar to the proposals of CERFI. Regardless of this, the relations between Lefebvre on the one hand, and the camp assembled around CERFI, Foucault, Deleuze and Guattari, on the other, were characterised by mutual aggression and lack of comprehension. To be sure, there are points in common, for instance their complex love–hate relationship with Marxism (Lefebvre was expelled from the Party in 1957), and they were all met with the same suspicion by official Party intellectuals. But even if the absence of any productive dialogue between them in this sense exemplified that fetishism of small differences that characterised the non-Party Left at the time, this should not lead us to overlook the essential theoretical differences. To clarify these divergences, while at the same time attempting to locate their point of origin, would be an essential task not only for a historical analysis, but also for what might still today be called a critical theory of architecture.

One recent attempt to straddle this divide can be found in Edward Soja, who attempts to bring Foucault and Lefebvre together in his conception of 'thirdspace' (Soja 1996), but the question is whether this might not risk erasing the particularities in their respective positions, above all their respective understanding of the historical dialectic, of the category of totality and the status of subjectivity. For Foucault – if we allow for the reconstruction of an argument that cannot be found as such in his writings – Lefebvre would be caught up in an illusory belief in the given, which makes him unable to see that subjectivity and individuality are themselves produced, and thus cannot immediately function as a lever for resistance, but require a historical and genealogical critique. Lefebvre, in those few passages in his writings where Foucault does appear, retorts that Foucault does not grasp the contradictory and open qualities of everyday spatiality (a point subsequently developed by Michel de Certeau in his work on 'everyday life', which in many respects attempts to straddle this divide), but derives it immediately from a kind of abstract diagram of power. It is symptomatic, so Lefebvre claims, that Foucault uses only the abstract concept *savoir*, and never speaks of knowledge as concrete, *connaissance*, which means that he is unable to bridge the gap between the theoretical sphere and the world of practical action, and thus fails to see the potential of the everyday as well as the decisive role played by capital as a dialectical totality in the Hegelian sense: an overarching structure resulting from the contradiction of its parts, while also determining the sense and direction that must be read into each contradiction for a theory to be possible as such.

This interrupted – or never begun – dialogue defines the parameters within which CERFI's investigations of urban space and collective facilities take place. While Lefebvre remains an indirect and mostly negative point of reference for them, Foucault's work is always central. From the early 1970s and onwards he directs several parallel research projects at the Collège de France dealing with the emergence of institutions such as the hospital as well as the politics of housing, and these intersect in many ways, including the personal, with the activities of CERFI.[7] During this period Foucault is attempting to think through, but also beyond (to a degree which is admittedly difficult to assess), the Marxist categories of social analysis: class, dialectical contradiction, determination in the final instance, the base–superstructure opposition, etc., all questions that his earlier work from the 1960s on madness, the clinic and 'epistemic orders' had left unanswered. His questions bear on the possibility of understanding the multiplicity of tactics and strategies that traverse the social field, on whether all the micro-assemblages to which they give rise and which function as the forcefield providing stability and movement to the 'order of discourse' can be understood solely through the meta-narrative of the development of capital. It is well known that in this period Foucault begins to understand power as coming from below, in terms of a 'microphysics' as he will say a few years later: the big, 'molar' macro-entities – state, capital, class – have to be dissolved into molecular functions. It is the latter that, through a long series of convergences, can explain the emergence of the former, not the former explaining the latter by orienting the movement of history toward a pre-given goal. There is no state, only processes of 'becoming-state', where the state may overtake and redirect processes that do not stem from its own interiority and that cannot be understood as expressions of its own logic. As we will see, CERFI's work on the city presents a particularly dense and nested version of these problems, both in terms of the relation between history and the production of new concepts, as well as regarding the way in which such conceptualisations themselves can make a difference in the world, for instance the status of intellectual work.

The City and Beyond

In Recherches, the preliminary results of the team's research into collective facilities are published as the first part of a more encompassing investigation that will remain unfinished: 'Genealogy of Capital'. Rather than a systematic theoretical exposé, the journal offers a series of essays, transcribed discussions, personal reflections on the internal erotic, financial and psychological tensions within the group itself (in a fashion typical of the period, these themes are entrusted to the female participants, while the men speak of serious, objective and theoretical things) and other texts of fragmentary character.[8] But despite, or perhaps because of, this stylistic heterogeneity, the journal is, as Daniel Defert claims in his essay 'Foucault, Space, and the Architects', 'one of the most interesting log books from the ideological crossings of those times', where one 'as if in a laboratory experiment watches the fissuring of Marxist analysis and the emergence of what would soon be named the "postmodern attitude"' (Defert 1997: 278). Regardless of whether the term 'postmodern' is adequate to the task of capturing this displacement, we can see the dismantling of a whole gamut of traditional urban and sociological categories, while the new analytical tools proffered remain highly insecure and tentative.

As Françoise Choay notes in her influential anthology from the mid-1960s, *Urbanisme: Utopies et réalités*, the architecture culture of the period was split between two main positions: a functionalism rooted in the Athens Charter devised by CIAM (Congrès Internationaux d'Architecure Moderne), and a culturalist attitude focusing on preservation of the cultural heritage (Choay 1965: 15ff.). The issue of *Recherches* opens by citing Choay's remarks (and placing Lefebvre in the culturalist camp without further ado), but it then proceeds to an analysis of these two solutions as mirror images of each other, both of which understand the modern city as fundamentally sick and thus also see it as their task to propose a solution. Both of them also see collective facilities in terms of consumption, where that which is consumed is either function/utility, or symbolic values.

A hidden precondition for there being an alternative in the first place is that one assumes the existence of a *subject of consumption* who would precede the facilities and that the consumption would occur within the register of representation. Now, this does not mean to invalidate any of these positions as such; instead the task must be to uncover an 'epistemological socle', i.e. the particular discursive conditions that make the very alternative possible in the first place. (The image of the socle is used by Foucault, both in *The Order of Things* and *The Archaeology of Knowledge*, and indicates that we are longer in search of a universal *ground*: while the ground is universal and transcendental, the *socle* is the condition of an actual instead of a merely possible knowledge; it is neither located in the depths of knowledge nor at the height of principles, but *in between*.) The point is to understand the city as production, and the collective facilities as the means of production. This is why the analysis, just like the genealogy proposed by Foucault, does not draw on the concept of ideology, which presupposes a set of already formed subjects with their respective representations of the world, but on the conditions for the 'machine' in which such subjects may be located, i.e. in the vocabulary of *Anti-Oedipus*, a schizoanalysis of the city. This would then imply that the city can be taken as a machine that produces itself: 'a signifying machine that does not signify, but gathers, connects, and redistributes all types of chains: productive, institutional, scientific, etc.' (Recherches 1973: 18).

The city is, however, not an ultimate category, but can itself be understood as a higher level of collective facilities which, in turn, is inscribed in a larger territorial organisation that again is part of an even larger system without any defined limits. The city becomes a fixating and stabilising machine, or a kind of relay or switch that on a certain level overcodes and connects flows that originate on a lower level and continue on a higher. This soon leads to the question of whether the category 'city' can be an adequate analytical category at all, which is the real topic of the seemingly abstruse arguments about whether the city and collective facilities deal in 'production' or 'anti-production' in a following section where the group begins to question its own claims: 'The first discussions, the first stutterings: is the city a productive force, or an anti-productive force?' (27–31). While the city, as we have seen, is a 'signifying machine', it is also bound up with the need of capital to produce its own limit, its own reterritorialisation, to avoid being completely fragmented and dispersed along the lines of flight that it also produces. At the end of this first discussion, Guattari intervenes with an argument that seems to wholly dethrone the city and the collective facilities as productive forces within the logic of capital:

Capital is also about anti-production; it too would erect pyramids if it could, but the pyramid of capital flees ahead of it, the signs branch out and flee in all directions. The body without organs of capital is the ideal to master the decoded flows: it is always one step behind machinism, after innovation [. . .] capitalists are there to prevent capital from expanding, but they don't succeed. The capitalist expropriates himself in the movement of capital – the capitalist class has the same function as an *Urstaat*.

The city is a spatial projection, a form of reterritorialisation, a blocking [. . .] The ideal of a reterritorialisation of the decoded flows is embodied in the ideal of an *Urstaat*. But this is impossible: the flows set in motion begin to function, to move. This is the collective facility. It begins to function on its own. It spreads out, it proliferates. The collective facility exists in order to hold something together that by definition cannot hold together. (Recherches 1973: 29)

Territory and Fixation

The following section in *Recherches*, 'The City-Metaphor', elaborates the conclusion that was already implicit, namely that the city is nothing but a metaphor, an empty container or a surface for the projection of various concepts whose proper function, however, has to be understood within a larger system. 'We used the word "city" for what is really relations of social production, forces of production, capital or even the state' (Recherches 1973: 35). The city, the authors remark, easily turns through a subtle displacement into a personification or a hypostatised historical subject endowed with a life of its own (as in, for instance, in the work of Lewis Mumford or Fernand Braudel). Instead, they propose, 'the discourse on urbanity should itself become the object of an archaeology, its reference should be deconstructed' (Recherches 1973: 36).

In Marx too they find indications of such hypostatising, for instance in *The German Ideology* or *The Communist Manifesto*. Both of them, notwithstanding their historicising of all categories, tend to understand the system country-city in an ahistorical fashion, which tacitly allows the form of the presentation to be organised according to an irreversible path leading from country to city, something which Marx famously characterises as the liberation from 'rural idiocy'.[9] What could equally well have been understood as oppositions between different cities within a given territory – for instance on the basis of conflicting interests of different producers – always comes to be overcoded by the abstract opposition country-city.

In CERFI's reading, it is highly significant that this is also the context in which Marx places the genesis of ideology. Resulting from the separation between material and intellectual labour, it has as its 'most essential precondition' the separation between countryside and city – 'the very passage from barbarianism to civilization', as *The German Ideology* has it. The theme runs through Marx's whole work and does not disappear in the later writings, which allows CERFI to argue against Althusser (and also *en passant* against Manuel Castells, whose 1971 *La Question urbaine* is heavily influenced by structural Marxism) and the thesis on an 'epistemological break' in Marx, where he would have freed himself from the dialectical and humanist metaphysics of his early writings, as well as against the dialectical humanist Lefebvre who refuses to acknowledge such a passage from 'subject' to 'system'. For Althusser, Marx's abandonment of concrete subjectivity in favour of an abstract and systematic totality means that individual experience can no longer be anything but an imaginary reflection, and we can now proceed to understand the individual as constituted via an 'interpellation' within and by ideology. For Lefebvre, this is a false view of the potential of everyday life, and ideology would rather consist of the dream of a 'pure theory' (and the corresponding dream of a pure subject capable of thinking it). But this stubborn opposition, the authors in *Recherches* claim, in fact hides the underlying points of fracture and allows them to be overlaid with a series of oppositions: nature–culture, barbarism–civilisation, knowledge–ignorance, impurity–purity, artificiality–authenticity, among others, which all remain caught within the same dualist model. Neither subject (experience) nor system (pure theory, structure) are sufficient concepts; instead we have to find a series of concepts that cut transversally through the opposition between the dialectic of experience and the structuralist system analysis, and open the opposition up to that which passes through both subject and system.

What we need to see, CERFI claims, is that there is no such thing as the city, an entity that would stand in opposition to an equally abstract countryside, but rather there is only a network of cities, which in its turn expands into a concept of territory, and it is this which might be the proper object of analysis. Two tasks are thereby crystallised: there is a need for, on the one hand, a theory of territoriality that accounts for both its openness (that it has no once-and-for-all defined limit) and its closure (the state overcodes a given territory, inscribes its signs onto it in order to make it into its own body), and on the other hand, an analysis that comes back to collective facilities, although no longer in terms of physical architectonic objects, but as complex assemblages of power and desire, i.e. as objects of what we, following Nietzsche and Foucault, could call a genealogy.

We may leave the development of the concept of territory aside here, even though many of the theses advanced in connection with territory would merit a discussion and could be fruitfully contrasted to Foucault's later lectures from the second half of the 1970s on 'Security, Territory, Population'. Here Foucault proposes an analysis of the genesis of the modern state apparatus by way of an interrogation of liberalism as a means to achieve a new type of control by stepping back from the processes inside society. This was a concern which remained absent from the horizon of CERFI in 1973, as it surely also was for Foucault at the time. In *Recherches*, the focus lies rather on a set of fixating and disciplinary mechanisms, as can be seen in the three points listed at the end of the third section (Recherches 1973: 93–4), and which summarise the territorial organisation of early industrial capitalism:

1. The city fixes the population around an industrial function, the example being mining cities in the north of France, which organise the habitation of the workers so that everything comes to revolve around the mine.
2. The city as a whole can therefore be seen as a collective facility for territorial fixation. A paradigm case of this would be, the authors note, Bentham's Panopticon model, where 'all the elements in the territory of the facility are monitored in such a way that they are all aware of it in every moment' (and here we may recognise a theme which Foucault would develop two years later in *Discipline and Punish*).
3. The family becomes an invested object and habitation comes to form a part of the system of collective facilities. Rather than a residual formation belonging to an earlier stage, the family is a new object produced at the initial phase of industrial capitalism, a kind of 'facility' in which desire may circulate in a new way, and which can become the point of departure for new processes of becoming-subject.

The Formation of Collective Facilities

At the outset, we noted that the analysis of collective facilities drew on a Lacanian distinction between needs (or explicitly stated demands) and desire. The radical thesis proposed at the later stage of the investigation is rather that the need for facilities is an illusion, or more like a retroactive rationalisation, a thesis to a great deal influenced by Foucault's investigations of how the discursive object 'madness' – an object we can talk about, analyse, fear, seek to control secretly or approach as a subversive force – is itself produced by the 'Great Internment', i.e. a physical institution that gives rise to manifold effects on all levels of knowledge instead of emerging as an answer to an already existing need. It is true that the population should not be understood as a passive and malleable mass; however, nor should its activity be understood in terms of given needs, but rather through the desires it sets in motion, and we have already discussed the wide sense in which desire is here to be understood.

Thus we should not understand institutions as responses to a need or as motivated by a function that would remain permanent throughout history: 'one can never explain a collective facility by its use in a system of needs; what has to be brought to light is the forceful gesture [*coup de force*] that gives rise to it as an instrument of subjection, dominance, and repression' (Recherches 1973: 109). This does not mean to deny function and use or to see them as mere ideologies but, the authors claim, to understand them as 'mechanisms of inscription that produce collective facilities as instruments of coding, internment, limitation, and exclusion of free social energy' (Recherches 1973: 109). This theory of collective facilities can be summarised with five central theses (Recherches 1973: 127–8):

1. The person or the subject, as that upon which the new facilities converge, is not an anthropological given, but an effect of the movement of the forces of the unconscious, which at the same time are social forces of production, registered and distributed over the surface of social institutions, where they determine a field of representation, which thus also comes to apply to the person or the subject.
2. The family is no more primordial than the person; the modern marital bond displaces the old large family and comes to play a decisive new role in the modern system of production.
3. Collective facilities inscribe, codify and give rise to a 'territorial fixation' of the flows that have been released by the destruction of the pre-capitalist order.
4. They produce normalisation on the basis of a whole gamut of distinctions: the healthy and the pathological, worker and unemployed, sane and insane, etc.
5. Social needs cannot explain facilities; instead, the formation state/capital produces, in one and the same movement, the facilities, the family and all the corresponding 'needs'. The 'genealogical turn', the authors claim, 'has as its aim to dissolve the objectivity of needs and the whole system that articulates it.'

As the discussions proceed, these general theses are tested in relation to the hospital and other medical facilities, schools and the educational system, the development of urban green spaces, and eventually in relation to the general discourse of planning. Throughout, these processes are seen in terms of 'normalisation' in a way that follows the path delineated in Foucault's early work on the history of madness and the birth of the clinic and that he was also developing concurrently in various research projects at the Collège de France. In the medical institution that emerges around the time of the French Revolution, the state begins to assume control over medicine as a means of surveillance and control, so that eventually 'medical space coincides with social space' (Recherches 1973: 151), which from the point of view of architecture means that the hospital as an enclosed space begins to be rethought as a mobile facility that extends throughout the city.[10] Similarly, the analysis of the school traces its development through its gradual removal from clerical authorities and its role in the constitution of a homogeneous and predictable workforce, and the way in which 'the physical space of the school works through the separation of the sexes, corporeal rigidity, the serialisation of children in a gridded space' (168), themes that would a few years later receive a systematic analysis in terms of 'docile bodies' in Foucault's *Discipline and Punish*. From the point of view of urbanism, the most relevant section is no doubt the one on 'green spaces' (169–74), which shows how this concept emerges in the writings of Georges-Eugène Haussmann, and was then continued through the Garden City movement up to Corbusier, as a kind of compensatory gesture that wants to assure that the logic of state and capital would be able to contain its exterior in a regimented and artificial interior nature.

Inserted in the beginning of this section (Recherches 1973: 129–45), there is yet another crucial and 'fabulous' discussion, which despite its 'harshness', as its title reads, does not succeed in 'penetrating the enigma of Capital' (*Une discussion fabuleuse ne parvient pas, malgré son âpreté, à percer l'enigme du capital*). While the inconclusive nature of the investigations presented are visible throughout and often made into a theme – this is indeed a 'log book', as Daniel Defert suggests – this is perhaps the place where inner contradictions come to the fore in a way that should still hold our attention.

This second discussion continues the theme of production and anti-production that in the first discussion was keyed to the city, now also in terms of circulation and non-circulation, and finally of the idea of the facility as such. The general issue seems to be the extent to which the 'axiomatics of capital' reaches into the other spheres (or, perhaps, the question of a relative autonomy of levels, using a more traditional Marxist vocabulary). At the end, the question is asked if even the very idea of axiomatic, as in the highly formal and abstract research of the Bourbaki group (an anonymous collective of mathematicians who devoted themselves to the project of founding mathematics on the axiomatisation of set theory), is already part of capital, along with all other theoretical models that attempt to analyse it, or if, as Félix Guattari – who throughout most of the discussion takes a highly critical stance towards the results produced so far[11] – suggests, intellectual work already points outside of the system. While it may be perverse to reduce the extreme complexity of the discussion, as well as the level of terminological inventiveness at which it takes place, to well-known agendas, the synthesis – to be a sure a 'disjunctive' one (to use the vocabulary of *L'Anti-Œdipe*) – of Marx's analysis of capital and Nietzsche's genealogy proved to be highly volatile: the relations between theory and practice or, on another level, between the analysis of historical material and the construction of new logical categories remain unresolved.

In the end, this implies not only that a genealogy of collective facilities does not provide us with any normative theory of the development of institutions, but also that it does not tell us what a good State, Society, or Man, ought to look like, and one must assume that the commissioners at the Ministère de l'Equipement were bewildered by the results presented in *Recherches*. But while these debates remained inconclusive, there are many zigzag lines that extend from this particular moment to our problems today, whose 'epistemological socle' remains to be uncovered.

Notes

1. For an overall study of the group's works, see Morford (1985). For two personal accounts that, among other things, discuss the special status given to the group by the free 'contract research' in France at the time, see Querrien (2002) and Fourquet (2002). Fourquet's text is available in a longer version in *Recherches*, No. 46 (1982).
2. In the 1953 Rome discourse, Lacan in fact uses three concepts: need (*besoin*), demand (*demande*) and desire (*désir*), the last being the void between the empirical, biological aspect of need and demand as verbalised, which leads to CERFI's use of the terms being slightly skewed. Just as in Lacan, they reject the idea of desire as an anthropological given, but then tend toward a radical constructivism. In this, they are in some respects close to Jean Baudrillard, who suggests that needs can only be understood as a system: 'in the same way that language does not exist because of an individual need to speak [. . .] "consumption" does not exist because of an objective need to consume'; needs are 'a function induced in the individuals by the internal logic of the system, or more precisely, they are

not a power to consume liberated by an affluent society, but a productive force demanded by this system's own mode of functioning' (Baudrillard 1972: 75, 87).

3. 'Généalogie du capital: 1. Les équipements du pouvoir', *Recherches*, No. 13 (1973), p. 15. This issue is henceforth cited in the text as 'Recherches 1973' with pagination; all translations to English by the author.

4. One must bear in mind that Foucault always remained sceptical toward desire as a universal category and the spontaneity it often seemed to imply, sometimes merging with the idea of an unmediated nature, as comes across for instance in his use of the term 'pleasure' in the first volume of the *History of Sexuality*. For Deleuze's comments on these disputes, see Deleuze (2003).

5. Lewis Mumford, cited in Deleuze and Guattari (1972: 165). The 'megamachine' is the term used by Mumford in his two-volume *The Myth of the Machine* (1967–70), to grasp the convergence of science, technology and power, to which he opposes a humanist resistance based in the experience of the self. While the vast historical sweep of Mumford's analysis, taking us from the pyramids of Egypt to the present, is consonant with Deleuze and Guattari, his claims about subjective interiority are obviously not.

6. The analogy between flows of information and capitalism obviously draws on a long lineage of cybernetic theory, but at this precise moment also gains traction because of technical changes like the computerisation of the stock exchange in the early 1970s. These ideas were at the same time systematically developed by Ernest Mandel, in his *Der Spätkapitalismus*, and they obviously also had profound repercussions on the basic concepts in Marxist theory after Althusser (see Jameson 1988).

7. During the early years, Foucault's research in these areas follows two main lines. The first deals with the emergence of the figure of the doctor and of medical knowledge as a form of public authority, and whose material correlate is the modern hospital as a place where patients can be studied in isolation from one another. In 1976 partial results of this project were published in the collected volume *Les machines à guérir (aux origines de l'hôpital moderne)*. The second line interrogates the 'politics of habitation' as it was formed during the first half the nineteenth century, and eventually results in two substantial collected publications edited by Foucault, *Généalogie des équipements de normalization: Les équipements sanitaires*, for which he provides the preface, and *Politiques de l'habitat, 1800–1850*, containing no written contribution by Foucault, even though his research directives seem to have influenced the essays in a decisive way (the research team behind this publication is also to a large extent the same as in *Les machines à guérir*). For a discussion of how these little-known research projects tie into Foucault's more general trajectory, see Wallenstein (2007: 382–94).

8. The theoretical contributions are unlike those that reflect on the group dynamic in the further sense that they are published anonymously, and while it would be possible to reconstruct individual authorship, I choose to treat the text as a collective product.

9. Samuel Moore's official translation, approved by Engels and since then the basis of innumerable editions of the Manifesto, reads: 'The bourgeoisie has subjected the country to the rule of the towns. It has created enormous cities, has greatly increased the urban population as compared with the rural, and has thus rescued a considerable part of the population from the idiocy of rural life (*Idiotismus des Landlebens*).' Moore's translation 'idiocy' has been questioned and 'isolation' would no doubt be closer to the Greek term *idiotes*, if this is what Marx and Engels had in mind. See, for instance, Hal Draper's new translation with comments in Draper (1998).

10. At another level, it also means that architecture begins to be understood as conditioned by a whole set of new forms of knowledge relating to statistics, natality and mortality rates, and to the surveying of the population as a living multiplicity to be grasped. In his contribution to the collected volume *Les machines à guérir*, which analyses the debates around the new kind of facility that was to replace the infamous Hôtel-Dieu after it was destroyed by fire in 1772, Bruno Fortier suggests that 'within the history of modernity the Hôtel-Dieu affair may be one of those moments when the architectural project is no longer exclusively understood in relation to history, but as a function of a double imperative: technical rationalisation and efficiency in matters of discipline, economy, and power' (Foucault et al. 1976: 46). For a discussion of the importance of these events for architectural theory, see Wallenstein (2009).

11. Apart from the particular, and to a contemporary reader sexist, gender structure that permeated the presentation in *Recherches*, there is also an ulterior dimension that could become the topic of a different reading, namely the role of Félix Guattari as the mostly absent father figure, and the even more remote and thus mysterious authority of Deleuze and Foucault, who at one point (Recherches 1973: 183–6) engage in the discussion, though seemingly without any contact with the others, a psychodrama sometimes referred to in the italicised sections written by the female CERFI members.

References

Banham, R. (1960) *Theory and Design in the First Machine Age*. London: Architectural Press.

Baudrillard, J. (1972) *Pour une critique de l'économie politique du signe*. Paris: Gallimard.

Choay, F. (ed.) (1965) *Urbanisme: utopies et réalités*. Paris: Seuil.

Defert, D. (1997) 'Foucault, space, and the architects', in *documenta X: Poetics/Politics*. Stuttgart: Canz.

Deleuze, G. (2003) *Deux régimes de fous*. Paris: Minuit.

Deleuze, G. and Guattari, F. (1972) *L'Anti-Œdipe*. Paris: Minuit.

Draper, H. (1998) *The Adventures of the Communist Manifesto*. Berkeley: Center for Socialist History.

Foucault, M. et al. (1976) *Généalogie des équipements de normalization: Les équipements sanitaires*. Paris: Ed. CERFI.

Foucault, M. et al. (1976) *Les machines à guérir (aux origines de l'hôpital moderne)*. Brussels: Mardaga.

Foucault, M. et al. (1976) *Politiques de l'habitat, 1800–1850*. Paris: Corda.

Fourquet, F. (2002) 'The story of CERFI', *Site*, 2–3: 12–13.

Jameson, F. (1988) *The Ideologies of Theory: Essays 1971–1986. Vol. 2, The Syntax of History*. Minneapolis: University of Minnesota Press.

Mandel, E. (1972) *Der Spätkapitalismus*. Frankfurt am Main: Suhrkamp.

Morford, J. (1985) 'Histoire du CERFI. La trajectoire d'un collectif de recherche sociale'. Unpublished Mémoire de D.E.A., École des Hautes Études en Sciences Sociales, available at IMEC, Paris.

Mumford, L. (1967–70) *The Myth of the Machine*. New York: Harcourt Brace Jovanovich.

Querrien, A. (2002) 'CERFI: four points', *Site*, 2–3: 11–12.

Recherches (1973) 'Généalogie du capital: 1. Les équipements du pouvoir', No. 13.

Recherches (1982) 'L'Accumulation du pouvoir, ou le désir d'Etat: Synthèse des recherches du CERFI de 1970 à 1981', No. 46.

Soja, E. W. (1996) *Thirdspace: Journeys to Los Angeles and Other Real-and-Imagined Places*. Cambridge, MA: Blackwell.

Stanek, Ł. (2011) *Henri Lefebvre on Space: Architecture, Urban Research, and the Production of Theory*. Minneapolis: University of Minnesota Press.

Wallenstein, S.-O. (2007) *Essays, Lectures*. Stockholm: Axl Books.

Wallenstein, S.-O. (2009) *Biopolitics and the Emergence of Modern Architecture*. New York: Princeton Architectural Press.

Chapter 9

Deterritorialising the Face of the City: How *Treponema pallidum* Planned Melbourne

Jean Hillier

John Batman, often recognised as the founder of Melbourne, Australia, fatally suffered from degenerative syphilis. The spirochaete *Treponema pallidum*, better known as syphilis, ravaged Melbourne in the early twentieth century. In its tertiary stage, syphilis can infect the brain or spinal cord, resulting in neurological disease, blindness, dementia and seizures. *Treponema pallidum* is highly mobile and may be transmitted through sexual encounter or congenitally. Highly resistant to most antibiotics, there remains no effective preventative vaccine (Margulis, in Teresi 2011).

Syphilis became a cause for international alarm in the late nineteenth and early twentieth centuries: 'There is nothing known to history – more appalling, more dangerous, and more terrible in its never-ending effect, to the general public than the disease of syphilis' (Fahey 1911: 931). For many years syphilis remained a mute force – the great unspoken – 'insidiously, silently stalking the unwary and rendering something more lasting than death' (Levine 2003: 43).

Debate about syphilis folded medical, economic, nationalist, religious and moral planes of reference together with those of an incipient town planning movement in Melbourne. The construction event of the Women's Venereal Disease (VD) Clinic in Little Lonsdale Street performs as Deleuzian monument confiding to the ear of the future an embodiment of affects that are at once past, present and eternally immanent (Deleuze and Guattari 1994: 176).

The Women's VD Clinic (Fig. 9.1) is a relatively mundane Victorian red-brick Georgian Revival-style building tucked away in a narrow backstreet of a former slum area of inner Melbourne. It is regarded as of little aesthetic value (Taylor 2012) and passers-by rarely give it a second glance. The building is not simply a historical remnant, however, but a monumental actualisation of the conjunction of medical and moral

Fig. 9.1 The Women's VD Clinic, Little Lonsdale Street, Melbourne (photograph by the author)

planes of reference and their encounter and folding together with the planes of reference of town planning in the late nineteenth and early twentieth centuries.

Heritage elements, such as the VD Clinic, are monumental not in the Nietzschean sense (Nietzsche 1983) because they conserve or preserve their time, but because they generate an affective rethinking of time and the nature of human and non-human life itself. Reading the VD Clinic as monument illuminates an 'agentic capacity not restricted to the human actor' (Bennett 2007: 133), a 'thing-power' (Bennett 2010) or 'material vitalism' (Deleuze and Guattari 1987: 411) which exerts forces and creates affects with regard to conceptualisation and production of the built environment. There is a 'thingness' to objects, such as the Clinic and *Trep. pall.*, beyond human capacity to construct them. They have their own infinite capacity to create encounters, relations and new planes of organisation.

While Deleuze wrote little about disease or illness itself,[1] concentrating on pathology and clinical psychotherapeutic practice, especially (literary) symptomatology, he regarded illness as a site for the merging of vital processes. I aim to move beyond a simple medical/moral dichotomy, to superfold together issues of science, eugenics, nationalism, economic and military efficiency and nascent town planning, unsettling the core agentive role of humans to highlight encounters and conjunctions of human and non-human assemblages represented monumentally by the VD Clinic. The planned landscape of the city is a facial assemblage, its skyline an expressivity (DeLanda 2006). The VD Clinic in Little Lonsdale Street is also a facial assemblage, as are the faces of the late nineteenth- to early twentieth-century women-in-prostitution it predominantly served.

In what follows, I introduce Deleuze and Guattari's concept of face. Faces are produced by abstract machines of faciality, as cartographic maps of relations between forces, while concrete machines, comprising assemblages of materialities and discursivities, socially organise or territorialise perceptions and meanings. I aim to render less opaque the conjunction of the concrete machines of despotic governmentality with the abstract machine of faciality which shaped these facial assemblages and, in this way, to problematise, deterritorialise and reterritorialise early town planning in Melbourne in order to enable a new sensibility of how Melbourne became planned.

Regarding the city of Melbourne as a plane of technical composition (Deleuze and Guattari 1994: 191–2), I outline the three planes of reference of medicine/health, morality/eugenics and what became town planning which folded together in the territorialised development of the late nineteenth- and early twentieth-century city. Transversal across the three planes, the unprepossessing red-brick Women's VD Clinic in Little Lonsdale Street signifies and monumentalises the importance of *Trep. pall.* in the planning story of Melbourne.

The activity of town planning in Melbourne today is still grounded in a system of land use zones which separate uses such as residential, medical and public parks into discrete spatial locations. Conservation of built heritage is also a key theme in the draft State Planning Policy Framework (DTPLI 2014). Heritage planning, however, typically captures and reproduces selected, contracted representations of past actualities. What interests Deleuze is how we might 'leave behind' the past as history, to create something new. How might history be active in the creation of life? Deleuze (1990) appropriates Nietzsche's (1983) 'history for life' by converting the Nietzschean history for the future into a philosophy for the future as a differential 'becoming/history'.

Since for Deleuze and Guattari (1994: 167) a monument is 'a bloc of present sensations', it can help us to fabulate not only the past but the present and the future, and thereby to influence the thinking and action of the present population. I suggest that heritage planning, of the Women's VD Clinic for instance, might engage the agency of materialities to stimulate people to think, both about the many pasts of Melbourne – about how the working-class women of 'Little Lon' were stereotyped as prostitutes, how eugenics was considered an acceptable 'solution' – and also about today's practices, nationally and internationally, of commercial, sexual exploitation of women, of trafficking, of blaming women for 'inviting' sex crimes and STDs and of State eugenic decisions to sterilise certain people.

I seek to utilise materialities of cultural heritage to confront hegemonic categorisations which inform our thinking and to identify new potentialities of becoming-woman, becoming-woman-in-prostitution.[2] In Deleuze's words, 'to think the past against the present, to resist the present, not for a return but "in favour, I hope, of a time to come" (Nietzsche): this means making the past active and present to the outside, in order that something new will finally happen, so that thinking always encompasses thought' (1986: 127, my translation).

Faciality and Machines

Deleuze and Guattari (1987) utilise the concept of the face to illustrate how processes of meaning-making are often constrained and consolidated into ordering, power-laden binaries of coding: us/them, acceptable/unacceptable and so on. Faciality thus serves as a means of identity management.

Faces take shape in assemblages of material and expressive connections in which humans, bacteria and other non-humans encounter and interact with each other. The face is produced by an abstract machine of faciality (Deleuze and Guattari 1987), the virtual structure of immanent relations which determines what faces are possible. Faces, therefore, are not ready-made, but rather the 'reactive effects of a process in which meaning is constructed through the association of elements into a coherent form' (Bignall 2012: 399). Processes of meaning-construction vary according to the particular assemblage of elements, their force relations and the 'assembly rules' (Bignall 2012) dominant at the time. As Deleuze and Guattari (1987: 181) comment, the face is 'a politics', manipulated, in Melbourne, by abstract machines linking unformed matters of bacteria and humans and non-formal functions of medicine, eugenics, town planning and so on.

A face comprises white walls of signification and black holes of sub-jectification. The white wall is a surface (such as the city) onto which signs (e.g. of *Trep. pall.*) are projected and from which they are reflected. The black hole is that invisible or unknown area behind the white wall where affect (generating disgust, anxiety and so on) operates. Faces are landscapes and landscapes are faces. MacCormack suggests that 'the landscape is also cultivated by a set of people who own, run and map the land' (2004: 137). In Melbourne, organisations such as the Victorian Town Planning and Parks Association (VTPPA) exemplify such cultiva-tion. Established in 1914 to lobby for the 'scientific regulation' of town planning (May and Reidy 2009: 98), the VTPPA's Committee com-prised educated, professional, reformist-minded members, including Dr Sir James Barrett and Professor Richard Berry, of whom more below.

Concrete machines construct a singular version of a thing (such as a disease or a place). They systematise and institutionalise particular ways of seeing and understanding through power-laden redundancies of rep-resentation (Hillier 2013). As oppressive (despotic) universal reference points, concrete machines reduce materialities of flesh, bacteria, bricks and so on to surfaces of interpretation or signifying machines channel-ling perception and behaviour: 'you will be a subject, nailed down as one' (Deleuze and Guattari 1987: 159).

Established sets of significations, such as the 'royal sciences' of bac-teriology, anatomy and town planning, predetermine the possibility of recognition and limit the potential for refiguring meanings (Bignall 2012) of bacteria and female prostitutes. In this manner, concrete machines (legislation, norms, standards, etc.) managed the conjunction of stratified authority with abstract machines of faciality. Advances in medical science, pride in new nationhood and a push for economic recovery in early twentieth-century Melbourne became associated with ideas such as 'purity of blood' and 'social inefficiency'.

Disease, Bodies and Space Conjoin Medicine, Morals and Planning

At the turn of the twentieth century, Melbourne's 'Little Lon' was a working-class area of immigrants living among manufacturing works, warehouses, shops and brothels. It was widely regarded as a slum and hotbed of vice by class-, gender- and faith-based moralists who declared 'war' on the area and its inhabitants. Little Lon became a venereal place where strata of race, class and gender were facialised by machines of health, eugenics and town planning.

In 1917–18 medical statistics estimated that some 7.5 per cent of the total population of Victoria were infected with venereal disease; there were 9,353 registered (plus an estimated *c.*70,000 unregistered) cases in Melbourne, roughly 10 per cent of the population. The monument of the Women's VD Clinic in Little Lon spatialises the early twentieth-century force relations between disease, bodies, politics and planning. As Huxley (2006:169) writes, practices of town planning emerged in Melbourne as a 'compilation of disparate rationales and justifications'. Planes of reference of medicine/health, moral purity/eugenics and town planning enfolded themselves through the intercession of assemblages such as the VTPPA and key committee members such as Barrett and Berry, while other discourses such as national defence (Smart 1998) and economic growth (Garton 1988) were also folded into the mix.

For Deleuze and Guattari (1994), a plane of reference relates to the differential field of potential transformations of material systems. It enables actualisation through the construction of functions of systems of coordinates, including the symptomatology and bacteriology of *Trep. pall.*, pharmaceutics, architecture, legislation and so on. Such functions are determinant of states of affairs, framing or limiting the conditions in which systems actualise in identifiable forms and configurations. The three planes of reference above form the bases for the establishment of various 'despotic' associations (such as the Women's Christian Temperance Union, the Association to Combat the Social Evil, the Board of Public Health, the Melbourne Metropolitan Board of Works, the Victorian Town Planning and Parks Association, the Metropolitan Town Planning Commission), various legislative measures (Act for the Conservation of Public Health 1878, Immigration Restriction Act 1901, Venereal Diseases Acts 1916, 1918) and various concrete structures (faith-based mission houses, children's playgrounds, kindergartens, hospitals and clinics).

Medical Plane of Reference: Healthy Bodies

Treponema pallidum is a spirochaete bacterium with long helically coiled cells. Free-living and anaerobic, *Trep. pall.* reproduces autopoietically through asexual transverse binary fission (cell division). Humans are the only known natural host for *Trep. pall.* Transmitted, particularly by males through sexual encounter, or pregnancy, it results in spontaneous abortion, stillbirth and congenital syphilis. The main problem with diagnosis of syphilis has always been that it initially manifests as a small, painless, non-itchy skin ulceration some 21–90 days after contact

(Kent and Romanelli 2008). The lesion gradually evolves into highly contagious ulcers. Since symptoms usually self-resolve after 3–6 weeks, many working-class sufferers often did not seek treatment. However, *Trep. pall.* can remain latent for several years and symptoms can recur between three and forty-five years after initial infection.

Such tertiary syphilis often involves the formation of soft, tumour-like balls of inflammation which can occur anywhere on the body (Kent and Romanelli 2008), especially, as in the case of John Batman, on the face. Such 'monstrous . . . welling up of the flesh' (Dixon and Ruddick 2013) was widely regarded as a moral as well as a physical degeneracy. Syphilis can also affect the central nervous system in the form of meningovascular syphilis (seizure), paralytic dementia and/or *tabes dorsalis* (syphilitic myelopathy), a degeneration of the sensory neurons affecting the entire body (Kent and Romanelli 2008).

While this symptomatology is known and readily accessible at the present day, *Trep. pall.* was not bacterially identified until 1905 (Franzen 2008),[3] after which time treatment tended to be with a highly toxic compound of mercury and chlorine (mercuric chloride) which could cause damage to the brain, kidneys and lungs. The first partially effective treatment (Salvarsan, an arsenic compound) was developed in 1910, though side-effects of convulsions, jaundice and liver damage were common and relatively high monetary costs were an impediment to its widespread use. Penicillin treatment commenced in 1943 (Franzen 2008). In the early twentieth century, *Trep. pall.* was associated with rampant contagion, a smooth space of rapidly spreading disease which appeared resistant to medical intervention. The outbreak of the First World War exacerbated the situation, with 25 per cent of Australian soldiers presenting with syphilis at enlistment (Shoesmith 1972). Doctors were perturbed by the high rates of infection as they recognised that cases were probably under-reported by at least 50 per cent. Syphilis rapidly became not only a medical problem but also one of national defence (Smart 1998): a veritable 'war machine invoked against the State' (Deleuze and Guattari 1987: 268), its 'anarchic chaotic tendencies . . . always threatening to disrupt the [State] order' (Bogue 2003: 118).

The development of methods of scientific measurement and collection of statistics reflected specific ways of thinking and intellectual techniques for striating what had previously been smooth spaces. Numbers implied objectivity, removed from political and other interests. As Foucault (1977) demonstrated, the rise of the calculable both individualises and normalises as individuals are allocated (stratified) according to their deviance (or not) from the norm. In so doing, scientific measurement becomes formalised as 'knowledge' and powerfully shapes, as a plane of reference, the ways in which choices are open – or closed – to actors, including medics, politicians and working-class women-in-prostitution. Scientific measurement performs as a machine of faciality, projecting calculation onto white walls of medical survey, constructing faces of the infected and, in particular, those presumed responsible for the infecting.

It was almost universally working-class women, and especially women-in-prostitution, who were held responsible for selfishly endangering economic, social and military health. During the First World War, having syphilis was regarded as a sign of 'disloyalty, betrayal, selfishness, and lack of moral rectitude' (Levine 2003: 146). Women's conduct, or rather that of their bodies, had to be acted upon, controlled and potentially transformed by medical (individual) and/or legislative (collective) biopolitical means.

As Anderson (2002: 44) points out, ideas abounded that those regarded as 'socially marginal, or outcast . . . nasty and uncouth, or lacking in civilization' might be responsible for 'the spread of invisible disease organisms'. Prostitution was thus reconfigured as a problem of hygiene and health. Scientific measurement 'was placing sex (sexual relations, venereal diseases, matrimonial alliances, perversions) in a position of "biological responsibility" with regard to the species' (Foucault 1978: 118). In early twentieth-century Melbourne, a medico-legal-town planning regime developed round women's bodies, syphilis and all they symbolised, determining that intervention was necessary for the future of white Australia (discussed below).

Material bodies were folded together with bodies of scientific knowledge, survey processes and practices: knowledge as a body of knowledge of the body. For Deleuze, the body is a machinic assemblage, not a singular ontological essence, but emerging in a series of affective and relational becomings (Duff 2010: 625). Material bodies were machinically facialised through encounters with powerful medical elements (such as bacteriologists, general practitioners, scientific calculation and so on), to be 'treated' accordingly.

The plane of reference for the diagnosis and treatment of syphilis, as indicated above, linked the tertiary stage to possible development of neurological problems, including paralytic dementia and *tabes dorsalis*. In Melbourne, as elsewhere, *Trep. pall.* and syphilis became linked to manifestations of insanity. In addition, prostitution and 'illegitimate' motherhood – both signs of sexual promiscuity – were linked with hereditary 'mental deficiency' and 'feeble-mindedness'. For Richard

Berry (1930), the solution was to eradicate the mentally deficient from the population through the systematic application of eugenics.

Moral Purity Plane of Reference: The Good Citizen

In early twentieth-century Melbourne, the medical profession was aligned with Christianity, temperance and propriety in general. The inclusion of moral arguments in medical debates about *Trep. pall.* was inevitable. Syphilis has always had (and still has for some) a moral as well as a medical face (see Foucault 2006: 83–7). It was regarded as not only attacking individuals but as weakening the white Australian 'race' and degrading 'national progress' (Garton 1988). Immediately following Australian Federation and the establishment of the Commonwealth in 1901, the Immigration Restriction Act (known as the 'White Australia Policy') was enacted to exclude unwanted (non-British or non-European) immigrants. The 'superior qualities' of the white Australian race were perceived as threatened by degeneration caused by imported diseases, dilution due to racial mixing and venereal disease.

Racial purity was linked with moral purity by many, including the Women's Christian Temperance Union and the Association to Combat the Social Evil. In debates about purity conducted predominantly within middle-class circles, women tended to be facialised through sex-role stereotyping, either as wife/mother or fallen woman/prostitute, moral or immoral. Eugenicists sponsored the establishment of clinics for 'race hygiene' and 'mental hygiene' (Watts 1994) through compulsory treatment and moral education. Patients needed specialised clinics in order to avoid morally infecting other, non-VD patients in general hospitals. 'Case-hardened' prostitutes were treated in VD clinics or 'locks'.[4]

Apart from treatment and education, the State attempted to territorialise the smooth space of *Trep. pall.* contagion through legislation. The Act for the Conservation of Public Health 1878 (informally known as the Contagious Diseases Act) and the Victorian Venereal Diseases Acts 1916 and 1918 represented direct attempts to suppress women-in-prostitution and control the spread of VD (Summers 1975) while protecting the interests of the larger, organised brothels (frequented by middle- and upper-class professional men). The Acts focused on women as the 'pool of contagion' (Levine 2003) and, in particular, the unregulated smooth spaces of 'amateurs', street-walkers or 'clandestines' who did not work in licensed brothels. Such 'disorderly female bodies' (Smart 1998: 11) – typically described as 'walking pestilences' (Wood 1909: 6) – needed to 'conform to the same sorts of standards as were imposed on other articles of consumption such as food and drink' (Wood 1909: 6, in Smart 1998: 11).

The concrete machines of legislation thus reduce the material bodies of women to 'articles of consumption' and immoral purveyors of disease. The facial white wall of unmarried working-class women in early twentieth-century Melbourne reflects signs projected by Progressive moral reformers and those concerned with the moral and racial purity of good Australian citizens. The women fall (or are rather pushed) into the black hole of subjectification as 'prostitutes', 'walking pestilences' and 'articles of consumption', defined solely in terms of their sexuality. Such a form of morality identifies the women not as bodies-in-the-making, but as fully-formed subjects of an already-constituted facialisation process. The women might be 'cured' or 'saved' through medical and educational 'treatment', but many faith- or temperance-based organisations nevertheless regarded them as irredeemable, meriting punishment by a debilitating disease: 'God's scourge for sinners' (Wyndham 2003).

Town Planning Plane of Reference: The Good City

Not all eugenicists advocated the segregation and/or sterilisation of 'mental defectives' and 'the feeble-minded', and there was a group of 'positive eugenicists' (Watts 1994) or 'reform eugenicists' (Jones 1999) active in Melbourne in the early twentieth century. Positive eugenicists were concerned with ensuring the propagation of a healthy white Australian race. James Barrett, who sympathised with eugenic beliefs, advocated prophylaxis, sterilisation, exercise and fresh air to combat the scourge of syphilis and to 'peopl[e] Australia with a healthy, vigorous, white race' (Barrett 1925, in Anderson 2002: 132). He urged 'the voluntary sterilisation of the more profoundly defective, a promotion of middle-class reproduction, and the development of infant welfare, kindergartens, playgrounds, Scouting, temperance, sexual hygiene, worker education, and a system of national parks' (Barrett 1918, in Anderson 2002: 160). Barrett presented the first of many public lectures on town planning in Melbourne in 1911 and founded the VTPPA in 1914.

The mute force of *Trep. pall.* in early town planning and the provision of standards for health and other welfare facilities is significant. Town planning, as a practice, has always been grounded in scientific planes of reference or regimes of rationality – architectural, engineering, medical and so on – and the values through which they are interpreted. Urban Melbourne became a laboratory for attempting to control *Trep. pall.* and all it symbolised. To the reformers, Little Lon was a place of physical and moral danger. It, and the bodies one might encounter there, were unordered, and unordered space was potentially dangerous, threatening 'contagion and dissent' (Levine 2003: 299). This was smooth space, to be striated, controlled and/or eliminated. Architecture, space and living arrangements thus took on a moral cast (Levine 2003: 315).

The Women's VD Clinic in Little Lonsdale Street references the physically planned striation of space, of women and of their bodies. It is a product of Deleuzian royal science: a hylomorphic model in which matter (bacteria, bodies, the city) are predetermined as homogeneous masses obedient to interventions and forms imposed externally. Royal, or State, science appropriates space through templates comprising a 'fixed model of form, mathematical figures, and measurement' (Deleuze and Guattari 1987: 365). Medicine and town planning are royal sciences surrounded by 'much priestliness and magic' (Deleuze and Guattari 1987: 373), utilised by the State to impose physical templates of the 'good city' onto early Melbourne, characterised by the planned provision of clinics, hospitals, playgrounds and parks.

A transversal reading of late nineteenth- early twentieth-century town planning in Melbourne can transform the mute forces of *Trep. pall.* into emergent twenty-first-century consciousness. In my reading, one plane of reference is not hierarchically absorbed by another, but all three are reciprocally implicated in the actualisation of Melbourne in a transversal movement which carries them all onwards a 'logic of the AND' (Deleuze and Guattari 1987: 25).

The 'problem' of *Trep. pall.* was constructed and made visible in different ways (through discourses of bacteriology, statistical methodology, morality, national defence and economic progress) by different agents (scientific experts, military and business leaders, politicians, faith-based and other pressure groups). 'These new professions sought to combat social problems by policies of preventive social intervention, bringing science to bear on the problems of economic organisation and moulding the private sphere of family and personal life in the interests of the broader "social good"' (Garton 1991: 340). Differences of opinion (such as those of negative and positive eugenics) were brought into some form of alignment, identifying common features of *Trep. pall.*, sexuality, sex work and town planning, which could then form the basis for exploring the smooth space of syphilis contagion and for devising physical strategies to striate and control it.

The role of the elite, educated middle class was pivotal to folding together the three planes of reference of medicine, eugenics and town planning in early twentieth-century Melbourne. The force relations of such intercessors served to affirm and intensify their values of life, health and body: good health, good citizens, good cities. On the white wall of the city, working-class women-in-prostitution were facialised as the antithesis of women such as Jane/Jean Greig and Edith Barrett on the VTPPA: sexually promiscuous v. modest/demure, diseased v. healthy, ignorant v. educated, alcohol-ridden v. temperant, faithless/debauched v. faith-full, morally evil v. morally good, feeble-minded or mentally defective v. intelligent, social defectives v. social paragons. Such dichotomies create a false exclusive difference (is/is not) and block true difference (and . . . and). The ideal woman's body was 'tight, contained, exercising full control over its boundaries and what comes inside and goes outside' (Lupton 1999: 130). Women may 'shit and fuck', as Deleuze and Guattari (1984: 1) famously write, but Victorian Melbourne was very particular about how and where they did so.

A Space Where Absent Presences Make Themselves Felt

A Deleuzian monument is concerned with the preservation of sensation (Deleuze and Guattari 1994), about shaping the past so that we can shape the present and future. We can thus begin to re-situate heritage planning not as an assemblage of passive objects, but as having a 'life' of its own. We need to tap into the virtual force of heritage, to 'tear it from its constituted time and open its constitutive time, its power to create time, not exist within time' (Colebrook 2006: 82–3). Heritage is both an actuality and a potential to become, what it may have been and what it might still be. An aim of heritage planning, then, would no longer be to (re)collect or (re)capture the past in some individual or collective consciousness or identity, but to explore potentialities and prevent closure. I argue that the Women's VD Clinic as heritage monument could open up the possible, perhaps centred on the features of faciality, through an encounter between visitors and passers-by and the women-in-prostitution of early twentieth-century Melbourne.

Following contested public consultation in 2014, the facade of the VD Clinic is being incorporated into the planning-approved extension of Victoria University in Melbourne. Perhaps this could be achieved in such a way that the bodies of absent women from Little Lon are made present in the built form, together with other texts (including documents, recordings, photographs, virtual reality and so on), to speak to visitors and passers-by in creative rapport (Guattari 2009: 67). This would be a form of topological heritage, folding together the material and the virtual, present and absent, where the VD Clinic, signifying the planes of reference underpinning early twentieth-century Melbourne town planning, is deterritorialised and reterritorialised by those who encounter it. This is not interpretation, but creative experimentation.

Thrift (1999: 310) suggests that 'places are "passings" that "haunt" "us"' and advises us to seek the 'ghostly signals' of what constitutes place: 'flashing half-signs ordinarily overlooked until that one day when they become animated by the immense forces of atmosphere' (1999: 313). Such 'flashing half-signs' may stimulate people to critique despotic, coercive power structures of late nineteenth-century colonialism, early twentieth-century Australian values and hegemonic narratives of medical, moral and physical (town planning) interventions by Progressives and others. The VD Clinic could perform as a counter-site to forces of violence and repression, stimulating alternative, sensory engagements, not only with the 'unconstituted' of dominant histories (trauma, pain, social engineering and so on), but also in the present.

The issue of eugenics is reappearing internationally. Australian Senate Committee inquiries into current practices of involuntary or coerced sterilisation on people with disabilities (Commonwealth of Australia 2013) have generated fresh debate about eugenics in the twenty-first century. Scientific advances in mapping human genomes and in genetic engineering, together with increasing prenatal diagnosis of gender and/ or foetal abnormalities, raise serious moral questions. Arguments in current debates resonate strongly with those voiced a century earlier in Melbourne.

In addition, the location of the heritage Women's VD Clinic, in what was the core area of brothels and sex work in early twentieth-century Melbourne, could trigger people to think about attitudes to adult entertainment premises today. Melbourne is home to 34 per cent of the sex businesses in Australia (IBISWorld 2013), strictly regulated by planning controls and health standards. Strict legislation reflects the conservative and highly moralistic attitudes still pervasive in Victoria (Maginn and Steinmetz 2015). The monument of the VD Clinic could, therefore, also trigger people to think about how societies have typically reduced sexuality to sex and women to purveyors of sex, whether as wives/partners, mothers or sex workers. Can we transform sexuality from being a 'dirty little secret' (Deleuze and Guattari 1984: 49) into a productive energy? Perhaps we can take Deleuze and Guattari's (1987) discussion of becoming-woman as a starting point for acknowledgement of the intensities and actualities that lie hidden in such insufficiently nuanced terms as woman, prostitute and sex worker.

While history as commemoration cannot express becoming (Rodowick

1997), the Women's VD Clinic offers an opportunity to embody history as conceptual creativity; it could allow alternative narratives of past-present-future, taking visitors and passers-by beyond the limits of their own lives to enter a 'zone of proximity' (Patton 2010: 123) with women-in-prostitution, for instance. It could open people to new personal, social or affective possibilities by stimulating them to challenge what they consider acceptable, right or just (Patton 2010: 156). As an experienced process of encounter, becoming may be triggered by the 'most insignificant of things' (Deleuze and Guattari 1984: 292), such as a photograph, audio recording or clinical record. Ethnographic details can reveal the worldliness, rather than the monstrous abnormality of people's – especially women's – struggles in early twentieth-century Little Lon.

The legacy of the planes of reference of medicine, eugenics and town planning is also represented in the mental and physical dispositions of the current despotic, universal reference points of zoning schemes for Melbourne. Health facilities must be located in a Public Use zone, open space in a Public Park and Recreation zone and so on. The first Open Space Strategy for the City of Melbourne (CoM 2012) cites physical and mental health and well-being – in particular, 'being outside in the fresh air and sunlight' (CoM 2012: 3) – as key objectives for open space provision, resonating strongly with the values of James Barrett and the VTPPA a century earlier. The VTPPA slogan 'Beautiful Cities for Beautiful Living' is equally applicable today in all its senses.

Conclusions

Medicine, morals and town planning all enfold both factual and normative claims about what constitutes improvement or betterment: better bodies, better cities. Betterment, however, generally entails less of some entities and more of others. In early twentieth-century Melbourne, this involved aims for less immigration, less venereal disease, less prostitution, less intemperance, less slum conditions and more moral and healthy living in more healthy environments. To this end, *Trep. pall.* was to be disciplined and eliminated through a biopolitics which folded together regimes of signification and planes of reference, translating them into practices of morals and hygiene education, medical treatment and healthy, planned environments. *Trep. pall.*, and by association working-class women, especially prostitutes, were facialised by abstract machines of medicine, eugenics and planning and concrete machines of legislation and standards.

A settlement founded by a syphilised male, Melbourne's relation with

Trep. pall. has long been one of symbiosis. The striated and closed space of the Women's VD Clinic set the medical and moral spaces of legislated 'treatment' against the smooth space of *Trep. pall.* contagion. It enfolds the disparate values, rationales and justifications that came to form the set of practices and legal regimes of town planning which shaped the early twentieth-century city. The legacy of the disparate rationales of the three planes of reference is evident today in the plane of composition that is Melbourne. The Women's VD Clinic, as Deleuzian monument, can potentially offer 'history in a spirited voice' (Stoler 2008: 198) – that of women-in-prostitution – at a site triggering fabulation of the past-present-future.

Acknowledgements

My thanks to Paul Mees and Margo Huxley for inspiration.

Notes

1. Note, however, 'M pour Maladie' in his interview with Claire Parnet (Deleuze and Parnet 1996).
2. Whereas 'prostitute' was the term predominantly used until the late twentieth century, I prefer to use 'women-in-prostitution' as it regards prostitution as a form of labour which may be chosen by women. The term recognises the different experiences and needs of women working in prostitution together with debates about free choice and coercion, abuse, exploitation and rights. I also recognise men-in-prostitution, but concentrate here on women monumentalised through the VD Clinic in Little Lon, Melbourne.
3. And not genomically sequenced until 1998.
4. More like a detention centre than a medical facility, the lock was a space for 'the removal of the morally as well as the medically dangerous' (Bashford 2004: 167).

References

Anderson, W. (2002) *The Cultivation of Whiteness.* Melbourne: Melbourne University Press.
Barrett, J. (Sir) (1918) *The Twin Ideals: An Educated Commonwealth.* London: H. K. Lewis.
Bashford, A. (2004) *Imperial Hygiene.* London: Palgrave Macmillan.
Bennett, J. (2007) 'Edible matters', *New Left Review*, 45, May/June: 133–45.
Bennett, J. (2010) *Vibrant Matter.* Durham, NC: Duke University Press.
Berry, R. (1930) 'The lethal chamber proposal', *Eugenics Review*, 22 (2): 155–6.
Bignall, S. (2012) 'Dismantling the face: pluralism and the politics of recognition', *Deleuze Studies*, 6 (3): 389–410.
Bogue, R. (2003) *Deleuze and Literature.* New York: Routledge.
City of Melbourne (CoM) (2012) Open Space Strategy, online at: http://www.melbourne.vic.gov.au/ParksandActivities/Parks/Pages/OpenSpaceStrategy.aspx (last accessed 12 December 2014).

Colebrook, C. (2006) *Deleuze: A Guide for the Perplexed*. London: Continuum.

Commonwealth of Australia (CoA) (2013) *Involuntary or Coerced Sterilisation of People with Disabilities*. Canberra: CoA; online at: http://www.aph.gov.au/Parliamentary_Business/Committees/Senate/Community_Affairs/Involuntary_Sterilisation/First_Report (last accessed 24 January 2014).

DeLanda, M. (2006) *A New Philosophy of Society*. London: Continuum.

Deleuze, G. ([1969] 1990) *The Logic of Sense*, trans. M. Lester and C. Stivale. London: Athlone.

Deleuze, G. (1986) *Foucault*, Paris: Les éditions de minuit.

Deleuze, G. and Guattari, F. ([1972] 1984) *Anti-Oedipus: Capitalism and Schizophrenia*, trans. R. Hurley, M. Seem and H. Lane. London: Athlone Press.

Deleuze, G. and Guattari, F. ([1980] 1987) *A Thousand Plateaus: Capitalism and Schizophrenia*, trans. B. Massumi. London: Athlone Press.

Deleuze, G. and Guattari, F. ([1991] 1994) *What Is Philosophy?*, trans. H. Tomlinson and G. Burchill. London: Verso.

Deleuze, G. and Parnet, C. (1996) *L'Abécédaire de Gilles Deleuze*, dir. P.-A. Boutang. Paris: Video Editions Montparnasse.

Department of Transport, Planning and Local Infrastructure (DTPLI) (2014) *Draft Planning Policy Framework*, online at: http://www.dtpli.vic.gov.au/_data/assets/pdf_file/0004/230998/PPF_Integration_VPP_all_clauses.pdf (last accessed 12 December 2014).

Dixon, D. and Ruddick, S. (2013) 'Monsters, monstrousness, and monstrous nature/s', *Geoforum*, 48: 237–8.

Duff, C. (2010) 'Towards a developmental ethology: exploring Deleuze's contribution to the study of health and human development', *Health*, 14 (6): 619–34.

Fahey, B. (Hon.) (1911) Speech, 13 September 1911, *Official Record of the Debates of the Legislative Council and the Legislative Assembly, 1911–1912*, vol. 108: 931, Queensland.

Foucault, M. ([1972] 2006) *History of Madness*, trans. J. Murphy and J. Khalfa. London: Routledge.

Foucault, M. ([1975] 1977) *Discipline and Punish*, trans. A. Sheridan. Harmondsworth: Penguin.

Foucault, M. ([1976] 1978) *The History of Sexuality, Volume 1*, trans. R. Hurley. New York: Pantheon.

Franzen, C. (2008) 'Syphilis in composers and musicians', *European Journal of Clinical Microbiology and Infectious Diseases*, 27 (12): 1151–7.

Garton, S. (1988) *Medicine and Madness*. Sydney: UNSW Press.

Garton, S. (1991) 'The tyranny of doctors', *Australian Historical Studies*, 24 (96): 340–58.

Guattari, F. (2009) 'So what', in S. Lotringer (ed.), *Soft Subversions: Texts and Interviews 1977–1985*, trans. C. Wiener and E. Wittman. New York: Semiotext(e), pp. 64–80.

Hillier, J. (2013) 'More than meat: rediscovering the cow beneath the face in urban heritage practice', *Environment and Planning D: Society and Space*, 31 (5): 863–78.

Huxley, M. (2006) 'The Soul's Geographer: Government and the Emergence of Town Planning in the Twentieth Century in England and Australia'. Unpublished PhD thesis, Milton Keynes, Open University.

IBISWorld (2013) *Brothel Keeping and Prostitution Services: Market Research Report*, ANZSIC S9534. Melbourne: IBISWorld.

Jones, R. (1999) 'The master potter and the rejected pots: eugenic legislation in Victoria, 1918–1939', *Australian Historical Studies*, 113: 319–42.

Kent, M. and Romanelli, F. (2008) 'Reexamining syphilis: an update on epidemiology, clinical manifestations, and management', *Annals of Pharmacotherapy*, 42 (2): 226–36.

Levine, P. (2003) *Prostitution, Race and Politics*. London: Routledge.

Lupton, D. (1999) *Risk*. London: Routledge.

MacCormack, P. (2004) 'The probe-head and the faces of Australia: from Australia Post to Pluto', *Journal of Australian Studies*, 28: 135–43.

Maginn, P. and Steinmetz, C. (eds) (2015) *(Sub)Urban Sexscapes: Geographies and Regulation of the Sex Industry*. London: Routledge.

May, A. and Reidy, S. (2009) 'Town planning crusaders: urban reform in Melbourne during the progressive era', in R. Freestone (ed.), *Cities, Citizens and Environmental Reform: Histories of Australian Town Planning Associations*. Sydney: Sydney University Press, pp. 89–118.

Nietzsche, F. ([1873] 1983) *On the Uses and Disadvantages of History for Life*, trans. R. J. Hollingdale. Cambridge: Cambridge University Press.

Patton, P. (2010) *Deleuzian Concepts*. Stanford: Stanford University Press.

Rodowick, D. N. (1997) 'The memory of resistance', *South Atlantic Quarterly*, 96 (3): 417–37.

Shoesmith, D. (1972) '"Nature's Law": the venereal disease debate, Melbourne, 1918–1919', *ANU Historical Journal*, 9: 20–3.

Smart, J. (1998) 'Sex, the State and the "scarlet scourge": gender, citizenship and venereal diseases regulation in Australia during the great war', *Women's History Review*, 7 (1): 5–36.

Stoler, A. L. (2008) 'Imperial debris: reflections on ruins and ruination', *Cultural Anthropology*, 23 (2): 191–219.

Summers, A. (1975) *Damned Whores and God's Police*. Ringwood, Vic.: Penguin.

Taylor, M. (2012) *Planning Scheme Amendment. C186 Central City Heritage Review 2011 to City of Melbourne Planning Scheme. Former Women's Venereal Disease Clinic 372–378 Little Lonsdale Street, Melbourne. Expert Evidence*. Melbourne: M. Taylor Architect and Conservation Consultant Pty Ltd.

Teresi, D. (2011) 'Lynn Margulis says she's not controversial, she's right', *Discover Magazine*, April, online at: http://discovermagazine.com/2011/apr/16-interview-lynn-margulis-not-controversial-right#.UuWn7hB9KUk (last accessed 12 June 2013).

Thrift, N. (1999) 'Steps to an ecology of place', in D. Massey, J. Allen and P. Sarre (eds), *Human Geography Today*. Cambridge: Polity Press, pp. 295–322.

Watts, R. (1994) 'Beyond nature and nurture: eugenics in twentieth century Australian history', *Australian Journal of Politics and History*, 40 (3): 318–34.

Wood, F. (1909) Speech reported in *The Truth*, 27 February 1909.

Wyndham, D. (2003) *Eugenics in Australia: Striving for National Fitness*. London: Galton Institute.

Chapter 10

The City and 'the Homeless': Machinic Subjects

Michele Lancione

The history of sociological thought is punctuated by a vast array of studies forming what one could call, in a Foucauldian way, the 'economy of homelessness': namely the 'knowledge of all the processes related to population in its larger sense' (Foucault 2000: 216–17). This 'economy' ranges from topics such as the causes of homelessness, the gender differences among homeless people and inquiries around the housing stock to, for instance, the role of neoliberal economies in reproducing the phenomenon. Despite this variety it is possible to recognise a common lacuna in the approaches adopted to investigate homelessness: the lack of thoughtful inquiries revolving around the ontology and epistemology of being (and becoming) a homeless woman or man. As Neale pointed out almost two decades ago, 'homelessness [. . .] has often been explained somewhat simplistically and atheoretically as either a housing or a welfare problem, caused by either structural or by individual factors, with homeless people deemed either deserving or undeserving' (1997: 48).

The main problem of this lack of theorisation is related to the kind of knowledge that the above 'economy' produces and re-produces over time. The translation of under-theorised academic work into research reports, policy-making and media portrayals contributes to a discourse on homelessness characterised by stigma, lack of agency and assumptions on homeless people's capabilities and will (Takahashi 1996). Although there are scholars who have been aware of this issue – see, for instance, the work of Veness (1993), Ruddick (1996), Gowan (2010) and Robinson (2011) – there have been few attempts to theorise what the American anthropologist Desjarlais has called 'the experience of homelessness', where 'experience' is not conceived 'as a universal, natural, and supremely authentic entity [. . .] but as a process built sharply out of cultural, historical, political and pragmatic forces' (1997: 10).

Tackling this theoretical and empirical challenge – which concerns both the ways one conceptualises 'homelessness' as well as the ways one approaches it in its unfolding – must necessarily begin from one of the most under-theorised aspects of the matter: quite surprisingly, that of the relationship between homeless people and the *city*. Although this relationship has been described by seminal anthropological works (Anderson 1999; Duneier 1999; Snow and Anderson 1993), and despite the recent shift promoted by the 'performative' scholarship in geography (Cloke et al. 2010; DeVerteuil et al. 2009), the 'homeless' and the 'city' still largely appear as two separate entities: at best, interweaving on the basis of utility and proximity; at worst, the one portrayed as just the backdrop for the other's actions. But what if urban homelessness is more than just a matter of location, of travel behaviours or of bounded control? What could be gained in treating the 'urban' and the 'homeless' as collective matters rather than discrete entities? And how could such a theoretical inquiry be effectively enacted in field research?

The following pages rely upon and expand the performative approach to homelessness, with the aim of offering a suitable way to 'breathe new life into understandings of the homeless city' (Cloke et al. 2008: 242). In order to do so, two interrelated adjustments are proposed: the re-conceptualisation of the city as a 'vitalist mechanosphere' and of the subject as 'post-human', and the implementation of a methodological approach based on the notion of 'tracing assemblages'. Key aspects of Deleuze and Guattari's work on subjectivity – rhizomatic thinking and becoming – as well as insights from the latest developments in urban theory will serve as guides for the proposed theoretical framework and its methodological implications. The proposed approach is then illustrated through narratives of observation carried out during a ten-month period of ethnographic fieldwork I undertook in Turin. These observations consist of field notes and exchanges with practitioners, gathered while volunteering in two different Catholic faith-based organisations (FBOs) (a morning soup kitchen and a shelter) and a public drop-in, as well as field notes based on the daily street journeys I undertook with several short- and long-term homeless individuals. The core of the proposed approach and its political value are summarised in the final section of this chapter.

A Vitalist Mechanosphere

The first step is to promote a topological and vitalist understanding of the city in order to show the heterogeneity of the components and forces that make up the urban. One promising resource toward this end is the emerging literature on urban assemblages, which sits at the intersection of Deleuzo-Guattarian thinking and Actor-Network approaches (Anderson and McFarlane 2011; Jacobs 2012; McFarlane 2011). Despite the disparities among its positions – for instance related to the theorisation of 'assemblage' (Greenhough 2011) – this literature proposes an ontological take on the city that 'does not presuppose essential and enduring identities' (Escobar 2007: 107). The city, according to this approach, is understood as a set of more-than-human articulations that are always open to the emergence of new events rather than as a determinable, human-driven, socio-spatial artefact. Farías and Bender elegantly summarise this when they argue that the city is 'a multiplicity of processes of becoming, affixing sociotechnical networks, hybrid collectivities and alternative topologies' (Farías and Bender 2010: 2). The aim of assemblage urbanism is not to arrive at a definition of *what* a city is: the aim is precisely to avoid a definition and to understand *how* a city is and, of specific interest for this chapter, to grasp *how* homelessness is.

Assemblage urbanism conceives the city as a mechanosphere of vitalist entanglements always open to possibility and change (Amin and Thrift 2002). In this sense the 'homeless city' ceases to be just a matter of places (sidewalks, train stations, public parks), services (soup kitchens, shelters, drop-ins), institutions and relations between people, as canonical scholarship has taught so far (see, for instance, Ravenhill 2008). Rather, it becomes a matter of entanglements between small objects and bodies, discourses and power, performances and blueprints for action – a universe of capacities that need to be traced in their contextual deployment. The homeless city is a rhizome of eventful post-human crossroads (Simone 2010) *within* which – and not only where – multifaceted experiences of homelessness are constituted.

In order to navigate this intricateness one needs a non-reductive, non-Cartesian account of subjectivity (Pile and Thrift 1995). Examples can be found in the work of diverse philosophical thinkers such as Lefebvre, Derrida, Butler and Foucault, who move away from the Freudian and Lacanian subject – a subject locked into phallocentrism and textuality – in order to account for the variegated 'contextuality' of the self (Wylie 2010). However, it is only with Deleuze and Guattari that such 'contextuality' is rendered visible and its complexity fully taken into account: the subject ceases to be *only* matter of text, body, rationality or power relations, but becomes understood as an ongoing, never-finished assemblage of the human, non-human, discursive, technical and potential matters making up the world (Deleuze and Guattari 2009). In other words, the subject is just one of the parts (breakable into smaller parts) of the mechanosphere described above. It is defined by it, it is made by it, it is constituted through it and it does constitute it: the subject is not determined by the strict boundaries of the rational self because rationality itself is just a product (and a producer) of countless other machines (Deleuze and Guattari 1977). Deleuze, and more particularly Guattari (2010), do not bring to the fore a definitive theory of the subject but allow us to navigate the broad rhizomatic canvas where the subject becomes with the other assemblage of the world. There are two important points to note here.

First, 'machines do not depend on *techne* [. . .] There are also technical, aesthetic, economic, social, etc. machines' (Lazzarato 2006: 1). This means, quite simply, that in the life of a homeless person the machines that matter are not only cars, mobile phones and electronic access-cards to service provision, but the concrete of the pavement, an overcrowded shelter and its smell of used linen and cheap soap, the weight of a heavy backpack, an abandoned railway carriage with its rust, shadows and creaks, the smile of a volunteer after a joke, the gesture implied in serving food, the furniture of an emergency shelter, or the inquisitive eyes of a social worker, a priest or a person passing by on the street. Second, and consequently, the (homeless) subject is 'collective': it is the expression of 'the heterogeneity of the components converging to produce subjectivity' (Guattari 1996: 193). This does not mean that the subject disappears in a collective mist, but simply that in order to grasp the subject one needs to look at the collective process of machinic affiliation through which subjectivity is constituted, challenged and reassembled. This means to understand the inner-self as an elongation of the mechanosphere and vice versa, in their productive constitutive tensions. Rosi Braidotti has depicted this process very clearly:

> [S]ubjectivity is a socially mediated process of entitlements to and negotiations with power relations. Consequently, the formation and emergence of new social subjects is always a collective enterprise, 'external' to the individual self while also mobilising the self's in-depth and singular structures. (Braidotti 2011: 18)

The shift from canonical homelessness scholarship is huge. The experience of homelessness cannot be understood any longer as a matter of personal culpability or lack of will, nor simply as the outcome of broader economic causes, but can only be grasped as an ongoing process of subject formation where the latter is always a collective endeavour – a matter of contextual material and discursive arrangements to be addressed in their processual heterogeneous becoming.

Tracing the Assemblages of Homelessness

The subject and the city cannot be mapped and navigated once and for all, but only traced in the provisional unfolding of what Deleuze and Guattari called 'the micropolitics of the social field' (1987: 7). But how might it be possible to investigate such micropolitics? The methodological approach that I have employed derives directly from the assemblage ontology, and in particular from assemblages' tetravalent systemisation (Deleuze and Guattari 1987). This aims to pay attention to the material (content) and immaterial (expression) elements that compose every assemblage, and to be ready to follow the different articulations that may occur in their becoming (territorialisation – deterritorialisation – reterritorialisation) (Dewsbury 2011). In tracing the assemblage of homelessness I therefore focused on the following three matters:

1. *Expression.* The discursive side of homeless people's everyday life. This includes both homeless people's accounts, as expressed in their own voice, and third-party depiction related to service provision, media portrayals and policies.
2. *Content.* The practice-based and performative side of homeless people's lives which includes the set of practices, materials and spaces consciously or unconsciously activated in their daily performances.
3. *Articulation.* The relational development of the assemblages emerging from each contextual content/expression dyad, which can follow paths of stabilisation (territorialisation) and destabilisation (deterritorialisation). Following its articulation one is able to show how the assemblage becomes ingrained in the everyday experience(s) of homeless people and how it challenges and changes their becoming.

Expression, content and articulation cannot be taken as established 'social facts', ready-at-hand in the field. What is expression at one point can easily become content at another: their distinction is blurred, and it must be so (DeLanda 2006). The fieldwork is in this sense a recollection of events, in which the triad above are just signposts to trace the action, not a 'container' of action itself (Harman 2009). But tracing the action is not enough. The key is to understand its relational becoming as 'micropolitical', meaning that at each and every moment things are capable of producing new things: new assemblages, new subjects and new urban machines. It is through the analysis of this production that critique becomes possible: the things that are produced, as well as the ways through which they are produced, are not neutral. Through their capacities and external relations they factually bring to the fore heterogeneous experiences of homelessness that are matters of trauma, fatigue or stress, but also of hope, joy and momentary escapes (lines of flight). The scope of approaching homelessness from the standpoint of the *vitalist city* and *post-human subject* is to reveal what effects these becomings have on homeless people themselves.

In order to both trace the assemblage of urban homelessness (via the retrieval of its expressions, contents and articulations) and to evaluate it through homeless people's own experiences, the field activity is of necessity ethnographic in nature. It is only through extensive participant and non-participant observations that one is able to perceive, experience and then describe the vast array of assemblages characterising homeless people's everyday life (Robinson 2011). These assemblages comprise discourses, practices, bodily performances, urban materialities, scheduling, affective atmospheres – to cite just a few of their elements, which are arguably hard to uncover with quantitative methods of investigation or by concentrating only on analysis of public policies (as the bulk of the literature on homelessness arguably does). In the end, tracing the assemblage of homelessness leads to a complex and unfinished map of the machinic subject: a cartography permeated by assemblages that are described in their capacity to create heterogeneous experiences through rupture, disjunction, painful alliances, solidifications and possible lines of flight.

One Example: Unfolding the Assemblage of Help

The vignettes reported below emerge from the investigation of a particular urban assemblage of homelessness: that of 'helping the poor'. This is a complex and variegated assemblage which is mainly brought forward by public and private institutions, where an increased role is played, at least in Europe, by FBOs (for an overview see Beaumont and Cloke 2013). The relevance of investigating this assemblage is twofold. First, the practices and discourses involved in 'helping the poor' do have a prominent role in shaping – for good or ill – one's own experience of homelessness. Second, the current literature on FBOs and homelessness arguably tends to overlook the more nuanced dynamics that underlie the provision of charitable services to homeless people, which are uncritically taken as 'good', being of their nature 'caring acts' of 'love' (Lancione 2014).

In what follows I concentrate on the assemblage of 'eating', analysing a specific service provided by a centre for homeless people managed by the Company of the Daughters of Charity of Saint Vincent de Paul (a society of apostolic life for women within the Roman Catholic Church), where I have been volunteering at least four days a week over a period of ten months. The centre is located not far from the main train station of Turin and consisted essentially of a couple of rooms, the bigger one filled with around twenty tables (four seats at each) and adorned with illustrations of Catholic prayers and holy scenes painted on the walls. The Vincentian nuns used this space to provide multiple services to homeless people: a morning soup kitchen (the only one available in the city, 250 breakfasts on average per day), distribution of sandwiches in the evening (around 150 units), free distribution of clothes, a free medical clinic, a counselling service and a monthly distribution of food parcels.

The Assemblage of Eating

An integral part of the assemblage of eating, both in the morning and in the evening service, was queueing. In the morning homeless people were waiting on the sidewalk in front of the FBO's building, sometimes up to two hours before the commencement of the service (Fig. 10.1). At 7 a.m. the main door of the centre was usually opened, allowing people to wait inside and to form another long queue at the door to the breakfast room. Even though they were in the end the same people, the two queues were fundamentally different. The first – on the sidewalk outside the soup kitchen – exposed homeless people both to environmental harshness and to the gaze of people and cars passing by, while the latter – within the premises of the building – allowed for a higher degree of privacy (especially in regard to the gaze of people and cars).

In those moments right before the commencement of the service, people were usually careful to maintain the position they had gained in the queue outside. As soon as the breakfast room was opened, however, people rapidly moved inside shouting at each other: a flux of bodies, bags, coats, smells and speech was then compressed in a tiny spatiotemporal context made up of a door passage and a few seconds. In this space arguments emerged very easily, since people often tried to cut in front of each other to get through before their peers. The fights always played out on a racial basis: the Italians would argue that the migrants

Fig. 10.1 Homeless people forming a long queue outside the Vincentians'
soup kitchen (photograph by the author (2010))

were trying to sneak into the room without respecting the queue, while
the migrants complained about how badly the man guarding the door
(always an Italian) was treating them. Arguments were even more
heated during the evening service, the distribution of sandwiches and

associated queue taking place outside the soup kitchen on the adjacent sidewalk. Here people were constantly fighting to retain their position in the queue, sometime defending a place that they had 'held' for someone else in exchange for favours. These arguments often ended in physical altercations, leading the FBO to suspend the evening service for several days in a row.

The breakfast was served each morning by two nuns and some volunteers (three or four persons including myself) between 7.30 and 8.30. The tables were made ready before the commencement of the service with a basket of bread, four cups with spoons and paper towels. Breakfast usually started with one of the nuns praying and giving a short sermon, most of the time about the meaning of poverty and the importance of Catholic charity. The following scene, which I have recorded in my field diary, is exemplary:

> One early December morning, a nun was talking to the homeless people seated in the soup kitchen (she usually did this just before serving the breakfast).
>
> *Nun*: 'We should always remind ourselves of the people who are less lucky than you and me. People in poor countries, with war. And we should never forget that Christ is close to them, as he is close to you too. The love of Christ makes us feel stronger and better, it is protective and warm . . .'
>
> *Homeless person, from the back of the room*: 'So Jesus Christ was not with me last night in the train station. It was damn cold!'
>
> [A ripple of laughter from the crowd]
>
> *Nun*: '. . . it is protective and warm. We should never forget that with the love of Christ we can overcome all difficulties . . .'

After the speech, the service took place. Volunteers were going around offering either tea or coffee, biscuits and, depending on the availability of the day, heated pizza, yoghurt or marmalade. Homeless people were entering and leaving continuously for one hour, in turn, creating a constant flow of bodies and backpacks, suitcases, umbrellas and other items (such as sheets of cardboard, books or plastic bags). People were mostly sitting in groups that tended to follow a pattern, in some cases according to the nationality of the individuals, in others the time they had been spending together in the street. They would sit very close to one other, usually still dressed in the same thick clothes that they had worn to get through the night. The proximity of bodies and things, the constant movement of people coming and going, as well as the movement of the volunteers into and out of the kitchen with trays and kettles, generated a peculiar chaotic atmosphere filled with repetitive movements, instructions from the nuns and the hubbub of people eating, drinking and bumping into each other. The smell of the soup kitchen was a damp one, of wet clothes, a hint of urine and hot reconstituted milk– the same smell over and over again for the months I have been going there. Sometimes the olfactory and auditory density of this ambience was broken by arguments, among homeless people, or by discussion concerning the service, between homeless people and the volunteers. Both were, however, managed in a matter of minutes, usually by the man guarding the entrance to the room.

The quality of the food was of great concern to the homeless people I encountered. Food was generally sourced from private donations – bakeries, supermarkets and private citizens – and was usually already beyond the expiry date printed on the package. The case of yoghurt in the Vincentian's soup kitchen records a practice common among such service providers in Turin (Lancione 2013). When yoghurt was available, usually served one day over its expiry date, the vast majority of homeless people would first check the date and then, if it had passed, either refuse it or take it but complain about it. Jokes about the laxative quality of the 'nuns' milk and coffee' were commonplace. Complaints about the hardness of the bread or the blandness of the biscuits were equally common. Such grumbling aside, people were not leaving food on their plates, but in fact often taking packets of biscuits with them for the day.

Eating was not only performed within the four walls of the soup kitchen, in isolation from the rest of the city. Besides the network of donations sustaining the service, one of the most peculiar aspects of this assemblage concerns the time one had to devote, and the space across which one had to travel, to access it. It involved a complex arrangement of bodies, buses and trains, schedules, money, services' opening times, personal preferences, etc. This assemblage of eating was, de facto, intimately part of a wider urban mechanosphere. One of the reasons why some individuals preferred to queue outside the soup kitchen very early in the morning was directly related to the opening times of Turin's public baths (at the time, usually from 9 a.m. to 12 p.m. only) or the similar opening times of other public services (like the office taking care of the city's social services to homeless people) and the fact that the only soup kitchen offering a hot lunch was open between 11.30 a.m. and 1 p.m. Without entering into details, *washing* and *eating* were two related urban assemblages that could be closely aligned and thus work together only through meticulous calculation, constant effort and reliance on other urban machineries (like public transport) (Lancione and McFarlane forthcoming).

Machinic Experiences

Eating in the soup kitchen is a socio-technical endeavour entangling homeless people with the materiality, discourses and ambience of the place. It is within these micropolitical articulations that the machinic nature of homeless people's subjectivity is assembled, challenged and reassembled, leading to sets of heterogeneous experiences of homelessness that cannot be accounted for by a priori theorisation or normative discourses. Bearing in mind that *eating* is only one of the assemblages making up the 'homeless city', three experiences brought forward by it seem worth highlighting.

The first can be called *the experience of feeling out of place*, and it is related to the sensation – consciously or unconsciously expressed by many short-term homeless people I have encountered – that the soup kitchen was not a 'place for them'. If the literature has touched upon this internal struggle – think for instance of those works highlighting the linguistic devices used by homeless people to 'take distance' from the peers they perceive as the 'real homeless' (Snow and Anderson 1987) – less has been said about the role of certain assemblages in reproducing a specific 'homeless atmosphere' that does affect how people feel and perceive themselves (Anderson 2009). Overcrowded rooms filled with noises, strong smells and anonymous encounters (both between homeless people and with the volunteers), as well as sermons restating each morning the discursive framework of the service provision (the 'poor' helped by charitable love), are just a few of the things which people had to confront in the analysed case. These elements, articulated with one another, produced a powerful affective atmosphere that for the short-term homeless people conjured a sense of disjunction with their perceived status as merely 'temporary homeless'. Some devised make-shift alternative behaviours by avoiding queueing outside the Daughters of Charity's premises (and the gaze of the passers-by) and the vast majority of them always tried to sit at tables with each other, in order to minimise contact with long-term street dwellers. However, as I witnessed many times, a simple disruption in the fragile equilibrium of these arrangements – for instance, the unavailability of sitting space close to the preferred companions – led those people into serious emotional distress. The 'homeless atmosphere' was always there, and the painful encounter with it almost unavoidable.

The second experience is closely related to the first one, and can be called *the experience of feeling homeless*. If short-term homeless people struggled to accept their new social identity – that of 'being homeless' – long-term ones were (uncomfortably) living with it. Although they neither minded showing their faces on the sidewalk nor cared about their seating arrangements, they were still negatively affected by the 'homeless atmosphere' of the soup kitchen. The case of the out-of-date food is a clear example. The habit of checking the expiry date on the yoghurt, as well as the constant complaining around the quality of the food, are tokens of a more profound sense of dissatisfaction and emotional distress regarding their condition. Take for instance what one of these people once told me:

> You see? I know it's good . . . it's only one day out of date [referring to the yoghurt] . . . But it's not good they give us this. See? Also when I collect the pack [a box containing food items distributed once a month in the same centre] it's the same story. Everything is European Union . . . Would you eat this stuff? I mean, of course you eat it . . . but it's not good, it's not right.

Small details like the packaging of food, the expiry dates or the fact that the bread was never fresh but already some days old, did matter for long-term homeless people because those things were constantly reminding them of their abnormality (Canguilhem 1989). As with the short-termers, this group too put up alternative deterritorialisations in order to avoid these feelings. Another long-term homeless person told me that he preferred to eat just once a day, using his own money, rather than frequenting the soup kitchens available in the city:

> The soup kitchen is not for me. The food, the people . . . I feel better in the bar, I can relax there. I look at the people. They got TV too! Cottolengo [another FBO soup kitchen in the city] is not for me. Too many people there. Too many immigrants. Have you ever been there? No, no, no. If I can, I eat kebab here [. . .] If not, I'd rather stay in the bar anyway!

The last experience worth noting here, one which was common both among short- and long-term homeless people, is that of *feeling under pressure*. This is a double-faceted experience related both to the timing of being homeless in the city and the encounters with different others. First, despite the popular view that homeless people have lots of free time on their hands, the opposite is often true. The timings of the available services generate a map that, if overlaid with that of the public infrastructure of the city and with that of physical and monetary limitations, reveals how homeless people struggle to find the appropriate time and resources to do everything. If one sleeps in a shelter, has to commute to the other side of the city to eat in a soup kitchen and must in between look for a job while also attending counselling meetings and other forms of help (like the distribution of second-hand clothes), the day is soon gone before one even realises it's already time to queue for the night shelter again. Second, emotional pressure and distress are constantly present in the overcrowded encounters between different others, with arguments and fights always ready to erupt. As I have seen many times, the intensity of these clashes actually rises in regulated contexts (such as soup kitchens and shelters) where normative atmospheres are more prominent, to radically diminish in contexts where homeless people organise themselves to achieve their own ends (such as looking for a job in the informal economy). The experience of 'feeling under pressure' is thus a complex entanglement within which the soup kitchen is just one knot, a knot that plays its role in ratcheting up the sensations of stress, displacement and time pressure constantly at play in the machinic lives of these people.

Openings

Despite the shortcomings of the services described above, homeless people were generally grateful for the provision of food and clothes by the Daughters of Charity at their centre. In fact, this and other services are of fundamental importance, since they often provide the only help available to this population. However, how the experience of homelessness is constituted within those services matters. It is only by revealing and acknowledging the nuanced dynamics at play in those spaces that homelessness can be appreciated in its multifaceted complexity. The literature has offered examples of critiques of this kind (see Allahyari 2000; Evans 2011; Johnsen et al. 2005) but more must be done to bring to light the grounded entanglements that are often overlooked by traditional scholarship.

The approach proposed in this chapter is all about this point: it is an effort to theorise and describe the assemblage of homelessness taking into consideration that homeless people, like anyone else, are subjects constituted within entanglements of a post-human kind, that escape normative categories, bounded spaces and self-centred narratives. The key is to bring together the *vitalist city* and the *post-human subject* and to account for the numerous assemblages that on a daily basis constitute heterogeneous experiences of homelessness. It is only there – within the machinic unfolding of those experiences – that one can note the partial deterritorialisations that might serve, if positively boosted, to provide alternative articulations. Starting from such deterritorialisations one could look forward to small-scale changes: a different configuration of tables, a shift in the blueprint governing the distribution of food, a more attentive relation to people and their individual needs, the redesign of services bearing in mind the intricate topologies of being homeless in the contemporary urban landscape – to cite just a few. Are these options enough to end homelessness? Certainly not. But they will be enough to shake the established ground that arguably tends – through its unquestioned arrangements – to 'institutionalise' homelessness and its people (Basaglia 1968; Lyon-Callo 2000).

The city and homeless people are one collective subject made up of a maelstrom of assemblages: a 'micropolitics' that Deleuze and Guattari, among other thinkers, allow us to navigate without fixing it, reducing it or adapting it (Guattari 2009). In the end, tracing, analysing and describing this complex cartography is a political task because it can foster cultural and practical changes. Mapping the homeless subject is, in this sense, a tripartite movement:

> first, towards redrawing the old maps in ways [...] that delegitimate the claims to truth of those maps which rely on an unspoken universal and universalised subject; second, towards the resymbolisation, resignification and parodic repetition of the maps that we already have; and, third, towards new maps of the subject [...] in order to re-establish tolerance towards different practices of body and subjectivity. (Pile and Thrift 1995: 50)

References

Allahyari, R. (2000) *Visions of Charity: Volunteer Workers and Moral Community*. Berkeley: University of California Press.

Amin, A. and Thrift, N. (2002) *Cities: Re-imaging the Urban*. Cambridge: Polity.

Anderson, B. (2009) 'Affective atmospheres', *Emotion, Society and Space*, 2 (2): 71–81.

Anderson, B. and McFarlane, C. (2011) 'Assemblage and geography', *Area*, 43 (2): 124–7.

Anderson, N. (1999) *On Hobos and Homelessness*, ed. R. Rauty. Chicago: University of Chicago Press.

Basaglia, F. (ed.) (1968) *L'Istituzione negata. Rapporto da un ospedale psichiatrico*. Torino: Einaudi.

Beaumont, J. and Cloke, P. (eds) (2013) *Faith-Based Organisations and Exclusion in European Cities*. Bristol: Policy Press.

Braidotti, R. (2011) *Nomadic Subjects*, 2nd edn. New York: Columbia University Press.

Canguilhem, G. (1989) *The Normal and the Pathological*. New York: Zone Books.

Cloke, P., May, J. and Johnsen, S. (2008) 'Performativity and affect in the homeless city', *Environment and Planning D: Society and Space*, 26 (2): 241–63.

Cloke, P., May, J. and Johnsen, S. (2010) *Swept Up Lives? Re-envisioning the Homeless City*. Chichester: Wiley-Blackwell.

DeLanda, M. (2006) *A New Philosophy of Society: Assemblage Theory and Social Complexity*. London: Continuum.

Deleuze, G. and Guattari, F. (1977) *Anti-Oedipus: Capitalism and Schizophrenia*. New York: Penguin Books.

Deleuze, G. and Guattari, F. (1987) *A Thousand Plateaus*. New York: Continuum.

Deleuze, G. and Guattari, F. (2009) 'Balance-sheet for "desiring-machines"', in S. Lotringer (ed.), *Chaosophy: Texts and Interviews 1972–1977*. Los Angeles: Semiotext(e), pp. 90–115.

Desjarlais, R. (1997) *Shelter Blues: Sanity and Selfhood Among the Homeless*. Philadelphia: University of Pennsylvania Press.

DeVerteuil, G., May, J. and von Mahs, J. (2009) 'Complexity not collapse: recasting the geographies of homelessness in a "punitive" age', *Progress in Human Geography*, 33 (5): 646–66.

Dewsbury, J.-D. (2011) 'The Deleuze-Guattarian assemblage: plastic habits', *Area*, 43 (2): 148–53.

Duneier, M. (1999) *Sidewalk*. New York: Farrar, Strauss & Giroux.

Escobar, A. (2007) 'The "ontological turn" in social theory: a commentary on "human geography without scale", by Sallie Marston, John Paul Jones II and Keith Woodward', *Transactions of the Institute of British Geographers*, 32 (1): 106–11.

Evans, J. (2011) 'Exploring the (bio)political dimensions of voluntarism and care in the city: the case of a "low barrier" emergency shelter', *Health and Place*, 17 (1): 24–32.

Farías, I. and Bender, T. (eds) (2010) *Urban Assemblages: How Actor-Network Theory Changes Urban Studies*. London: Routledge.

Foucault, M. (2000) *Power: Essential Works of Foucault, 1954–1984, Volume 3*, ed. J. Faubion. London: Penguin.

Gowan, T. (2010) *Hobos, Hustlers and Back-sliders: Homeless in San Francisco*. Minneapolis: University of Minnesota Press.

Greenhough, B. (2011) 'Assembling an island laboratory', *Area*, 43 (2): 134–8.

Guattari, F. (1996) 'Subjectivities: for the better and for the worse', in G. Genosko (ed.), *The Guattari Reader*. Oxford: Blackwell.

Guattari, F. (2009) *Chaosophy: Texts and Interviews 1972–1977*, ed. S. Lotringer. Los Angeles: Semiotext(e).

Guattari, F. (2010) *The Machinic Unconscious: Essays in Schizoanalysis*. London: Semiotext(e).

Harman, G. (2009) *Prince of Networks. Bruno Latour and Metaphysics*. Melbourne: Re.Press.

Jacobs, J. M. (2012) 'Urban geographies I: still thinking cities relationally', *Progress in Human Geography*, 36 (3): 412–22.

Johnsen, S., Cloke, P. and May, J. (2005) 'Day centres for homeless people: spaces of care or fear?', *Social and Cultural Geography*, 6 (6): 787–811.

Lancione, M. (2013) 'Homeless people and the city of abstract machines: assemblage thinking and the performative approach to homelessness', *Area*, 45 (3): 358–64.

Lancione, M. (2014) 'Entanglements of faith: discourses, practices of care and homeless people in an Italian city of saints', *Urban Studies*, 51 (14): 3062–78.

Lancione, M. and McFarlane, C. (forthcoming) 'Infrastructural becoming: sanitation and the (un)making of life at the margins', in I. Farías and B. Anders (eds), *Urban Cosmopolitics*. London: Routledge.

Lazzarato, M. (2006) 'The machine', *Transversal*, 10: 1–6, online at: http://eipcp.net/transversal/1106/lazzarato/en/print (accessed 21 March 2014).

Lyon-Callo, V. (2000) 'Medicalizing homelessness: the production of self-blame and self-governing within homeless shelters', *Medical Anthropology Quarterly*, 14 (3): 328–45.

McFarlane, C. (2011) 'The city as assemblage: dwelling and urban space', *Environment and Planning D: Society and Space*, 29 (4): 649–71.

Neale, J. (1997) 'Homelessness and theory reconsidered', *Housing Studies*, 12 (1): 47–61.

Pile, S. and Thrift, N. (eds) (1995) *Mapping the Subject: Geographies of Cultural Transformation*. London: Routledge.

Ravenhill, M. (2008) *The Culture of Homelessness*. Aldershot: Ashgate.

Robinson, C. (2011) *Beside One's Self: Homelessness Felt and Lived*. New York: Syracuse University Press.

Ruddick, S. (1996) *Young and Homeless in Hollywood: Mapping Social Identities*. New York: Routledge.

Simone, A. (2010) *City Life from Jakarta to Dakar: Movements at the Crossroads*. London: Routledge.

Snow, D. A. and Anderson, L. (1987) 'Identity work among the homeless: the verbal construction and avowal of personal identities', *American Journal of Sociology*, 92 (6): 1336–71.

Snow, D. A. and Anderson, L. (1993) *Down on Their Luck: A Study of Homeless Street People*. Berkeley: University of California Press.

Takahashi, L. M. (1996) 'A decade of understanding homelessness in the USA: from characterization to representation', *Progress in Human Geography*, 20 (3): 291–310.

Veness, A. R. (1993) 'Neither homed nor homeless: contested definitions and the personal worlds of the poor', *Political Geography*, 12 (4): 319–40.

Wylie, J. (2010) 'Non-representational subjects?', in B. Anderson and P. Harrison (eds), *Taking-Place: Non Representational Theories and Geography*. Farnham: Ashgate.

Chapter 11

Cut-Make-and-Trim: Fast Fashion Urbanity in the Residues of Rana Plaza

Maria Hellström Reimer

Aeon: the indefinite time of the event, the floating time that knows only speeds and continually divides that which transpires into an already-there that is at the same time not-yet-here, a simultaneous too-late and too-early, a something that is both going to happen and has just happened.

Deleuze and Guattari (1987: 262)

Incidents, Accidents

'"It's absolutely amazing!" The first visitor to the new shopping centre cannot hide her enthusiasm, her eyes sparkling at the shower of golden discount coupons' (*Sydsvenska Dagbladet*, 25 October 2012). The new commercial facility presents itself as part of a natural circuit, its elevators embedded in lush greenery, its open spaces framed by rippling waterfalls. Even the public lavatories express the same environmental concern, with bird tweets and other animal sounds activated as you lock the cubicle door, all according to one early reviewer whose inaugural visit to the privy was greeted by an intimate 'cock-a-doodle-doo' (Fürstenberg 2012).

The impressive opening of Emporia took place in October 2012 in Malmö, Sweden. Located close to the Öresund Bridge, in the transnational metropolitan area often referred to as Greater Copenhagen, the new shopping destination is one of the most extravagant and extensive in Europe. Architectonically spectacular and environmentally certified, the three-storey complex is an award-winning piece of green investment.[1] Access is easy; you can arrive at the site by public transport or even by bike if you wish; most likely you enter from the new station square through the imposing 'Amber Entrance', or, if you still prefer coming here by car, the glimmering blue 'Sea Entrance' facing the main parking will provide as grandiose an ingress; a deep, translucent cavity in the sienna-coloured glass facade, an enticing orifice, exerting a cen-tripetal force. The most idiosyncratic mode of entry, however, is via the six-acre public rooftop park, which can be accessed by either car or foot via an exterior stairway. While the park allows for a more relaxed passage into the emporium and its 200 stores and restaurants, it also buffers the consuming experience, making clear that consumption is only one part of the Emporia vision.

The commercial centre is conceived as an experiential totality, where architecture, design, art and environmental efforts 'go hand in hand to create a delightfully uncomplicated retail sanctuary', as it says on the company's webpage (http://www.emporia.se). The idea is for visitors 'to feel as though they are embarking on a journey into a world of unique opportunities' (http://www.steenstrom.com). And in this respect, the green and rolling rooftop park (Fig. 11.1) is the crowning achievement, its hilly topography elegantly masking the ventilation infrastructure which feeds the interiors with fresh air. Covering the entire roof of the complex, the park is not simply an adventurous amenity but provides important insulating and draining ecosystems services. It constitutes a diverse biotope and a habitat for birds and insects, as well as a socially recreational space for shoppers and residents in the new and 'climate-smart' city district of Hyllie (http://www.hyllie.com/climate).

Alongside state-of-the-art energy supply systems and ambitious recy-cling schemes, the park thus contributes significantly to the shopping centre's unique environmental certification.[2] Yet, as much as its colour-ful sedum slopes and biodiverse expanses add to the environmental credibility of the centre, they also present what in marketing language is called a USP, a 'unique selling point'.[3] For the random visitor, the park is the environmental bonus, which, besides offering inviting wooden decks and grand vistas of the surrounding peri-urban landscape, also presents an array of spatial experiences, from the eco-pedagogical 'wild corner' and 'the garden of the senses' to activities such as rabbit jumping, pony riding and beekeeping.[4] So far, the only flaw in this consumerist-envi-ronmentalist wonderland has been an oversensitive fire alarm system, which has on several occasions prompted an emergency evacuation, temporarily emptying the entire complex of its massive throng of visi-tors, even on the day of the opening.

* * *

A year or so after my first visit to Emporia, I find myself in a totally different location. It is a hot day in July, and I am travelling along the main street of Savar, an *upazila* or county in the Dhaka district of

Fig. 11.1 Rooftop garden, Emporia Shopping Centre, Malmö, Sweden (design by Wingårdh Architects; photograph by Perry Nordeng)

Bangladesh. A historically significant site on the north-western outskirts of the capital and just next to the green groves of the Jahangirnagar university campus, the municipality is today a booming industrial area in what is perhaps the world's most expansive urban conglomeration, whose population is increasing by close to 2,000 people a day.[5] And the urbanisation is palpable. On both sides of the main road, concrete, multi-use formations of various shapes are going up, clad in signboards and scaffolding and with uneven rebar roof-top vegetation aspiring towards the sky.

The streetscape is hectic, with waiting rickshaws, informally erected tea stalls and heaps of farmers' produce all jostling together. It takes some intrepid creativity to find a parking space. As my driver pulls over, carefully negotiating the broken edge of the tarmac, I try to locate what I expect will be a marked cut in the informal urban fabric. For what brings me to this intense neighbourhood is not simply its material accretion, but rather what I know to be a disruption in its flows. Only a bit more than a year has passed since the disastrous collapse of Rana Plaza, an eight-storey edifice, which contained among other facilities several garment factories producing clothing for as many as twenty-eight different global brands.[6]

The site is unassuming. From the street, there is not much to indicate the incident, except for the fence along the empty lot, a shiny screen of new corrugated metal sheets, held together in an ad hoc fashion by tangled wires. There is, however, a gap in the fence, indicating the existence of a subdued yet insistent stream of visitors. On the day of the collapse, 24 April 2013, there had been a totally different kind of tension around. The day before, during inspection, major cracks had been discovered in the construction, and the building was immediately evacuated. The next morning, the many thousands of workers (the majority of them women) accordingly gathered outside of the facility, reluctant to begin the new day's shift. Now, according to the management, the structural defects had disappeared overnight and safe working conditions were guaranteed. While this did not convince the employees of the commercial facilities on the ground floors, the situation for the poorly paid garment workers was different. Threatened with significant income loss, they saw no other option than to enter the building. But just as thousands of sewing machines were again up and running, one of the frequent power outages occurred, bringing on line the diesel generators located on the recently added top floor (Siegle with Burke 2014). This time, however, the vibrations from the back-up power supply system caused the entire building to collapse, the eight floor plates dropping one on top of the other. As if choreographed, the crumpling confirmed what everybody already somehow knew – that the load bearing construction was deficient, that it was poorly reinforced and of second-class concrete, that the building stood on swampy, undrained ground and that it was for some reason three stories higher than legally permitted. And so it happened that Rana Plaza, through its caving in, more or less instantly crushed 1,134 people and severely injured 2,515.[7]

The site of the collapse is, however, not entirely unmarked (Fig. 11.2). There is a blue signboard with contact information in Bangla and English for the 'Coordination Cell for Rana Plaza Victims'. There are also some posters and banners, informal petitions, moderate yet incontestable. As I slip through the fence, the feeling of neglect is replaced by one of material affect. To the left of the jerry-built edifice is a dark, irregular crater filled with muddy water and greenish algae florishing in the heat. Around the pool, a lunar landscape of crushed cement, mixed with rags that still show their original colours and quality. And I am not alone. Along the shores of the pit, on top of this uneven mass of rubble, I discern single figures and small groups of visitors who, in varying degrees of openness and pain, are making their presence felt.

A celebrated shopping mall and an insignificant garment factory, the

Fig. 11.2 Rana Plaza's aftermath (photography and collage by Safia Azim (2013))

former secure and certified, sheltered under greenery; the latter hastily erected with second-rate material on shifting ground. Two sites far apart yet connected, one suspects – but how? As stops along historical trade routes? As nodes in a global supply circuit? As markers in a venturous developmental game with supply and demand? By chance or not at all? In an attempt to contextualise the Rana Plaza collapse and other recent workplace mishaps, a Bangladeshi minister suggested that '[t]hese are individual cases of . . . accidents. It happens everywhere' (Hossain and Alam 2013). Contemporary society is never completely reliable, never fully proof against the material *forces majeures*. Yet, the marketing director of the company behind the flagship commercial amenity of Malmö's new urban development gives voice to a different concern. 'Unfortunately,' he said in a recent interview, 'the general image of shopping centres is probably that they are the complete opposite of environmental responsibility. But there is no such contradiction, [as] the shopping centre [. . .] constitutes a very efficient and thus a very socio-economically and environmentally judicious type of marketplace'.[8]

In between the two settings – the shopping centre and the factory – a number of classical 'urban' questions arise concerning means of spatial production and modes of urban becoming. On the one hand, the gulf between the two sites seems to confirm the idea put forward by Rem Koolhaas and others of the end or the disintegration of the modern metropolis as a rationally situated 'encoding [of] civilizations on their territory' (Koolhaas with Mau 1995). On the other hand, in exposing an unsettling disparity of material conditions the potential interrelation also substantiates the notion of a hyper-capitalist urbanity as proposed by Harvey and Sassen among others (Harvey 2007; Sassen 2010), fulfilling Marxist forecasts of a globally distributed, highly asymmetrical production of localities, now more than ever sifting 'winners' from 'losers' (Sassen 2010: 23).

Despite offering a generous panorama over southern Scandinavia, what is less obvious from the environmentally certified Emporia rooftop is its extended milieu, its larger systemic setting and its sustaining modes of production. The main question spanning the abyss is therefore one of contemporary city becoming – of extended material entanglement, of interdependencies across distances, of action and impact. Is the quivering instability of the marketplace-factory setting really accidental, or is it instead inevitable, and therefore the very incentive for a responsible urbanity? In the following, I will approach this question through the insightful work of Deleuze and Guattari on capitalist modes of societal production and their process-oriented extrapolation of Marxist historical materialism. Initially, I will turn to their problematising of intentionality and agency through the ideas of desire and machinic assemblages. I will then discuss dependency and responsibility, with the point of departure in all-pervasive capitalist circumstantiality.

Entanglements, Offshoots

To a certain extent, contemporary urbanity is already 'Deleuzo-Guattarian'. Prioritising flows over demarcations, infrastructures over edifices, repetitive branding over fixed identities, it might seem completely *Anti-Oedipal*, liberated by capitalism from its own territorial unconscious, from the coded constraints and culpabilities of former urban typologies and from the modernist demands of progression: 'Since the urban is now pervasive, urbanism will never again be about the "new", only about the "more" and the "modified"' (Koolhaas with Mau 1995). Emancipating as this might sound, cities continue to monumentalise themselves as mega-technical nodes and flagship constructions, at the same time obscuring what are increasingly extended supportive works of extraction and production. While clearly explained by Deleuze and Guattari in terms of a 'schizophrenizing' process (Deleuze and Guattari 1977: 339), cities remain surprisingly indifferent to the critical side effects of this unhinged development. Deleuze and Guattari's theorising of capitalist societal production may have been driven by their dedicated affirmation of capitalism's complex appeal. Yet, it was equally motivated by a deep frustration with the chasm between thinking and social mobilisation, and especially philosophy's inability to act. What Deleuze and Guattari developed in *Anti-Oedipus* and later in *A Thousand Plateaus* is therefore first and foremost an all-encompassing *diagnostic* of a pervasive global economic shift as it was taking off. Their thinking is a 'symptomatology' (Deleuze and Guattari 1990: 237) of forces, a hands-on approach operating on and cutting directly into the ambiguous and emergent body of capitalism. Unfolding from their clinical inquiry is thus a 'material ontology of becoming' (DeLanda 2002: 51; Lenco 2014: 141), insisting on the univocal and horizontal entanglement of bodies, occurrences and processes.

This ontological levelling has direct repercussions for the material conception of the city and, consequently, for the following discussion. Through the case of Emporia and Rana Plaza, the intention is to actualise a capitalist horizontality, a plateau of relationships and routings as they unfold 'between workshop and wardrobe' (Siegle with Burke 2014). Addressing the urban mode of production in its entirety and through its extremities, it might be possible also to speak to its potential exhaustion including its repetitious 'schizzes' (Deleuze and Guattari 1977: 39), the incidental breakdowns and ruptures unmasking its interdependent mechanisms, whether accidentally or responsibly.

This is also where the work of Deleuze and Guattari provides not only a theory but a circumstantial diagram of the variables of social production, especially in its capitalist appearance. The point of departure of Deleuze and Guattari is capitalism as a fundamental break with previous coordinating, territorialising and hierarchising forms of social configuration, the main shift being capitalism's variability; its decoding and deterritorialising of matter and bodies into flows, driven as much by non-coded desire as by codified intentions. Desire is a vital force, constituted neither by lack nor by purposiveness, an emergent energy, gathering and differentiating, associating undifferentiated flows and simultaneously dissociating customary movements, enabling things and matter to escape ordering and enter into new affiliations. 'Desire constantly couples continuous flows and partial objects that are by nature fragmentary and fragmented. Desire causes the current flow, itself flows in turn, and breaks the flows' (Deleuze and Guattari 1977: 5). The productive aspect of flowing desire is the 'machine'. Intervening into flows in certain operative or 'playing' combinations, like for example the mouth, the machine facilitates directed, productive action (Deleuze and Guattari 1977: 8). In a similar sense, 'fashion' is a machine, combining flows of material and social desire into new looks, new identities, new constellations, and ultimately new desires. 'The machine' is thus not a metaphor: 'Something is produced: the effects of a machine, not mere metaphors' (Deleuze and Guattari 1977: 9).

When Deleuze and Guattari describe capitalism in terms of a civilised 'desiring-machine', they refer to this specific execution of power as cuts into existing social orders, as a decoding and deregulating play with flows of matter and bodies as well as currencies and capital. If this dynamic between desire and machinic cuts constitutes one fundamental dimension of capitalist social production, the dynamic between actuality and virtuality constitutes another, similarly non-dualistic and non-dialectical. The actual–virtual plane thus unfolds as a modifying forcefield of continuously actualising/stabilising and virtualising/mobilising processes. There is no pure actuality and, consequently, no independent virtuality, but simply emergent tendencies of becoming-other and becoming-concrete. The actual and the virtual constitute charged polarities, giving rise to movements and sustaining drives. This flattened, de-hierarchised relationship between the actual and that which is latent is fundamental in a capitalist, horizontalising logic, the principle of which coincides with the methodological ideal of Deleuze and Guattari. As expressed in the introduction to *A Thousand Plateaus*, the ultimate means of interrogation would be 'to lay everything out on a plane of exteriority' (Deleuze and Guattari 1987: 16),[9] to make everything accessible on a plane of total, relational configurability. Every complication of flows, every machinic intervention, thus comes into being as an actual-virtual *layout*, in French *agencement*, in the English edition of Deleuze and Guattari's work translated as *assemblage* (Bennett 2005; Anderson et al. 2012) – as a co-incidence of material contiguities and cuts, expanses, positions and relations.

Calling attention to the marketplace–factory relationship is obviously an attempt to actualise the larger, world-embracing capitalist layout that today conditions the urban socius. Realised to its full potential in the 'fast fashion' business model,[10] capitalism does indeed expand as a flattening decoding of flows, optimised through computer-aided design, global procurement and bar code inventory management, and further deterritorialising through outsourcing, subcontracting and offshoring. Emporia and Rana Plaza are but partial elements in this distributing and complicating, indeed urbanising arrangement, the specific layouts of which largely remain inconspicuous. Yet moments of exposure occur, described by Deleuze and Guattari as interruptive incidents of material breakdown.

In desiring machines everything functions at the same time, but amid hia-
tuses and ruptures, breakdowns and failures, stalling and short circuits,
distances and fragmentations, within a sum that never succeeds in bringing
various parts together so as to form a whole. That is because the breaks
in the process are productive, and are reassemblies in and of themselves.
(Deleuze and Guattari 1977: 42)

While desiring flows are the fuel of the capitalist machine, the collapse is its actual–virtual working gears, which so far from impeding
development in fact enable shifts and re-routings. The question is only
how this inherent presence of breakdown or counter-actualisation, this
risk or probability of interruption, influences the contemporary urban
machine as a productive totality of matter and agency, causality and
responsibility.

Cut-Make-and-Trim

The distributed production-consumption chain of the ready-made
garment is today an essential driving force of contemporary urbanity,
and since the late 1990s is increasingly dominated by large multinational
retailers with the ability to dictate the terms of short lead times, huge
orders, lowered wages and prices, and constant flows of new designs.
While the average clothing item today is the result of an increasingly
segmented manufacturing process of up to a hundred operations from
material sourcing to store shelf (Siegle with Burke 2014), the duration of
this operational chain reaction is reduced to no more than three weeks.
Enabling consumers to enjoy 30–50 micro seasons a year, instead of the
summer and winter collections of days gone by (Siegle with Burke 2014;
Taplin 2014: 78), this speedy process obviously has knock-on effects
also for urban space. A manifestation of continuous material becoming,
fast fashion is also labour intensive, dependent in both the production
and consumption phases on young and stress-resistant bodies with
nimble hands or good looks. Referred to as the Cut-Make-and-Trim
complex (Siegle with Burke 2014), the fashion machine is speedily
cutting, making and especially trimming both social desire and urban
space, productively optimising and reinforcing accumulative currents.

Although dependent on social fluidity, this Cut-Make-and-Trim
aggregation is still highly material, an industry propped up by a cheap
workforce that nevertheless needs to keep growing at 8 per cent a year.
It is also sustained by a complex set-up of non-human sub-components,
such as cotton plantations, looms and weft knitting machines, dye-
works, containers, billboards and retail display systems, coordinated

by a huge number of entrepreneurial subcontractors, continuously optimising sources and taking advantage of fluctuations. Increasingly segmented, the entire set-up depends on an 'operational separation' (Taplin 2014: 78), in Marxist terms referred to as the historical process of 'primitive accumulation', the first decoding stage of separating people from the means of gaining a livelihood (Sassen 2010: 25), and later, in a transferred sense, of distancing 'investors' from the local and material circumstances of surplus value production. As this capitalising machine is further advanced, its disruptive 'schizzes' are being increasingly dispersed thus furthering capitalism's fundamental shift away from codified intentionalities towards the decoded playing out of probabilities.

The collapse of Rana Plaza rendered this complex set-up somewhat more explicit, unveiling a pervasive affirmation of socio-material volatility. Not surprisingly, this also complicated the ensuing discussion of causes and culpabilities. While the triggering factor seemed to be the vibrating generators, they initiated a rupturing event that eventually raised awareness of a wider set of circumstances that would otherwise have remained concealed, in political theorist Jane Bennett's words a 'vibrant' material eventfulness (Bennett 2005, 2010). In a world consisting of complex and deregulated material gatherings, agency is not rationally directed but distributed, even across 'the human-nonhuman divide' (Bennett 2005: 446). Matter and material things are not obstacles or passive support structures but have an agential capacity of their own. With reference to the major electricity blackout that struck North America in 2003, Bennett ascribes also to coal, generators and shutdown valves the ability to act. The idea behind this 'new' materialist argument is potentially to draw materiality, in an even more explicit way than did Deleuze and Guattari, into the agential domain of politics. Analysing the electrical grid, Bennett specifically focuses on how the deregulation of the energy market separated the production of electricity from its commercial distribution and use, and as such opened up new scope of action for non-human actors such as electrons, and – perhaps more importantly – electricity companies. While the intention with the deregulation was to enable both electrons and corporations to play with or compete for the most economic of trajectories, it also generated unexpected 'loop flows', improbable systemic fluctuations and, eventually, collapse.

Equally deregulated and distributed across materialities and territories, the complex of fast fashion perhaps needs no help to find its way into the domain of politics. Even before Rana Plaza, its political implications were obvious – its asymmetrical distribution of resources, its exploitation of human bodies, its damaging environmental effects. What has become conspicuous is rather how, as a 'civilised capitalist machine', it has systematically distributed its schizzes, deregulated its flows and decoded its actions, and this on a global level. Therefore, while it is important to politicise materiality, thus increasing awareness of the material agency brought into play by the capitalist machine, it is also essential to materialise its increasingly evasive trans-agency. What is pursued throughout *Capitalism and Schizophrenia* is precisely an attempt to rematerialise the decoding, deterritorialising and dematerialising capitalist machinery, to make graspable the fluctuating, self-regulatory coincidences of natural 'markets'. Beyond the reach of meddling political regulators, such assembled markets lend themselves to far-reaching 'axiomatisation', probabilistic and speculative projections of the relationship between actuality and virtuality (Deleuze and Guattari 1980: 79). Axiomatisation drains desiring flows of inert social and material specificity and replaces any remaining circumstantial code with 'derivative' micro-machines, new productive 'lines of flight' (Deleuze and Guattari 1987: 89), further decoupling assets from assurances.

Capitalism is in this sense different from other historical orders like 'primitive territorial machines' or 'despotic machines' in that it is always directed towards the activating of a totality of possible effects, and thus as destructive as it is constructive. In the diagnosis of Deleuze and Guattari, there is therefore a recurrent emphasis on what in the original French is referred to as *agencements*, machines of rupture *and* stabilisation, of actual *and* virtual formation. *Agencements*, or 'assemblages', are thus 'affective' rather than 'effective', productively playing out the contingency of a totality, and as such affirmative of both social and material becoming.

More Than Butterfly Effects

The role of becoming is particularly apparent in the case of fast fashion, which comes into existence through a play with modes and with the outmoded, and this through affective pushes of relationships, boundaries and margins. The specific circumstantiality of fast fashion depends on a 'floating time' described by Deleuze and Guattari as a time 'that knows only speeds and continually divides that which transpires into an already-there that is at the same time not-yet-here, a simultaneous too-late and too-early, a something that is both going to happen and has just happened' (Deleuze and Guattari 1987: 262). It is a kind of ahistorical spatio-temporality allowing for abundance to come into play, the non-linear, vibrant causality of 'releasing' and 'unwinding' recognised by Bennett (Bennett 2005: 458) – a blind and forgetful loop-flow causality giving rise to increasingly detached yet systemically conditioned 'butterfly effects' (Lorenz 1963). And these collateral effects, rather than a systemic deficiency, should be seen as enabling, pointing to the fact that, as Deleuze expressed it, 'relations are always external to their terms' (Deleuze 1991: 66), that relations between entities are not exhausted by the specific configuration. Yet, as critics of new and vitalist forms of materialism have pointed out, while recognising material agency might be a way to highlight the relevance of a relational and thus political ecology, it runs the risk of simply expanding causality, thus disregarding the diverse, historical modes of political becoming, the specific 'complexities, frictions, intractabilities, and conundrums of "matter in relation"' (Abrahamsson et al. 2015: 13).

In the case of Emporia and Rana Plaza it is obvious how an overemphasis on material agency may result in a problematic concealing of frictions and intractabilities and a subsequent diffusion of accountability. Legal actions have been commenced against certain individuals, such as Sohar Rana, the owner of Rana Plaza, and some of the subcontractors and engineers, including the mayor of Savar who signed the disastrous building permit (Mustafa and Islam 2013; Fidh Report 2014). But other influential actors in the supply chain, including immensely profitable corporations like Benetton and Carrefour, continue to deny involvement and thus remain unaffected, unwilling to contribute to the Rana Plaza Arrangement Victims Fund (Siegle with Burke 2014). What these actors say in their defence is that they were unaware of and therefore not part of the assemblage in question, a deficit of awareness that in this case constitutes a fundamental, deterritorialising principle.

So, while workers in Bangladesh fight for the recognition of their bodies as something more than volatile flows of matter, Emporia dresses up in a green and environmentally certified outfit, enthusiastically embracing local bee colonies but consciously unmindful of its remote 'butterfly effects'. With the capitalist transformation of the industry–marketplace complex into a general, transactional busy-ness, it is indeed problematic 'to yield the term *agency* to humans alone' (Bennett 2005: 461). Yet while, according to geographer Sue Ruddick, the large 'tent' of assemblage thinking also allows for political mobilisation of things, it simultaneously gathers a polarised crew of agitators, on the one hand 'neo-vitalists' and on the other 'neo-Marxists' (Ruddick 2012: 208). While the former focus on the affirmation of pulsating life, the latter maintain that affirming contingency 'can never be a goal in and of itself' (Braun 2011: 391). Similarly, in her critique of applied assemblage thinking, political theorist Isabel Garo points to a certain 'indistinction' (Garo 2008: 58), where Deleuzian assemblage politics, instead of referring back to 'a common causality, which can be clearly demonstrated' (Garo 2008: 58), runs the risk of moving in 'a closed circuit [. . .], by way of selected practices, from theory back into theory' (Garo 2008: 55). The source of confusion might in this respect be the paradoxical way in which politics unfolds in Deleuze and Guattari as both de- and repoliticization – both as a rejection of the institutional game of politics as coordinated social struggle and as an affirmation of political action in terms of transversal, molecular energy exchange. As a micropolitics, their schizoanalytical assemblage thinking is therefore neither a politics in miniature nor a politics of isolated things, but a politics that in relation to dominating flows is minoritarian, materially irruptive and spatially deviant.

Concluding Remarks

While Emporia's rooftop park is again budding, the question of the centre's circumstantiality remains, and with it the question of accountability. What is its scope of action, its range of effect? As a celebrated exemplar of an urban becoming that claims to be 'smart', it takes on the challenge of managing its own downsides. Environmentally certifying its coming into being, it has acknowledged its responsibility, its effects upon wider flows of resources and matter. Yet, at the same time, its recognition of circumstantiality is limited, unmindful of the totality of its expansive social and material derangement. While in the Mango store of Emporia a new shipment of fashionable cotton tops of the latest cut is selling out, and this for less than two euros each, its backwash subsists in the Rana Plaza pit – a schizoid, corporate and environmental ripple, conflating desires and debts. A suspicion surfaces that fast fashion and the quick-response business models of today are the privileged and established modes of urban becoming, consumer driven and busy, yet opaque as concerns their distributed material impact. As emphasised by Ian Taplin (among other sociologists), 'the apparent dilution of accountability' needs to be addressed (Taplin 2014: 79). It may be that the Rana Plaza collapse and its aftershocks will draw attention to the limits of smartness, of corporate social responsibility and of environmental certification protocols. It may also shed some light on a skewed urbanity that, despite claims to the contrary, irresponsibly privileges the marketplace over the factory, the consumer over the worker and business over environment, and indeed to such an extent that it is misleading to talk about butterfly effects.

While the juxtaposition of Emporia and Rana Plaza is motivated by a wish to situate the city in a wider political ecology, it is also an attempt to examine the scope of dependency and responsibility and to raise the inconvenient issue of guilt. While it is clear that the world is an abundant eventfulness of flowing forces more or less successfully managed by a 'capitalist machine', it is equally clear that there is a need to attend to the asymmetrical ways in which it is playing out its powers. Against this background, simply 'blaming' according to the most immediate causal chain of action will not do. Instead, we need to imagine and consider what the urban machine as a totality may allow, taking into account 'the affordance' (Gibson 1979: 27; Abrahamsson et al. 2015: 15) or the totality of circumstantial offerings of the assemblage as a whole, including also its potential loop-flows. We might, for example, pause to acknowledge the fact that our shopping habits affirm the complex of fast fashion, that we as consumers are also answerable and ultimately, as Taplin suggests, would 'bear some responsibility for its adverse consequences' (Taplin 2014: 80), for which the systemic services of the Emporia rooftop will compensate only marginally, if at all. At the end of the day, we find ourselves looking out not over a smart city district but over a muddy puddle, lined with a mixture of concrete and rags – a schizoid instance of a Cut-Make-and-Trim urbanity which, despite fatal breakdowns, continues to ignore its own accelerating debts.

Notes

1. Designed by Wingårdh Architects and certified according to the British BREEAM protocol, Emporia has been awarded several prizes, including first prize in the World Architecture Festival, Shanghai, 2013, the winner of the Mapic Award 2013 and the MIPIM Award 2013, and second prize in the Retail and Leisure International Global Award 2014. The owner is the retail company Steen & Strøm, itself owned by French Klépierre, in turn controlled by American Simon Property Group, the world's largest real estate company, focusing on retail real estate, primarily regional malls (PrNewswire 2014). See also http://www.steen-strom.com and http://www.breeam.org.
2. The rating according to the BREEAM protocol is 'very good', which is the average on a five-level rating scale. The detailed information behind the rating is not publicly accessible.
3. According to the Steen & Strøm official webpage, Emporia attracts around ten million shoppers yearly and generates a €222 million turnover.
4. Rabbit jumping and pony riding were activities offered during a study visit undertaken by the author in July 2013. As for beekeeping, see http://www.emporia.se/Nyheter/Datum/2014/8/Bikupor-pa-Emporias-tak/.

5. In 2014, Dhaka has an estimated population of 16.9 million and an estimated annual growth rate of 3.6 per cent. See UN World Urbanization Prospects, 2014 Revision, p. 26, online at: http://esa.un.org/Unpd/Wup/Highlights/WUP2014-Highlights.pdf (accessed 18 November 2014).

6. Brands include (among others) Walmart, Primark, Benetton and Mango, the last of which has its own outlet at Emporia. For a more detailed list, see Clean Clothes Campaign, online at: http://www.cleanclothes.org/ranaplaza/who-needs-to-pay-up (accessed 18 November 2014).

7. The Rana Plaza collapse is the deadliest garment factory accident in history and 'most deadly structural failure in modern times' times' (BBC website, 3 May 2013, online at: http://www.bbc.com/news/world-asia-22394094). Statistical information provided by the Rana Plaza Coordination Committee, online at: http://www.ranaplaza-arrangement.org/.

8. Charles Larsson, Steen & Strøm, in an interview with the author, 9 June 2014.

9. 'L'idéal d'un livre serait d'étaler toute chose sur un tel plan d'extériorité, sur une seule page, sur une même plage: événements vécus, déterminations historiques, concepts pensés, individus, groupes et formations sociales.' While they here use the verb *étaler*, this passage is very elucidating as to their idea of active layout, of *agencement*. Deleuze and Guattari (1980/1987:16).

10. *Fast fashion* – 'lean retailing' and a 'quick response model of production', pioneered by among others Inditex (through Zara), a model dramatically limiting stockpiles and reducing time between initial design and arrival in store, effectively increasing turnover. For a thorough discussion, see Taplin (2014).

References

Abrahamsson, S., Bertoni, A. and Mol, F. (2015) 'Living with omega-3: new materialism and enduring concerns', *Environment and Planning D: Society and Space*, 33: 4–19.

Anderson, B., Kearnes, M., McFarlane, C. and Swanton, D. (2012) 'On assemblages and geography', *Dialogues in Human Geography*, 2 (2): 171–89.

BBC (2013) 'Bangladesh building collapse death toll passes 500', published on BBC website, 3 May, online at: http://www.bbc.com/news/world-asia-22394094 (accessed 28 February 2015).

Bennett, J. (2005) 'The agency of assemblages and the North American blackout', *Public Culture*, 17 (3): 445–65.

Bennett, J. (2010) *Vibrant Matter: A Political Ecology of Things*. Durham, NC: Duke University Press.

Braun, B. (2011) 'Book review forum: Jane Bennett – A Political Ecology of Things', *Dialogues in Human Geography*, 1 (3): 390–3.

DeLanda, M. (2002) *Intensive Science and Virtual Philosophy*. New York: Bloomsbury.

Deleuze, G. ([1953] 1991) *Empiricism and Subjectivity – An Essay on Hume's Theory of Human Nature*. New York: Columbia University Press.

Deleuze, G. (1990) *The Logic of Sense*. New York: Columbia University Press.

Deleuze, G. and Guattari, F. ([1972] 1977) *Anti-Oedipus: Capitalism and Schizophrenia*. New York: Penguin Books.

Deleuze, G. and Guattari, F. ([1980] 1987) *A Thousand Plateaus: Capitalism and Schizophrenia*. Minneapolis: University of Minnesota Press.

Deleuze, G. and Guattari, F. (1980) *Milles Plateaux: Capitalisme et Schizophrénie*. Paris: Éditions de Minuit.

Fidh – International Federation for Human Rights (2014) 'One year after the Rana Plaza catastrophe: slow progress and insufficient compensations', online at: https://www.fidh.org/IMG/pdf/20140422_bd_ranaplaza_qa_en.pdf (accessed 28 February 2015).

Fürstenberg, C. (2012) 'Färg och fågelkvitter' ['Colour and birds' tweets'], Sydsvenska Dagbladet, 25 October, online at: http://www.sydsvenskan.se/malmo/farg-och-fagelkvitter/ (accessed 29 November 2014).

Garo, I. (2008) 'Molecular revolutions: the paradox of politics in the work of Gilles Deleuze', in I. Buchanan and N. Thoburn (eds), Deleuze and Politics. Edinburgh: Edinburgh University Press, pp. 54–73.

Gibson, J. J. (1979) 'The theory of affordance', The Ecological Approach to Visual Perception. Boston: Houghton Mifflin.

Harvey, D. (2007) 'Neo-liberalism and the City', Studies in Social Justice, 1 (1): 2–13.

Hossain, F. and Alam, J. (2013) 'Bangladesh building collapse death toll tops 500: engineer whistleblower arrested', Huffington Post, 2 May, accessed 19 November 2014.

Koolhaas, R. with Mau, B. (1995) 'What ever happened to urbanism?', S, M, L, XL. New York: Monicelli Press, pp. 959–71.

Lenco, P. (2014) '(Re)-introducing Deleuze: new readings of Deleuze in international studies', Millennium: Journal of International Studies, 43 (1): 124–44.

Lorenz, E. N. (1963) 'The predictability of hydrodynamic flow', Transactions of the New York Academy of Sciences, 25 (4): 409–32.

Mustafa, S. and Islam, S. (2013) 'Profile: Rana Plaza owner Mohammad Sohel Rana', BBC News Asia, 3 May, online at: http://www.bbc.com/news/world-asia-22366454 (accessed 15 December 2014).

PrNewswire (2014) online at: http://www.prnewswire.com/news-releases/simon-property-group-recognized-for-leadership-in-sustainability-and-reporting-transparency-by-cdp-and-gresb-276972691.html (published 24 September 2014, accessed 19 November 2014).

Ruddick, S. (2012) 'Power and the problem of composition', Dialogues in Human Geography, 2 (2): 207–11.

Sassen, S. (2010) 'A savage sorting of winners and losers: contemporary versions of primitive accumulation', Globalizations, 7 (1): 23–50.

Siegle, L. with Burke, J. (2014) We Are What We Wear: Unravelling Fast Fashion and the Collapse of Rana Plaza. London: Guardian Shorts.

Sydsvenska Dagbladet (2012) 'Emporia flödade i guld' ['Emporia flooded in gold'], Sydsvenska Dagbladet, 25 October, online at: http://www.sydsvenskan.se/sok/?q=emporia,+invigning&p= (accessed 29 November 2014).

Taplin, I. M. (2014) 'Who is to blame? A re-examination of fast fashion after the 2013 factory disaster in Bangladesh', Critical Perspectives on International Business, 10 (1/2): 72–83.

Websites

BREEAM official website, at: http://www.breeam.org (accessed 18 November 2014).

Clean Clothes Campaign, online at: http://www.cleanclothes.org/ranaplaza/who-needs-to-pay-up (accessed 18 November 2014).

Emporia official website, online at: http//www.emporia.se (accessed 29 November 2014).

Rana Plaza Coordination Committee, online at: http://www.ranaplaza-arrangement.org (accessed 19 November 2014).

Steen & Strøm official website, online at: http://www.steenstrom.com (accessed 19 November 2014).

UN World Urbanization Prospects, 2014 Revision, online at: http://esa.un.org/Unpd/Wup/Highlights/WUP2014-Highlights.pdf (accessed 18 November 2014).

Chapter 12

The Haifa Urban Destruction Machine

Ronnen Ben-Arie

> The city of Paris entered the twentieth century in the form which Haussmann gave it. He revolutionized the physiognomy of the city with the humblest means imaginable: spades, pickaxes, crowbars, and the like. What destruction was caused by even these crude tools! And as the big cities grew, the means of razing them developed in tandem. What visions of the future this evoked!
>
> Benjamin (2003: 52)

Destruction has been a mode of operation of city development at least since the latter's modern emergence. Walter Benjamin identifies the crucial moment with Haussmann's project for creating the grand boulevards of Paris. The development of technological capacities was indeed essential for the feasibility of the project (Buck-Morss 1989: 317), but according to Benjamin there was more to it. He realises the project as a conjunction of the 'fraudulent speculation' based economy of the time, which caused the displacement of the urban proletariat, and the goal to 'secure the city against civil war' (Benjamin 1999a: 12).[1] Thus modern urbanism has entangled the economic and the military since its inception, urban development alongside destruction and violence. Following Benjamin, Andrew Herscher suggests that 'the destruction inflicted in the course of Haussmann's modernisation of Paris was not peripheral, but rather a distinctive and significant dimension of the project of modernisation' and that urban destruction should be considered as 'one of modern urbanity's very manifestations' (Herscher 2007). To paraphrase Lefebvre, it might be said that in order to understand the modern city and urban space, we should analyse the social destruction of space, that is the productive dimensions of the destruction of urban space.

This chapter aims to examine the ways in which destruction operates within urban space and urban development through the exploration of one specific urban space, the downtown of the city of Haifa in Israel-

Palestine, which in recent years is undergoing a massive rehabilitation project. I will consider the ongoing destruction of this urban space as it operates and is modified with time, in relation to different and changing contexts and for different and changing functions. Following Ann Stoler's assertion that destruction is 'a corrosive process that weighs on the future and shapes the present' (Stoler 2008: 194), I will consider urban destruction as a becoming rather than a fixed or finalised condition. This will enable me, on the one hand, to avoid what Gastón Gordillo identifies as the ruin fetish, which tends to conceal the evidence of destruction (Gordillo 2014: 261), and to relate to the ongoing operation of ruins and destruction in the production of an urban space entangled with different subjectivities, on the other. In order to do this I will use Deleuze and Guattari's concept of the machine to conceptualise the function and operation of destruction as part of the production of urban space.

Machines are prevalent throughout the writings and thought of Deleuze and Guattari. Desiring-machines, abstract machines and war machines are probably the most famous concepts but there are of course many more. From the opening lines of *Anti-Oedipus*, where machines are first presented as an alternative to the Freudian id (Deleuze and Guattari 1977: 1), machines have had different meanings and served different functions for them. As Todd May observes, the machine in their work is a concept that can be situated at the level of the individual, the society, the state, the pre-individual, among groups and between people, and across these various realms (May 2005: 122). Nonetheless, I would like to expand on some of the concept's general features that are relevant and helpful in the current exploration. For Deleuze and Guattari, machines are all about production, and a machine is always a multiplicity. They assert that *'we are misled by considering any complicated machine as a single thing*; in truth it is a city or a society ... We see a machine as a whole' (Deleuze and Guattari 1977: 285; italics in original). Machines are multiplicities of connections and interactions between heterogeneous elements, components and other machines, which are producing new connections, new arrangements and new machines. As Guattari explains in a short text entitled 'On Machines', '[t]he essence of the machine is linked to procedures which deterritorialise its elements, functions and relations of alterity' (Guattari 1995b). Thus machines have no identity or stability; it is not about 'the production *of* something *by* someone – but production for the sake of production itself' (Colebrook 2002: 55; italics in original). The distinction Deleuze and Guattari make between machinic enslavement and social subjection is important in this regard. Machinic enslavement takes place when human beings are constituent parts of a machine that they compose together with other things, and which operates as a higher unity that controls and directs its components. In social subjection, a higher unity rather constitutes the human being as a subject linked to an exterior object of which he or she is no longer a component but a user. The difference is between being subjected to the machine and being enslaved by the machine (Deleuze and Guattari 1987: 456–7). Maurizio Lazzarato explains that while social subjection produces an 'individuated subject', machinic enslavement has to do with Deleuze's dividual[2] which is contiguous with machines (Lazzarato 2014: 25–6). It is not about making use of machines, but rather about being '*a point of conjunction or disjunction* in the economic, social, or communicational processes' (2014: 26; italics in original). Machinic enslavement operates through desubjectivation and the deterritorialisation and decodification of subjects and objects, that is with decoded flows of molecular components and potentialities of non-individuated and asignified subjectivity. Social subjection, according to Lazzarato, imposes molar hierarchies by converting and reducing multiplicity to a series of dualisms. Against that, taking into account the operation of machinic enslavement provides the possibility for 'converting the machinic dimension into forms of subjectivation that critique, reconfigure, and redistribute these molar dualisms' (2014: 35–6). Machines operate through breaks and interruptions of flows of matter and energy and, as Guattari asserts, a machine is 'shaped by a desire for abolition. Its emergence is doubled with breakdown, catastrophe' (Guattari 1995a: 37).

Machines are always open for change and transformation and ready for the creation of new connections. The concept of the machine might seem very similar to that of the assemblage, but Deleuze and Guattari make a distinction between them, giving the machine the prerogative of transformation within and of assemblages:

> [A] machine is like a set of cutting edges that insert themselves into the assemblage undergoing deterritorialisation, and draw variations and mutations of it. For there are no mechanical effects; effects are always machinic ... What we call *machinic statements* are machine effects that define consistency or enter matters of expression. (Deleuze and Guattari 1987: 333; italics in original)

Mechanisms are closed specific functions with pre-given outcomes (Colebrook 2002: 56). Machines, on the other hand, are productive in unpredictable ways (May 2005: 125). As Bogard puts it, machines are not to be assimilated to 'mechanist or vitalist forms, or to any concept that would essentialise either them or the assemblages they compose' (Bogard 2009: 16). Machines function within assemblages, setting them in processes of transformation through the production of new connections and relations between flows of matter and bodies and flows of statements and expression, that is producing new machinic assemblages of content and new collective assemblages of enunciation (Deleuze and Guattari 1987: 43–5, 88). That is why Guattari asserts that machines are more than just technological tools, but are rather social entities, with the city being an example for such a mega-machine, one that 'develops *universes of reference* – ontological heterogeneous universes, which are marked by historic turning points, a factor of irreversibility and singularity' (Guattari 1995b; italics in original).

In what follows, these basic features of the concept of the machine, namely that 'each machine has a composition, function, and potential' (Goodchild 1996: 49), will anchor an analysis of destruction as a machine which operates, through its connection and relations to other machines, in the production of the urban space and its materiality, its different subjectivities and the different possible modes of collective existence that might actualise with it. This schizoanalysis of the urban space will attempt to offer an alternative and to challenge more commonly used conceptualisations of urban destruction, specifically those of urbicide as political violence and creative destruction as an economic system of development.

Destruction's Surplus Value

The city of Haifa is the third largest city in Israel, the major metropolis of the north of the country, and one of its two main seaports. In recent years, the municipality has been promoting a neoliberal-oriented rehabilitation project for the city's downtown area. The municipality's project aims to rebrand and revive the city's old downtown, hoping that this will encourage private investors and developers to come in and stimulate a real estate market which has been almost non-existent for many years. As can be seen in the municipality's statement of intentions:

Haifa's Downtown which is located 2 minutes walk from Haifa Port was built in the mid eighteenth century. As years passed, the coastal strip has developed into a harbour and the city has become the area's thriving commerce centre. During the British Mandate, the downtown area had a significant economic momentum. The modern sea port, launched in 1933, has become the entrance gate for numerous Jewish immigrants and an anchor for international corporations. With Israel's establishment, commercial and residential areas have migrated towards the higher neighbourhoods of the city, while the downtown has begun to fade away.

50 years later, a new era has started to blossom with the launch of the unique urban rehabilitation project, which is taking its shape nowadays. Planned by Haifa Municipality, the downtown area will be transformed into a lively student-centered compound, combining cultural life, entertainment and commerce. You are invited to meet the colourful people and to soak in the special atmosphere that downtown Haifa offers to its guests. (Haifa Municipality 2012)

This official narrative tells the common story of a city's downtown, which has been through familiar processes of decline and decay and is now ready for an active intervention of rehabilitation. As is well articulated in the municipal statement, it is a transformative intervention that is directed towards the built environment as well as its inhabitants. Walking through downtown Haifa, signs of destruction, desolation and neglect are everywhere. Ruins, half demolished houses and empty and deserted buildings are clearly in evidence, side by side with new, modern, mostly office buildings. All these are apprehended as the physical stratum on which manipulation is needed in order to produce a new desired urban space. But this also entails a transformation of the meanings attributed to the urban space and the subjectivities that are part of it, as well as the modes of existence it aims to create and promote. This is apparent both in the municipality's campaign, which aims to rebrand the area as a hip neighbourhood, and in that of the private developers involved. Municipal signboards and public presentations of future renovation plans show a clean, designed and well-cared for environment, in contrast to the decay and neglect of the existing reality. Developers' advertisements for new housing projects are directed to 'cool artists and sophisticated lawyers' and signs posted on desolate buildings offer to pay in cash for properties that are 'deserted/problematic/wrecked/ occupied by squatters'. This is intended as a straightforward process of gentrification, which, on the one hand, makes clear who are the desired inhabitants of the renovated urban space and what is deemed to be their lifestyle and appropriate environment; on the other hand, it is obvious who is to be excluded and removed – those who have inhabited the area throughout its deterioration.

In this narrative, destruction operates as the base condition, one which calls for intervention. It is the physical infrastructure on which capital surplus can be produced. In Marxist and neo-Marxist theories it is conceptualised as 'creative destruction', which 'is embedded within the circulation of capital itself', as David Harvey puts it – 'A prime force pushing capitalism into periodic paroxysms of crisis' (Harvey 1989b: 106). According to this logic, destruction serves as a basis for future economic growth and the creation of surplus value. A phase of urban destruction and decay is considered essential in order for real estate values to radically decrease, so as to enable the maximisation of future profits for private investors and developers. This lays the ground for economists like Joseph Schumpeter to glorify those 'heroic creative destroyers', such as Haussmann in Paris and Robert Moses in New York, who pushed forward the 'benevolent capitalistic development' (Harvey 1989b: 17). In a neoliberal economy, it is private entrepreneurs who are invited by the local authority to fulfil this role, by creating new complex governance-economy relations and market-based regulatory arrangements, such as public-private partnerships, that facilitate the necessary conditions for profitable development options (Brenner and Theodore 2005; Harvey 1989a). It is through destruction and violence that the urban space is restructured, transforming not only the built environment but also its inhabitants and agents of transformation. Creative destruction of the urban space most commonly involves the characterisation of the poor, the underprivileged and the marginalised as unwanted, accompanied by their physical exclusion and dispossession (Harvey 2008: 33), while on the other hand distinguishing who and what the regenerated milieu is meant for and who can be part of its production, be it private developers or artists lured by the available deserted spaces.

This kind of theorisation is very powerful in explaining processes of urban development and redevelopment, as well as the gentrification that often accompanies these processes. The conceptualisation is based on translating violence and destruction into an economic system and coding it as exchange values, and by signifying destruction by its economic values, a whole set of hierarchised social values is also being produced. What it fails to do is to take into consideration the origins of destruction that lie outside the economy and financial crises, and to account for the continuity of its operation. This lack is also strikingly apparent in Haifa municipality's official narrative.

In the municipality's statement, 'the downtown has begun to fade away' in a rather mysterious way and for reasons that are not made explicit. But the text conceals two clues that might help us figure this out. First, the sentence 'With Israel's establishment, commercial and residential areas have migrated towards the higher neighbourhoods of the city, while the downtown has begun to fade away' implies that this fading away was correlated somehow with the establishment of the state of Israel; and second is the surprising absence of the Palestinian population of the city and its relations with the city's Jewish population, something which on other occasions is often referred to as evidence for the alleged coexistence and peace that have prevailed in Haifa for more than a hundred years. Indeed, much of the history of the development of the city's downtown, including the destruction that took place some 65 years ago, is omitted from the official narrative.

Destruction as Political Exclusion

The origins of Haifa's development as a modern city date back to the time of the Ottoman Empire when the city was rebuilt by Daher el-Omar, an autonomous Arab ruler of northern Palestine during the mid-eighteenth century, in a sheltered location alongside a new seaport. By the beginning of the twentieth century, the city's population was increasing faster than that of any other city in the region, and with the help of foreign investment it grew rapidly, connected by a new railroad line to the Hejaz Railway in the east as well as to a modernising harbour. Under British rule, the city became the Empire's major economic and administrative hub in the eastern Mediterranean. The harbour was expanded and deepened, new railroad tracks along the coast were built leading to Cairo and Beirut, and a pipeline bringing oil from Iraq served as a basis for the establishment of refineries and heavy industry. All this made Haifa the primary gateway to the Mediterranean and was the basis for the city's growth and expansion. The population grew steadily as rural Palestinian workers became urbanised and Jewish immigrants flowed in by sea. During the thirty years of the British Mandate, the city's population increased from around 20,000 to almost 150,000 and its composition changed from a vast majority of Palestinians to a situation of near-parity between the Palestinian and Jewish residents (Yazbak 1987).

Although known at the time for the relatively good relations and municipal cooperation between its Jewish and Palestinian populations, the city developed clear distinctions between the neighbourhoods populated mostly by Palestinians and those populated by the Jewish. The Palestinian population inhabited the lower parts of the city, in the old city and the surrounding neighbourhoods, and the Jewish population lived mostly in the new neighbourhoods that were being built higher on the slopes of Mount Carmel. This topographically divided situation became crucial in the 1948 war and its aftermath. The war that swept the country and concluded in the establishment of the state of Israel and the destruction and expulsion of most of the Palestinian people did not spare Haifa, and had harsh consequences for its urban space and population (Khalidi 2008). With the conquest of the city by the victorious Jewish forces, only 3,000 out of around 70,000 Palestinian residents remained. All the rest became refugees, some in other Palestinian cities and rural areas while many left for Lebanon and elsewhere (Morris 2004: 99–109). The remaining Palestinian population was concentrated in two bounded neighbourhoods on the outskirts of the city centre (Goren 1999). In the few weeks that followed, the new state's government, supported by the local municipality, took advantage of the new situation in the lower parts of the city, which remained almost entirely deserted and already severely damaged by artillery attacks that had taken place during the fighting, and demolished hundreds of Palestinian homes and properties, leaving vast parts of the city's downtown in ruins (Goren 1994).

Details of a May 1948 discussion in a special committee appointed to attend to the issues of Palestinians that remained in the city after fighting had ended testify to the new policy adopted for the city's downtown:

> The exodus of the Arab population from Haifa and the almost complete evacuation of the downtown area . . . offer an unprecedented opportunity for conducting preservation works linked to demolition. These works have the power to fundamentally fix the security conditions, the transportation arteries and the sanitary condition in the city. The fact that the buildings designated for demolition were vastly damaged during the war and must be demolished according to the dangerous building by-laws, is in a way a relief and gives an additional argument for the implementation of the required works . . . The acknowledgment that the city could not stay desolated and deserted for long, facing the waves of immigration that we are all anticipating, and of the return of many of the Arabs who abandoned Haifa, should invigorate us to execute all the required actions without any delay . . . (Quoted in Goren 1994: 6)

Interestingly, the act of destruction, aimed at preventing refugees from returning and reclaiming their houses and stabilising the tremendous demographic transformation the city underwent, was justified, and even implemented, by means of another logic, that of urban planning. On top of considerations of national struggle, there were also public health and safety, transportation and urban development needs to be addressed in anticipation of a population influx. And indeed, the new administration was fortunate to have at its disposal urban plans already prepared by British planners that provided a professional and official basis for the demolition of large parts of the old city. As early as the 1930s, British officials and planners were concerned with the old city's urban fabric and physical condition and its incompatibility with the contemporary model of urban development, and attempted to enforce on the area modern regulations of town planning that could only be implemented through demolition of the old fabric, as happened in many places throughout the world (Kolodney and Kallus 2008). The plans they drew up in pursuit of those objectives were later used in the destruction of the old city as carried out by the new Israeli state, although the actual scope of destruction went beyond what was originally envisaged. Thus we can see how the new political order that emerged after the war appropriated for its own needs and purposes a destruction apparatus already developed by modern urban planning in the production of a new urban space in Haifa. The destruction of the old city left not only a severe rupture in the urban fabric. Now, with the harbour disconnected from its main supply routes due to the closed borders of the new state and the depletion of the inhabitants and users of the old city, urban development was relocated to the Jewish quarters on higher ground. The old downtown was left deserted and in decay for many years, and though some parts have been rebuilt, it still remains as evidence of the violence that took place.

The extensive destruction of the Palestinian parts of the city and the almost total expulsion of the city's Palestinian population – and with that, the extinction of the possibility for a shared mode of existence between Jews and Palestinians – were crucial in the production of the new formation of Haifa as a Jewish city and, on a larger scale, of Israel as a Jewish state. Other major cities throughout the country shared a similar fate, culminating, as Manar Hassan asserts, in the destruction of the Palestinian city and Palestinian urban society (Hassan 2005). According to Hassan, this was highly instrumental in the evolution of the Palestinian society after the war as mostly rural, patriarchal and backward, a society which was politically excluded and inert for many years. Destruction as 'urbicide', that is the killing of the urban space, operated as part of the establishment of the new political order after 1948, an order that is founded on the extinction of the Palestinian collective existence and much of its physical actualisations.[3] The establishment of the state of Israel based on these lines had formalised and consolidated forces of violence, annihilation, exclusion and separation, while eliminating other possibilities that had been actualised in the city until then.

According to this theorisation, the destruction and annihilation of one mode of existence and possible collectivity is necessary for the establish-

ment and preservation of another, and as long as the victorious collectivity, be it national or any other, desires to prevail, it will continue to deny
any sign of all other alternatives. The logic of this conceptualisation is
based on the coding of destruction and violence along the molar lines
of collective identities and their alterity and exclusion. But as we have
seen, the actualised operation of destruction can be transferred from one
assemblage of enunciation to another: in this case, from that of urban
planning to national identity exclusion, and then on to that of economic
dispossession. Destruction, as a machine, operates and functions within
different social assemblages; it is being actualised in different ways by
connecting to other social machines such as war and urban renewal, and
it bears different significations within these assemblages. Nonetheless,
it is insufficient to understand the operation of destruction only within
the frame of the current reality, while ignoring the ways previous modes
of destruction continue to unfold within the production of the urban
space. The deserted and neglected neighbourhood that is now the object
of urban regeneration plans has its origins in the acts of destruction that
took place in the past for different reasons and according to different
desires. Failing to understand this poses the risk of overlooking all the
actual effects of destruction, and as a consequence a failure to attend
to all its possible implications. To conclude this chapter, I will consider
such possible shortcomings by reflecting, very briefly, on the short story
'Returning to Haifa', written in 1969 by the Palestinian author Ghassan
Kanafani, and the implications it might hold for understanding the city's
reality today.

Machinic Destruction

In Kanafani's story, a Palestinian couple from Ramallah, Said and
Safiyya, journey to their hometown of Haifa almost twenty years after
they left it during the 1948 war. This is made possible due to the opening
of the borders as a consequence of the 1967 war and the Israeli occupation of the West Bank. As the plot develops, we learn that the aim of
their journey is not merely to visit their forsaken city and abandoned
home, but also to try and find their eldest son whom, to their sorrow,
they mistakenly left behind as a five-month-old baby as they fled the city
amid the commotion of the fighting.

As they approach the city, Said, who is driving the car, feels that
he knows his way through the streets as though nothing has changed,
although he last travelled along them many years before. He feels that
he still knows every curve and turn, and that the city as he encounters it

now is actually the living memory of a past that all at once comes back to him, 'sharp as a knife' (Kanafani 2000: 152). The memory of the city intertwines with the memory of Khaldun, the son who was left behind, as a moment of fixation, which remained inerasable in the continuous flow of change that is life, affecting and dominating all that followed without itself being altered, and a memory that is a focal point of the desire for return to the past that has gone but keeps on living unchanged.

Arriving at their abandoned home, Said and Safiyya realise that it is now occupied by Miriam, a Jewish woman who came to Haifa as an immigrant around the time they were forced to leave, and who received from the new authorities their house to live in as well as their baby child to raise as her own son. In the house, they find that much has remained as they left it, with their furniture being used by the new residents. As in many other places in Israel (and around the world), houses that were not demolished, at least not right away, were used by the state for housing newly arriving immigrants.

Although Miriam also seems to mourn the past that has gone with the possibilities that it enveloped, saying sorrowfully that after the war there is in Haifa a 'true Sabbath, but there is no longer a true Sabbath on Friday, nor a true one on Sunday' (2000: 168), it is made clear that a return to the past is not an option for her. When the son, now a soldier in the Israeli army, returns home, his adoptive mother leaves it to him to choose between his biological parents, strangers to him now, and the parents who have raised him as their own son. Said, who is frightened by the possible outcome – knowing that, just as he felt renounced by the city and his home, his son might now do the same – tries to persuade Safiyya to leave the place and 'go back to the past' (2000: 172). For him, this means now relinquishing the hope they once had for a return, and also to avoid confronting the future that might bring with it even more destruction and sorrow. Towards the end of the story, Said realises that his hope to return to his past hometown and homeland is worthless, and that his younger son is right to look for it instead in the future, which for him means to take up a weapon and fight for his homeland, as part of the Palestinian liberation movement. This now seems to him to be the only option that might open a way for change.

The logic of the story is the logic of exclusive identities that require an exclusive urban space. Although there are signs of simultaneous existence, like the matching of Said's memories of the city of the past with the actual streets of the present, or the dual identity of the abandoned son who was adopted, in the end choices must be made between strict identities that cannot coexist. For Said, there is no place in the city for its past, and he and Safiyya must once more leave behind their home and their son, who must now make a choice and maintain a different identity in order to stay in the city. Understanding the city this way leaves no room for the emergence of possibilities other than those delineated by rival identities, and overlooks the complexities of the production of urban space.

In this regard, what would be more adequate and helpful is a detailed analysis of the ways that the appropriation of deserted Palestinian houses and their re-inhabitation by new immigrants lead to the production of subjectivities and of social collectives that do not easily conform to prescribed exclusive binary national identities and loyalties.[4] One good example is Yfaat Weiss' research (Weiss 2011) on the evolution of the Wadi Salib neighbourhood in Haifa after 1948, and the ways in which it became the scene for one of the first and most significant cases of civil revolt in Israel. It explores the entangled and conflicted modes of the social production of urban space, and may also shed light on contemporary possibilities for political coalitions that could resist current modes of neoliberal urban development. On the other hand, it is also worthwhile (as I have discussed elsewhere: Ben-Arie 2013) to explore the ways in which existing objections to urban development in Haifa often overlook the origins of the destruction of the city's downtown and conform to the neoliberal logic. This was particularly apparent in one of Haifa's most active and dominant civil movements of recent years, which focused on issues of development of the downtown area and was known as the Movement for the Return of the City to Haifa. It disregarded the fact that the city whose return was hoped for is not the city that once actually existed and thrived in Haifa's downtown, that is the Palestinian city which was demolished and deserted, but rather an imagined European city, one which in many ways conforms to the development plans of the municipality.

The urban space and the modes of existence that are part of it and which it enables are transforming all the time, and of course the past cannot be reinstated. As I have shown in this chapter, destruction is a potent power in the production of urban space, not only through its signified forms, in this case economic, political and professional, but also as asignified non-identitarian flows of matter and energy. This machinic destruction interrupts and breaks processes of development and creation of stable identities, undermining possible stabilising closures and making way for unforeseeable turns. Exploring and mapping the modes by which destruction functions in the evolution of the urban space of Haifa does make it clear that it is not possible to fully attend to the current functions of the destruction of space while ignoring its modes of operation in prior formations and the desire invested in them and their ongoing effects. There might still be hope that by acknowledging the different modes of operation and the different ways destruction is appropriated and functions time and again, new and better possibilities might open up and be realised through the reproduction of the urban space.

Notes

1. On this point, Benjamin also cites Le Corbusier's assertion that 'the avenues [Haussmann] cut were entirely arbitrary: they were not based on strict deduction of the science of town planning. The measures he took were of a financial and military character' (Benjamin 1999b: 125).
2. See Deleuze (1995).
3. Urbicide, as Nikolina Bobic asserts, is a 'flexible concept' (Bobic 2014) which can indicate, and has been used for the conceptualisation of, many different cases of destruction of the urban built environment and of social collectivity, at different scales and times. I refer here to its conceptualisation as political violence which is realised through urban destruction and collective national exclusion. For more on the different uses and conceptualisations of urbicide see Graham (2004a, 2004b) and the symposium dedicated to the debate around the concept in *Theory and Event*, 10 (2) (2007). For more on the use of the concept in the context of Palestine, see also Abujidi (2014) and Pappé (2006).
4. For such analysis from a different location, see the work of Yael Navaro-Yashin on Northern Cyprus (Navaro-Yashin 2009).

References

Abujidi, N. (2014) *Urbicide in Palestine: Spaces of Oppression and Resilience*. London: Routledge.

Ben-Arie, R. (2013) 'Neoliberal Resistance and the Repressed Destruction of a City'. Unpublished paper given at the Royal Geographical Society Annual Conference, London.

Benjamin, W. (1999a) 'Paris, the capital of the nineteenth century (exposé of 1935)', in *The Arcades Project*, trans. H. Eiland and K. McLaughlin. Cambridge, MA: Harvard University Press, pp. 3–13.

Benjamin, W. (1999b) *The Arcades Project*, trans. H. Eiland and K. McLaughlin. Cambridge, MA: Harvard University Press.

Benjamin, W. (2003) 'The Paris of the Second Empire in Baudelaire', in *Selected Writings: 1938–1940*, trans. H. Eiland and M. W. Jennings. Cambridge, MA: Harvard University Press, pp. 3–92.

Bobic, N. (2014) 'Operations of Force: NATO, Belgrade and the Inflection of Urbicide'. PhD dissertation, University of Sydney.

Bogard, W. (2009) 'Deleuze and machines: a politics of technology?', in David Savat and Mark Poster (eds), *Deleuze and New Technology*. Edinburgh: Edinburgh University Press, pp. 15–31.

Brenner, N. and Theodore, N. (2005) 'Neoliberalism and the urban condition', *City*, 9 (1): 101–7.

Buck-Morss, S. (1989) *The Dialectics of Seeing: Walter Benjamin and the Arcades Project*. Cambridge, MA: MIT Press.
Colebrook, C. (2002) *Gilles Deleuze*. London: Routledge.
Deleuze, G. (1995) 'Postscript on control societies', in *Negotiations 1972–1990*, trans. M. Joughin. New York: Columbia University Press, pp. 177–82.
Deleuze, G. and Guattari, F. (1977) *Anti-Oedipus*, trans. R. Hurley, M. Seem and H. R. Lane. London: Penguin Books.
Deleuze, G. and Guattari, F. (1987) *A Thousand Plateaus*, trans. B. Massumi. Minneapolis: University of Minnesota Press.
Goodchild, P. (1996) *Deleuze and Guattari: An Introduction to the Politics of Desire*. London: Sage.
Gordillo, G. (2014) *Rubble: The Afterlife of Destruction*. Durham, NC: Duke University Press.
Goren, T. (1994) 'Account of the disappearance of the 'Old City' from the Haifa landscape, 1948–1951', *Horizons in Geography*, 40–1: 57–82 (in Hebrew).
Goren, T. (1999) 'Changes in the design of the urban space of the Arabs of Haifa during the Israeli War of Independence', *Middle Eastern Studies*, 35 (1): 115–33.
Graham, S. (ed.) (2004a) *Cities, War, and Terrorism: Towards an Urban Geopolitics*. Malden, MA: Wiley-Blackwell.
Graham, S. (2004b) 'Postmortem City', *City*, 8 (2): 165–96.
Guattari, F. (1995a) *Chaosmosis*. Bloomington: Indiana University Press.
Guattari, F. (1995b) 'On machines', trans. V. Constantinopoulos, *Journal of Philosophy and the Visual Arts*, 6: 8–12.
Haifa Municipality (2012) 'Downtown Haifa', online at: http://downtown.co.il/en (accessed 1 April 2015).
Harvey, D. (1989a) 'From managerialism to entrepreneurialism: the transformation in urban governance in late capitalism', *Geografiska Annaler, Series B: Human Geography*, 71 (1): 3–17.
Harvey, D. (1989b) *The Condition of Postmodernity: An Enquiry into the Origins of Cultural Change*. Cambridge, MA: Blackwell.
Harvey, D. (2008) 'The right to the city', *New Left Review*, 53: 23–40.
Hassan, M. (2005) 'City ruination and the war against memory: the victorious and the defeated', *Theory and Criticism*, 27: 197–207 (in Hebrew).
Herscher, A. (2007) 'Urbicide, urbanism, and urban destruction in Kosovo', *Theory and Event*, 10 (2); online at: https://muse.jhu.edu/journals/theory_and_event/v010/10.2herscher.html.
Kanafani, G. (2000) 'Returning to Haifa', in *Palestine's Children: Returning to Haifa & Other Stories*, trans. B. Harlow and K. E. Riley. Boulder: Lynne Rienner, pp. 149–96.
Khalidi, W. (2008) 'The fall of Haifa revisited', *Journal of Palestine Studies*, 37 (3): 30–58.
Kolodney, Z. and Kallus, R. (2008) 'From colonial to national landscape: producing Haifa's cityscape', *Planning Perspectives*, 23 (3): 323–48.
Lazzarato, M. (2014) *Signs and Machines: Capitalism and the Production of Subjectivity*, trans. J. D. Jordan. Los Angeles: Semiotext(e).
May, T. (2005) *Gilles Deleuze: An Introduction*. Cambridge: Cambridge University Press.
Morris, B. (2004) *The Birth of the Palestinian Refugee Problem Revisited*. Cambridge: Cambridge University Press.
Navaro-Yashin, Y. (2009) 'Affective spaces, melancholic objects: ruination and the production of anthropological knowledge', *Journal of the Royal Anthropological Institute*, 15 (1): 1–18.
Pappé, I. (2006) *The Ethnic Cleansing of Palestine*. Oxford: Oneworld Publications.

Stoler, A. L. (2008) 'Imperial debris: reflections on ruins and ruination', *Cultural Anthropology*, 23 (2): 191–219.
Weiss, Y. (2011) *A Confiscated Memory: Wadi Salib and Haifa's Lost Heritage.* New York: Columbia University Press.
Yazbak, M. (1987) 'The Arab immigration to Haifa: 1933–1948', *Katedra*, 45: 131–46.

Chapter 13

Imagining Portland's Future Past: Lessons from Indigenous Placemaking in a Colonial City

Janet McGaw

Contemporary cities, such as Portland, Victoria, are complex assemblages, produced through multiple subjectivities and both human and non-human ecologies over different temporal cycles and geographical relations, made manifest through diverse materialities. Although these systems necessarily intersect, this chapter will argue that in colonial centres, where settler histories are short, they have generally evolved in ignorance of one another. Tales have been told and maps have been drawn that Gilles Deleuze and Félix Guattari would describe as 'root-books' and 'tracings'. The root-book begins with the seed of an idea. As it sprouts and develops it equally burrows down, ever deeper through the strata, to stabilise it in the foundations of its subject. The tracing is a 'map' that privileges one type of knowledge over all others. In so doing a tracing 'rejects redundancies and propagates them. What the tracing reproduces of the map . . . are only the impasses . . . or points of structuration' (Deleuze and Guattari 1987: 13).

There are many 'root-books' on Portland, Victoria. Each one is thoroughly grounded, rigorous and scholarly, adhering to the interiorities of the conventions of its discipline. Noel Learmonth's history of the town written for its centenary, for example, is a chronology of English settlement. Susan White's geological study of the underground karst landscape beneath Portland's surface, a system of limestone caves populated with stalactites and stalagmites formed over millennia, is researched and described from a different scholarly tradition. Although roots and branches might spread, they always emanate from the one trunk – the focused lens of their discipline. Other books on Portland, like the revisionist histories of Henry Reynolds, Jan Critchett and Geoffrey Blainey, are secondary grafts – what Deleuze and Guattari call 'radicle-systems' or 'fascular roots' – that take the history of the region in a new direction (Deleuze and Guattari 1987: 5). While they adhere to the conventions of historical scholarship they include the multiple stories of Aboriginal clans in Portland alongside the dominant settler narrative.

The various 'maps' that represent the geography of Portland – physical, cultural and political – are similarly bound by disciplinary conventions. On the whole, they are what Deleuze and Guattari, following Deligny, would call 'tracings' rather than true maps (Deleuze and Guattari 1987: 14). A tracing, like a 'root-book', is an exercise in arborescent thinking, laying down patterns that are familiar, known and coded with an inherent structure. The mid-nineteenth-century squatter's map by Hamm and subsequent selection map by McHutchison privilege the names of early settlers and their property boundaries, while maps such as the geological survey of the Nelson–Portland region are tracings of the geological substrata of Portland. These orthographic representations of Portland follow singular lines of inquiry.

Portland's future is a 'wicked problem' (Rittel 1973: 160), as unpredictable as any city in this age of climate change, environmental degradation and population explosions. Wicked problems, according to Philippe Vandenbroeck, cannot be addressed through linear thinking or structuralist modes of research (Vandenbroeck 2013). Wicked problems require lateral thought and interdisciplinary collaboration. Rather than burrow, therefore, this chapter slips sideways, following the flickers in the periphery, foraging on the surface wherever the flights of thought lead. Vignettes of Portland from different disciplinary perspectives – history, geography, anthropology, archaeology, urban planning, industry and science – and different temporal periods are montaged together. Excavation follows, taking unexpected pathways through fault lines discovered along the way. Through this process a new and unexpected Portland emerges. Although a (haec)ceity, a city that is wholly specific to its time and place, Portland has lessons to offer other small coastal cities in the age of the Anthropocene that will be explored in conclusion.

Becoming Portland: Entangled Tales of Smooth Migrations and Settler Striations 1802–35: Edges, Building and Cultivation

Lieutenant James Grant was the first to sail past Portland in 1800 on behalf of the new colonial government through the 'just discovered' Bass Strait that unexpectedly divided Tasmania from the mainland. He named and surveyed (albeit inaccurately) Portland Bay and the adjacent coast line (McMartin 1966: 468). Two years later Captain Nicolas Baudin surveyed the territory on behalf of Napoleon, renaming the harbour Baie Tourville at the same moment that Matthew Flinders was mapping the edge more precisely on behalf of the British Crown (Learmonth 1934: 7–15). The first colonial 'instruments of capture' – compass, circumferentor, sextant and quadrant – were deployed by early maritime surveyors to plot the coast in relation to the sun, the horizon and the magnetism of the planet.

Most history books declare Edward Henty as Portland's first settler, journeying from Western Australia via Launceston in search of farmland in 1834 (McCrombie 1858: 18; Turner 1904: 78; Kiddle [1962] 1967: 31; Dingle 1984: 21). However, sealer William Pelham Dutton claimed in 1874 to have beaten Henty to it, arriving in 1828. Still others have dated European settlement to 1826 (Learmonth 1934: 33). Dutton claims to have built his house from 1831 to 1832, sustaining himself on potatoes and other vegetables he planted in his garden (Dutton 1874), while Henty is recorded to have built his house in 1835 from stone, for-tified with glass shards on the top of the wall to keep out the 'the natives' (Learmonth 1934: 57). The second 'instruments of capture' were the axe, the handsaw, the hammer and the plough – tools that were used to fell the forests, construct fences and dwellings and replace endemic vegetation with European vegetables.

Henty's glass topped wall was not an isolated practice. Architectural historian Karen Burns has uncovered evidence of other early settler barns and houses in Tasmania and Western Victoria that were selectively sited on naturally fortified tracts of land, with an absence of windows, the inclusion of gun slots and gun loops, and with ventilation shafts lowered to shoulder height to accommodate the shaft of a rifle (Burns 2010: 73). Australia's early settler architecture provides evidence of deliberate spatial and material territorialising practices that anticipated subsequent violent deterritorialisation of pre-existing Indigenous cultures.

Sixteenth Century – 1844: Smooth Explorations and Occupations

It is believed that explorers and traders from China, the Americas, Portugal and Holland, as well as England and France, had been flowing past the Portland region via the smooth space of the sea from the six-teenth century, well before European settlement. By 1791 sealers and whalers were taking up seasonal residence on the coastline (Learmonth 1934: 18). Within a decade, trade was well established; eleven vessels from England, France and the United States were recorded meeting there in 1804.

By 1836, explorer Thomas Mitchell penetrated the interior, making a smooth journey overland from the east, naming the landmarks he saw along the way to honour 'pioneers', colonial authorities and explorers who were anxious to attach themselves to the strange land. According to Indigenous historian and novelist Tony Birch, the name Mt Dispersion records the site at which a group of seven Jardwadjali men were 'dispersed' through gunshot by Mitchell's party, achieving 'permanent deliverance of the party from imminent danger' (Birch 2003). While Mitchell and his men have been honoured with a commemorative track along with fifty cairns to remember their passing, no built form remembers the violent erasure of the Jardwadjali men. By 1837 the inland region of 'Wannon country' was claimed as a permanent settlement, and within the space of three years eighty-five pastoral stations were established (Critchett 1992: 25). In 1842 Governor La Trobe wrote that 'the savage tribes are not only upon our borders, but intermingled with us in every part of this wide district' (Critchett 1992: 23).

William Learmonth claimed the last station available at Darlot Creek in 1844. He writes in his journal:

> runs are now so very scarce to be had near the settled districts. I fortunately heard of one situated at Darlots Creek, only 17 miles from Portland and 35 from Port Fairy. The only reason why this fine run had not been occupied long before was on account of the natives, who are said to be very troublesome there, harbouring in a country close by not penetrable by a horse on account of rock &c. They are in great force, but lately have been quiet. (Learmonth 1844)

Conflict intensified between settlers and the Gunditjmara, continuing across the Portland Bay district for almost two decades. William Learmonth, like the others before him, was quick to entreat Governor La Trobe and Police Magistrate Foster Fyans for support in withstanding Aboriginal reprisals against the theft of their land despite the fact they had no licence to be there from colonial authorities either. Official responses varied. At time they were reproached and entreated to avoid violence; at other times they were offered police support.

1840–2: Grids, Centres and Peripheries

Within a few years hasty efforts were made to striate space with cadastral surveys and legislation to bring 'clarity' to land ownership (Critchett 1992: 87–113). Colonial surveyor Charles James Tyers was engaged in 1840 by Governor Sir George Gipps to 'fix the 141st meridian of longitude, the boundary between New South Wales [the region of Victoria was an extension of New South Wales at this point] and South Australia' and to impose a grid of property boundaries and streets over the 'unauthorised settlement' in Portland, by then an already established township. Tyers describes his survey as 'an account of the part of the country between Melbourne and the Glenelg . . . [using] triangulation, and chronometer and lunar observations undertaken' (Tyers 1839). He followed the same general principles deployed in other colonial cities in Australia, marking the site with a rectangular grid positioned adjacent to a fresh waterway, leaving space within the township for future private land and civic buildings and 'other Public Works of utility and general convenience' (Lewis 1995: 26) and demarcating what could be called gaps in a colonial Cartesian grid.

Tyers' survey was for the township and state boundaries alone, leaving the pastoral lands surrounding – Mitchell's 'Wannon Country' – free from the segmentarity of the State until 1862, when a survey was prepared for the first Land Bill. This and the subsequent Land Selection Acts that followed further divided Portland's peripheries into (mostly) orthogonal allotments for farming. This worked well where the country was flat or slightly hilly, but failed in the more mountainous regions to Portland's east, according to Barbara Minchinton. As Thomas Baker (cited by Minchinton) wrote in 1895, 'Whenever [I s]ee a straight road on a plan in such country I [take] it as a certainty that it crosses impassable places' (Minchinton 2011).

Deleuze and Guattari write 'the smooth always possesses a greater power of deterritorialisation than the striated' (Deleuze and Guattari 1987: 480) and the primary action 'of the State is to striate the space over which it reigns . . . to vanquish nomadism . . . and . . . establish a zone of rights over an entire "exterior"' (Deleuze and Guattari 1987: 385). In the case of Portland we see the reverse is equally true. The nomadic flow of global migration was the tactic of the State. The striations of grids and urban centres which the State later imposed may have territorialised colonial space but it equally deterritorialised Aboriginal space. At times we see smooth forces in the ascendancy with squatters claiming land in advance of approval by the colonial government through a range of tactics: violence, erasure, friendship, conjugal relations and disease. But equally, illegitimate squatters called on the State for support when it suited them. Grids remain 'holey' (Deleuze and Guattari 1987: 500) to this day, incomplete and unsettled by topography and ecologies.

What shapes and practices constitute these 'holes'? Interstices in settler occupation took various forms – some linear, some pocket sized, others vast areas of land – but they are similarly constituted with pre-colonial ecologies that have been undisturbed by agriculture or urbanisation: the linear reserves for future rail lines and roads, easements along waterways, cemeteries and some state and national forests remain outside both striated and smooth practices of land acquisition. Fenced off early in European settlement and never subject to fertilisers or cultivation, they support the few remaining examples of remnant biodiversity in Victoria (*Catalyst* 2011). According to Denis Byrne, many of these interstitial spaces also supported Aboriginal occupation and journeying long after the cadastral system of property ownership was introduced into Australia (Byrne 2010).

What matter(s) in the Port's Land: Indigenous and Settler Material Resources

4,700 BCM: Stone and Fire

While histories – both 'root' and 'radicle' – reveal a complex web of territorialisations and deterritorialisations through the colonial era, other disciplines cast their net over different temporal periods. Anthropology draws on oral histories from living Aboriginal people that can date back ten thousand years (Benterrak et al. 1996: 33–4). Archaeology uses scientific methods of radiocarbon dating and other types of geological analysis to uncover the same histories through a different epistemology.

Coutts et al.'s seminal archaeological study of the Western Districts of Victoria in 1977/78 provided the first scientific evidence of an extensive Aboriginal stone settlement, challenging the claim that Aboriginal people were 'nomadic' (Coutts et al. 1977/78: 17–58). Subsequent work by archaeologist Heather Builth in 2002 showed that this village was built around eel farming covering an area of 75 square kilometres in the 'stony rises' of the Tyrendarra lava flow around Mt Eccles (*Budj Bim*) north-east of Portland. It has been dated at 6,700 years old and is believed to be one of the five oldest sedentary settlements in the world (Builth 2002). The aquaculture system connected Darlot Creek – where William Learmonth later settled in 1844 – to Lake Condah and surrounding wetlands with stone channels and weirs and woven nets for trapping eels, used continuously up until European settlement. Rock shelters at Cape Bridgewater were occupied 12,000 years ago and there is evidence of shell middens indicating continuous occupation of the coastline for at least 8,000 years (Musuem Victoria). Indigenous Australians were part of the first diaspora of Homo sapiens from Africa between 62,000 and

75,000 years ago, at least 24,000 years before the diaspora that gave rise to contemporary Europeans and Asians (Rasmussen et al. 2011: 94–8). Australian Aboriginal people have the longest continuing culture on the planet. Of the 250 Aboriginal tribal groups across Australia, 38 occupied the region we now call the state of Victoria. The Portland region is home to the Gunditjmara.

Eugene von Guérard's 1858 painting of the hill surrounding the Mt Eccles crater, rendered within two decades of colonisation of the Portland district, records evidence that the Gunditjmara deliberately organised the landscape also. Historian Bill Gammage compared the painting, which shows a landscape patterned with belts of trees and broad strips of cleared grasslands, with his own photograph of the same landscape from 2011, which shows a forested wilderness (Gammage 2011). Pre-colonial Indigenous people across Australia had an understanding of fire, humidity, wind and plants as interdependent ecologies. Fire, when deployed as a land management tool during specific atmospheric conditions – certain humidities, particular wind speed and direction and optimal temperature – both clears the land of excess leaf and bark litter and activates fire-dependent seeds. The practice of periodic erasure has material effects: it improves supplies of native fruits and tubers, and produces grasslands that support large marsupials. Retaining belts and clumps of trees between grasslands, in turn, provides habitat for smaller marsupials, shelter for campsites and cover for hunting. Perfectly timed fire regimes created possibilities for abundant ecosystems, the by-products of which could be used for making shelters, garments, ritual objects and tools. In contrast to settler building materials, which were chosen because they were inert, resistant to the weather, pre-colonial Indigenous building materials were understood to be part of a living ecological and meteorological cycle.

Dreamtime: sacred and living ecologies

Anthropologist Aldo Massola recounts the Mara *Dreaming* story, an oral creation story of how *Mondilibi* (Flat Top Hill, another volcanic outcrop) came into being (Massola 1968: 29–31). The story tells of the journey of an ancestral being along the Hopkins River creating the landforms as he goes.[1] In part of the story, the smoke of a fire is seen coming from the mountain top. It is a story of ethics, of how one is to treat one's mother-in-law and animal totems. But it also makes 'sense' of the volcanic landscape, demanding that it be treated as a sacred site. *Dreaming* stories such as these establish reciprocal rights and responsibilities to the landscapes they record. Often described as *songlines*, vectors with intrinsic energy, directionality and pace that navigate specific paths through the land connecting points where apical ancestors are emplaced, these *Dreaming* stories are different from settler striations yet they are equally organising, repeated 'on country' in the same way across countless generations. Unlike western knowledge, which has been freely transmitted through text since the invention of the printing press, Aboriginal knowledge is carried by tribe, clan and individuals. 'Public' songs would be known by whole tribes, but others were 'owned' and handed on only to select individuals at initiation. Although not hierarchically organised, power – *pouvoir* (Massumi 1987: xvii) – was explicitly exercised through story ownership.

Gammage argues that 'the *Dreaming* is saturated with environmental consciousness. Theology and ecology are fused ... Ecology explains what happens, the *Dreaming* explains why it happens' (Gammage 2011: 133). The ecological template of clearings, edges, belts and clumps, produced through Indigenous fire regimes that Gammage describes, were configured around *songlines*. Both fire regimes and *songlines* were dynamic, created through the cyclic performance of events. But equally they were structured: not with geometry but around complex living and sacred relational ecologies.

800,000 BCE–18,000 BCE: Volcanoes and Karsts

Volcanic activity in the Portland region, such as the one described in the story of *Mondilibi*, dates from around 27,000–18,000 BCE according to geologists who have uncovered thermoluminescence dates on the scoria, used radiocarbon dating for materials buried by the ash, and analysed pollen and sedimentary organic material from the floor of craters (Sherwood et al. 2004: 69–76). Volcanoes provide a ready supply of easily collected stone and produce rich nutritious soils for plants to thrive. These have been important provisions for both Indigenous people and settlers alike.

But beneath Portland is a topography produced not by fire, but by water over the past 800,000 years. Susan White uncovered a hidden karst landscape under the town of Portland in 1984 (White 1984). It is the largest karst formation in the state. The particular layering of soft water-soluble limestone beneath a volcanic basalt surface has enabled the tidal waters from the Glenelg River to carve deep subterranean caves and the trickling surface water to form stalactites and stalagmites. The 'intervening tract of poor country' that Governor Gipps described in

1840 was probably produced by these chasms. Soil moisture drains into the space below, leaving the surfaces dry.

This same soft substrate produces a fragile coastline. A coastal engineering study done by consultant AECOM has identified areas of the Portland coastline as subject to 'high coastal hazard risk' (AECOM 2010). Coastal scientist Andrew Short argues that erosion began when a breakwater was completed in 1960 to expand the port of Portland, interrupting the easterly flow of sand to the Dutton Way beach (Short 2008). The beach retreated, threatening the properties and road, so a bluestone seawall was constructed in 1970. This wall has been gradually extended for 4.5 km as erosion has continued. Glenelg Shire's Strategic Future Plan from 2009 identifies the fragile coastline as well as numerous sinkholes and basins and the extent of land subjection to inundation and potential flooding as contemporary threats to building development. The port's land, formed over millennia from rising seas and volcanic eruptions from folds of limestone and granite and riddled with fault lines, subterranean karsts and water holes, is now a fragile, unstable terrain on which to build.

1944–2014: Economics and Industry

In the postwar period the Victorian State government made a decision to invest in developing global trade, and Portland was identified for a deep-water port because of its strategic location halfway between Adelaide and Melbourne, its natural harbour and surrounding wool, timber and fishing industries (Learmonth 1960). Works were completed in 1960 and industry followed. In 1979 Alcoa announced it would build the state's second aluminium smelter in Portland, opening in 1986. It is now Australia's third largest smelter with the majority of its product destined for export. It is the largest user of energy in the state, of which 85 per cent is produced by burning brown coal. This industry makes a significant ongoing contribution to Australia's greenhouse gas production. Although Portland's international shipping harbour currently handles six million tonnes of bulk commodities in annual throughput it remains a small city by any standard, with a relatively static population of 10,000.

With the recent signing of the free trade agreements with China, Korea and Japan, however, significant implications are forecast for industry, agribusiness and population in Portland and its surrounds as trade through the port increases rapidly (Prime Minister of Australia Media Office 2014). Over the past decade food and agricultural prices have soared in China, the largest nation on the planet (International Food Policy Research Institute 2012). Agricultural trade with Australia is key to China's strategy to maintain food security for its people. The farmlands of the Portland region specialise in wool production, dairy and beef, and live animal exports are expected to rise. A sale of 4,000 sheep destined for 'breeding improvement farms' near a northern Chinese province in Mongolia was recently brokered by national rural services provider Elders. Sheep were acquired from 70 farms around Australia and held in quarantine for a month in Condah in preparation for export (Marshall 2014). The new interest in dairy products in China is similarly anticipated to substantially increase export production in the region served by Portland's port.

Transformations of the landscape are now produced by substantially larger tools than those used by early settlers. As ecologist Eugene F. Stoermer and atmospheric chemist Paul Crutzen have argued, human intervention in the landscape has produced more substantial geological transformations than those caused through natural processes since the Industrial Revolution (Subcommission on Quaternary Stratigraphy 2013). The Holocene has been superseded by the Anthropocene. Cranes, dredging equipment, excavators, trenchers and geological drills are the contemporary instruments that continue to transform the waterways, coastline and landscape of the Portland region for agriculture and industry. In Australia biodiversity is locally threatened through the land clearing and mono-cropping that is necessary to support agriculture supplying ballooning populations in a global market. These are transformations to the periphery upon which a city's viability is contingent. We are coming to understand that human interventions since the Industrial Revolution are increasingly rendering the planet uninhabitable. Scientists are predicting a sixth mass extinction event within the next 300 years unless there is radical change to the way humans inhabit the earth (Dirzo et al. 2014).

Imagining Portland's Future Past:
Old Knowledge, New Futures

What are Portland's future prospects in the face of such loss of biodiversity, pollution and environmental degradation? Its uncertainty is shared by many small coastal cities facing the threat of rising sea levels, expanding global trade and exponentially growing populations. Chris Ryan, director of the Victorian Eco-innovation Laboratory (VEiL) argues that catastrophe stories by the climate science community have done little to change global energy consumption and greenhouse gas emissions. Rather, the stories have led to psychological disempowerment and inertia among ordinary citizens. Overcoming these feelings of hopelessness is now as much a challenge as technological change (Ryan 2013).

The 'roots' and 'tracings' this chapter has followed so far can tell us only so much about Portland. Historians, anthropologists and scientists are shaped by the epistemological limits of their own discourses. Politicians, industrialists and global traders are equally blinkered by the remits of their professions and economic agendas. On their own they lead to only partial understandings of Portland as a milieu. So how do we stitch the 'plateaus' together? Peg Rawes has challenged those who design, build, live in and write about built environments to consider them instead as 'relational architectural ecologies' (Rawes 2013a: 1–18), that is places that are at once social, political, economic and environmental. Philosopher Rosi Braidotti has argued, following Deleuze, Guattari, Haraway and others, for 'nomad' thinking to construct a fluid, 'geo-politics or an eco-philosophy' that considers positive points of interrelationship between humans, ecologies and technologies (Braidotti 2013: 21–39). Drawing on feminist discourse, she suggests that a focus on connectedness rather than catastrophe is affirmative, creative and enabling.

VEiL has developed a model of cross-disciplinary urban design praxis grounded within communities that focuses what is *'permissible, desirable and possible'*. They call it 'eco-acupuncture' (Ryan 2013: 189–200). The Laboratory works first on changing community perceptions and then, through multiple small-scale design interventions, on *building urban resilience*. Locating abandoned, undesirable or leftover spaces within a city as sites for intervention is an important starting point. As we have seen, the spatial practices deployed in Portland's colonial settlement unfurled across the surface of the landscape leaving many gaps. I would like to suggest that the 'holes' between settler striations offer a spatial prospect for Portland's future. Similarly, the surface which appears now to be collapsing conceals material possibilities for redemption.

In a corner of Portland's Henty Park behind a cyclone wire fence sits one such interstitial space, an abandoned geothermal bore and pump that once delivered space and water heating to Portland's police station, hospital, library, arts centre, municipal offices, civic hall and public swimming pool. The geological instability that produced the volcanic landforms visible on the surface is an endless source of geothermal energy deep in the ground below. The geothermal bore was dug in 1983, 1,400 metres deep into the Dilwyn aquifer, drawing 60°C water in a loop past civic buildings. But it was decommissioned in 2006 when the local council and water authority was separated into two jurisdictions. Wannon Water argued at the time that the decision to close it would deliver major long-term environmental and social benefits by ensuring water security for the region, but others have questioned the wisdom of this decision made in isolation from other systems. Now fossil fuels are used to heat these facilities at a cost of 300,000 AUD per year (Weaver 2011). Turning on geothermal power in Portland again is both permissible and possible.

Portland is home to another renewable energy venture. With a coastline exposed to the southern ocean, Portland receives strong and consistent southwesterly winds. Built over four sites, Pacific Hydro is one of the largest wind farms in Australia. Extending and capitalising on the renewable energy resources hidden under the surface and in the skies would go some way to addressing the carbon footprint of Portland's aluminium smelter.

Meanwhile, the Glenelg Shire launched a new planning scheme in 2013 that demands nomad thinking of a different kind. In recognition of the fragility of Portland's coastline, new dwellings on private land along Dutton Way are required to be 'relocatable' (Dowling 2014). This is a nation first. While Portland was shaped equally, as we have seen, by smooth migrations and colonial striations, the cadastral system of property presumes sedentism rather than nomadism. Perhaps this foreshadows a 'future past' that echoes Indigenous practices, a model of building that enables cycles of seasonal journeying rather than the fixity of permanent occupation.

Rawes and Braidotti have argued that feminism has been an enabler of relational ecological thinking (Rawes 2013a: 17; Braidotti 2013: 30–1). And yet feminist discourse continues to be largely framed within a western 'world view'. In coloniser settler nations Indigenous ways of knowing and doing are a pre-existing eco-sophy. Aboriginal knowledge systems are place-based, local and holistic. *Dreaming* stories (lore which carried law) simultaneously remembered processes of formation of the land, its ecological complexity, social relations and the best processes for managing the health of the land. As Gammage writes:

> The *Dreaming* is comprehensive . . . It gives and explains a role to every part of creation, and decrees how each must act. This does not stifle human curiosity, but innovation and creativity become means not ends, eddies not the pool, and do not disturb a sense that the fundamentals of existence are beyond challenge or improvement. (Gammage 2011: 124)

The *Dreaming* challenges designers and planners of cities to understand the 'pool' first before initiating change. This is not to advocate returning to some pre-colonial moment; rather, it echoes Braidotti's notion that 'futurity is non-linear' (Braidotti 2013: 37). One of Portland's specificities is a depth of Indigenous knowledge that immediately enables its future to be developed around complex understandings that have been developed over deep time.

Gunditjmara people continue to live in Portland and the surrounding Glenelg region. An Aboriginal mission was established at Lake Condah in 1867, only thirty years after settlement of the region. It remains another 'hole' in the settler fabric. The Winda-Mara Aboriginal Corporation in conjunction with Gunditj Mirring on behalf of the Gunditjmara people oversees the Tyrendarra Indigenous Protected Area (which forms part of the *Budj Bim* National Heritage Landscape) (Department of Environment and Water Resources), located on Darlot Creek, a tributary of Lake Condah, upstream from the land William Learmonth 'selected' in 1844. The land is part of major *Dreaming* trails and remains an important ceremonial site. It was one of the first sites to be included in the National Heritage Register in 2004. A cultural rehabilitation plan has been developed that includes restoring the woodlands and wetlands ecosystems that were destroyed by settler land clearing practices. Restoring biodiversity in a region that is increasingly challenged by agricultural practices of mono-cropping genetically modified products is an essential step in Portland's environmental futures.

Verena Andermatt Conley writes that Guattari's manifesto *Les Trois Ecologies* written twenty-five years ago foreshadowed the challenges of the ecological movement (Andermatt Conley 2013: 275–87). Indeed, his argument that improving natural ecologies would be predicated on first reconstructing the subject and social relations was seminal. In colonised nations where settler histories are short and Indigenous histories are ancient, reconstructing social relations between Indigenous people and settler Australian citizens might well be the best path for forging an eco-sophical approach as we reshape our cities for the future.

Note

1. On the advice of Rueben Berg, Director of Indigenous Architecture and Design Victoria (a Gunditjmara man), I have erred on the side of caution and refrained from including the details as it is unclear whether this is a private or public *story*.

References

AECOM Australia, Pty Ltd (2010) *Coastal Spaces – Inundation and Erosion – Coastal Engineering Study*, 7 July; online at: http://www.glenelg.vic.gov.au/Files/Portland_Engineering_Study_Final_Report.pdf (accessed 16 September 2014).

Andermatt Conley, V. (2013) 'The ecological relation', in P. Rawes (ed.), *Relational Architectural Ecologies*. London: Routledge, pp. 275–87.

Benterrak, K., Muecke, S. and Roe, P. (1996) *Reading the Country: Introduction to Nomadology*, rev. edn. Fremantle: Fremantle Arts Centre Press, pp. 33–4.

Birch, T. (2003) '"Nothing has changed": the making and unmaking of Koori culture', in M. Grossman (ed.), *Blacklines: Contemporary Critical Writing by Indigenous Australians*. Parkville: Melbourne University.

Blainey, G. (2013) *A History of Victoria*, 2nd edn. Cambridge: Cambridge University Press.

Braidotti, R. (2013) 'Posthuman relational subjectivity', in P. Rawes (ed.), *Relational Architectural Ecologies*. London: Routledge, pp. 21–39.

Builth, H. (2002) 'The Archaeology and Socioeconomy of the Gunditjmara: A Landscape Analysis from Southwest Victoria, Australia'. PhD thesis, April.

Burns, K. (2010) 'Frontier conflict, contact, exchange: re-imagining colonial architecture', in M. Chapman and M. Ostwald (eds), *Imagining: Proceedings of the 27th International Conference of the Society of Architectural Historians, Australia and New Zealand (SAHANZ)*. Newcastle, NSW, Australia, 30 June – 2 July, p. 73.

Byrne, D. (2010) 'Nervous landscape: race and space in Australia', in T. Banvanua Mar and P. Edmonds (eds), *Making Settler Colonial Space: Perspectives on Race, Place and Identity*. London: Palgrave Macmillan.

Catalyst: Sweet Solution for Woodlands (2011) Television broadcast, Australian Broadcasting Corporation, Sydney, 7 July; online at: http://www.abc.net.au/cata lyst/stories/3263957.htm (transcript accessed 4 April 2014).

Coutts, P. J. F., Witter, D. C. and Parsons, D. M. (1977/78) 'Impact of European settlement on Aboriginal society in Western Victoria', *Records of the Victorian Archaeological Survey*, 4: 17–58.

Critchett, J. (1992) *A 'distant field of murder': Western District Frontiers 1834–1848*. Melbourne: Melbourne University Press.

Deleuze, G. and Guattari, F. (1987) *A Thousand Plateaus: Capitalism and Schizophrenia*, trans. B. Massumi. Minneapolis: University of Minnesota Press, p. 13.

Department of Environment and Water Resources, Australian Government (2007) 'Tyrendarra: Volcanic Plains, Victoria', *Indigenous Protected Areas*, 7 February; online at: http://www.environment.gov.au/indigenous/ipa/declared/tyrendarra. html.

Department of Primary Industries (1994) 'Map 48, Warrnambool-Mortlake, MGA Zone 54', *Geodetic Datum of Australia*. Melbourne: Victoria State Government.

Dingle, T. (1984) *The Victorians Settling*. McMahons Point, NSW: Fairfax, Syme & Weldon Associates, p. 21.

Dirzo, R., Young, H. S., Galetti, M., Cebellos, G., Isacc, N. J. B. and Collen, B. (2014) 'Defaunation in the Anthropocene', *Science*, 345: 401–6.

Dowling, J. (2011) 'Is this the solution to the impact of climate change?', *The Age*, 30 July; online at: http://www.theage.com.au/victoria/is-this-the-solution-to-the-impact-of-climate-change-20110729-1i4cj.html (accessed 16 September 2014).

Dutton, W. (1874) 'Who is the oldest colonist?', *Portland Guardian and Normanby*

General Advertiser, 2 October; online at: http://trove.nla.gov.au/newspaper/ (accessed 16 September 2014).

Gammage, B. (2011) *The Biggest Estate on Earth: How Aborigines Made Australia*. Crows Nest, NSW: Allen & Unwin.

Hamm, T. (1851) *Ham's squatting map of Victoria (Port Phillip District, New South Wales) [cartographic material]: carefully corrected to this date from the Colonial government surveys*. Crown Lands Commissioners & explorers maps, private surveys, &c.; online at: http://nla.gov.au/nla.map-f895 (accessed 2 June 2014).

International Food Policy Research Institute (2012) *Food Security Portal: China: Country Resources*; online at: http://www.foodsecurityportal.org/china/resources (accessed 3 January 2015).

Kiddle, M. ([1962] 1967) *Men of Yesterday: A Social History of the Western District of Victoria 1834–1890*. Melbourne: Melbourne University Press.

Learmonth, N. F. (1934) *The Portland Bay Settlement: Being the History of Portland, Victoria from 1800–1851*. Portland: Historical Committee of Portland.

Learmonth, N. (1960) *The Story of a Port: Portland, Victoria*. Portland: Portland Harbour Trust.

Learmonth, W. *Journal of 1844*, quoted in N. F. Learmonth (1934) *The Portland Bay Settlement*. Portland: Historical Committee of Portland, p. 233.

Lewis, M. (1995) *Melbourne: The City's History and Development*, 2nd edn. Melbourne, Vic.: City of Melbourne.

McCrombie, T. (1858) *The History of the Colony of Victoria: From Its Settlement to the Death of Sir Charles Hotham*. Melbourne and Sydney: Sands & Kenny.

McHutchison, D. (1862) *Victoria shewing the approximate position of the ten millions of acres proposed to be open for selection under clause 10 of new land bill*. Melbourne: Victoria Department of Crown Lands and Survey.

McMartin, A. (1966) 'Grant, James (1772–1833)', *Australian Dictionary of Biography*, Vol. 1. Melbourne: Melbourne University Press, pp. 468–9.

Marshall, A. (2014) 'Sheep exports take next Steppe', *Farm Weekly*, 4 September; online at: http://www.farmweekly.com.au/news/agriculture/sheep/general-news/sheep-exports-take-next-steppe/2710738.aspx.

Massola, A. (1968) *Bunjil's Cave: Myths, Legends and Superstitions of the Aborigines of South-East Australia*. Sydney: Lansdowne Press.

Massumi, B. (1987) 'Notes on the translation and acknowledgements', in G. Deleuze and F. Guattari, *A Thousand Plateaus: Capitalism and Schizophrenia*, trans. B. Massumi. Minneapolis: University of Minnesota Press, pp. xvi–xix.

Minchinton, B. (2011) 'The trouble with Otway maps: taking up a selection under *Land Act 1884*', *Provenance: The Journal of Public Record Office Victoria*, no. 10; online at: http://prov.vic.gov.au/publications/provenance/provenance2011/trouble-with-otway-maps (accessed 25 March 2014).

Museum Victoria (n.d.) 'A Victorian Timeline', *Bunjilaka*; online at: http://museum victoria.com.au/pages/2326/bunjilaka-glossary-timeline.pdf (accessed 3 January 2015).

Prime Minister of Australia Media Office (2014) 'Landmark China-Australia Free Trade Agreement', 17 November; online at: https://www.pm.gov.au/media/2014-11-17/landmark-china-australia-free-trade-agreement/ (accessed 3 January 2015).

Rasmussen, M. et al. (2011) 'An Aboriginal Australian genome reveals separate human dispersals into Asia', *Science*, 6052: 94–8.

Rawes, P. (2013a), 'Introduction', in P. Rawes (ed.), *Relational Architectural Ecologies*. London: Routledge, pp. 1–18.

Rawes, P. (2013b) 'Architectural ecologies of care', in P. Rawes (ed.), *Relational Architectural Ecologies*. London: Routledge, pp. 40–55.

Reynolds, H. ([1981] 2006) *The Other Side of the Frontier: Aboriginal Resistance to the European Invasion of Australia*. Sydney: UNSW Press.

Rittel, H. (1973) 'Dilemmas in a general theory of planning', *Policy Sciences*, 4: 155–69.

Ryan, C. (2013) 'Eco-Acupuncture: designing and facilitating pathways for urban transformation, for a resilient low-carbon future', *Journal of Cleaner Production*, 50: 189–200.

Sherwood, J., Oyston, B. and Kershaw, A. (2004) 'The age and contemporary environments of Tower Volcano, Southwest Victoria, Australia', *Proceedings of the Royal Society of Victoria*, 116 (1): 69–76.

Short, A. (2008) 'Impact of Coastal Erosion in Australia', 3 November; online at: http://www.coastalwatch.com/environment/4524/impact-of-coastal-erosion-in-australia (accessed 16 September 2014).

Subcommission on Quaternary Stratigraphy (2013) 'Working Group on the Anthropocene: What Is the Anthropocene?', last updated 1 August 2014; online at: http://quaternary.stratigraphy.org/workinggroups/anthropocene/ (accessed 31 March 2014).

Turner, H. G. (1904) *A History of the Colony of Victoria: From its discovery to its absorption into the Commonwealth of Australia in two volumes*, Vol. 1. London: Longmans, Green & Co., p. 78.

Tyers, C. J., Letter to Gipps and Preface to Journal of Expedition to Portland Bay, 10 October 1839 to 5 March 1840; quoted in N. F. Learmonth (1934) *The Portland Bay Settlement: Being the History of Portland, Victoria from 1800–1851*. Portland: Historical Committee of Portland, p. 111.

Vandenbroeck, P. (2013) 'Working with wicked problems: Philippe Vandenbroeck at TEDxUHowest', 19 June; online at: https://wwww.youtube.com/watch?v=A5P5kDxY3zU (accessed 16 September 2014).

Weaver, A. (2011) 'Portland's untapped energy awaits rediscovery', *The Standard*, 24 May; online at: http://www.standard.net.au/story/792189/portlands-untapped-energy-awaits-rediscovery/ (accessed 16 September 2014).

White, S. (1984) 'Karst Landforms and Their Relationship to Pleistocene Dune Ridges, Bats Ridge, Portland, Victoria'. MSc thesis, University of Melbourne.

Chapter 14

Folded Ground: Escape from Cape Town

Catharina Gabrielsson

> This is how it should be done: lodge yourself on a stratum, experiment with the opportunities it offers, find an advantageous place on it, find potential movements of deterritorialization, possible lines of flight, experience them, produce flows of conjunctions here and there, try out continuums of intensities segment by segment, have a small plot of new land at all times.
>
> Deleuze and Guattari, *A Thousand Plateaus* (2004: 178)

1.

The veld seems flat in this part of the Cape, marked by red soil, naked rock and low sparsely growing vegetation. The landscape undulates softly towards the mountains that rise abruptly, their rugged surfaces laid bare as if jerking themselves out of the grip of the Earth. But the flatness is deceptive. Here and there are ridges and cracks where the shrubbery thickens, marking the proximity of water that over millennia has carved out hollows in the terrain. It is a landscape to hide in, a landscape to master or to die in. Already in October at the advent of spring, the morning sun is strong enough to make you abandon your plans and turn back. This was once the foraging landscape of the Cape San, indigenous hunter-gatherers who were gradually pushed back by pastoralist tribes before being brought to extinction by white settlers in the early twentieth century.[1] The folded ground belonged to the First People, to those who stayed behind, when everyone else drifted northwards in what by all accounts must be regarded as the first wave of colonisation inflicted upon the world. It is a prime example of nomadic space, the basis for a subsistence economy and a way of life stemming from the dawn of human existence.

The trajectories that led me to these grounds – to what appears like a crystalline return to origins – are a meshwork of incidents, interests and work-related striations. Following the advice of Deleuze and Guattari, I'm here to maintain my 'small plot of new land' in the reckless pursuit of an ongoing project whose aims and outcomes are uncertain. This divergence from my formal profile (elaborated on in countless funding applications) did not come gently, however. If escape is a process of simultaneously losing oneself and forming oneself differently, it necessitates a rupture, the violence of a gap (Malabou 2008: 73). Lines of flight are infinitely more painful than the soft slippages implied: I'm here to escape from Cape Town following an accident that in an instant shattered my capacities for researching the city.

Far too little has been written on how crime and violence influence the conditions for producing knowledge about the city. Surely there's a history remaining to be written on how the affect of danger – whether anticipated, projected or real – has shaped conceptions about cities and modern planning, ranging from the prohibition of public gatherings and condemnation of the urban poor to 'defence by design'. Hence trauma is normally projected onto the other – the victims of abuse, war or terrorist attacks – rather than approached as *integral* to science: the element of coldness, indifference and distance to the world that characterises not only trauma patients (Malabou 2012: 24) but also objective knowledge. Does western science emerge from trauma – embedded in that painful process of distancing mind from body, culture from nature, human from animal? It decisively has a hold on a molecular level, pertaining to researching bodies. For trauma enters discreetly into research, whether as the precautionary 'where, how and when' that influence findings and frame the conditions for fieldwork, or as an accomplished fact – as part of the researcher's mental fabric.

In her work on the brain, Catherine Malabou analyses how trauma – identified as the core of psychic suffering, whether caused by sociopolitical events, cerebral injuries or pathologies – has the effect of dissolving the unity of self, turning you into *someone else*. This formative capacity of the wounded brain – Malabou's 'destructive plasticity' – is token for a continuous adaptation and development that circumscribes the brain as work in a double sense: *our* work, as formed by impressions and experiences, and its cerebral manner of working, of *doing* (Malabou 2008: 4). Posing this 'work' as the basis for self at once undermines and calls into question any distinction between society and biology as makers of human consciousness. In its most extreme, trauma is a transversal experience par excellence, the inverse of Félix Guattari's example of a person transformed by learning to drive a car (Guattari 1995: 17–18). The rush of energy and sudden empowerment to move freely

– hence to leave, abandon, arrive and attain – has its counter-form in the incapacitation of the traumatised body. Struck by accident, a victim of crime, your capacity for thinking, sensing and moving in the city is completely transformed. Your senses of spatial orientation and temporal recollection are drastically impaired, altering your sense of self in ways that unsettle your perception of others who may, or may not, constitute a repeated threat. Having learnt from experience that walking alone in the allegedly post-apartheid city is tantamount to becoming-animal, in the most literal way possible, becoming-prey – as one removed from the flock, the easy capture of one too old, too young, too weak or sick – I made my escape into the desert.

What does it mean to escape the city into the desert? How can the relationship between them be described? If the city is defined by striation, as Deleuze and Guattari repeatedly assert – a sedentary space 'striated by walls, enclosures, and roads between enclosures', a metric space 'counted in order to be occupied' (Deleuze and Guattari 2004: 420, 399) – the desert, like the sea, is a smooth space: 'an intensive rather than extensive space, one of distances, not measures and properties' (Deleuze and Guattari 2004: 528). In constituting a refuge, an abstract void, the vast expanse of the desert seems hitched into a negative clause with civilisation, a transcendental image of sacrifice, redemption, asceticism and purity that resounds through Judeo-Christian culture. The Byzantine anchorites, for instance, could withdraw into a mountain cave and sustain life there for years. Withdrawal served the obvious purpose of isolation from social life, but the extreme ascetic practices (prolonged fasting, exposure to heat and cold, loading the body with iron weights, etc.) were also producing isolation in another sense: isolating the spirit from the body by 'denouncing the flesh'. Thus forging a subjectivity distanced from all things human, attaining a position outside or above society, the anchorites could return to the city as important public figures, conducting themselves with 'the objective authority of a councillor devoid of earthly interests, a mediator without human loyalties' (Rosenqvist 1981: 12, my translation). The movement between the desert and the city, in this case, is thus also a career move, involving power and influence. Recognising the thickness of the desert 'void' immediately complicates the relationship of simple opposition between smooth and striated space.

But the relationship between the city and the desert is also replete with revolutionary implications. Surrounding the events of May 1968 was the circulation of the slogan 'Sous les pavés, la plage!' Connecting the beach beneath the pavement to the freedom of a natural state –

whether beyond, prior to or underneath the oppression of society – evokes the revolutionary romanticism of Rousseau. The theme reappears in SUPERSTUDIO's 'moderate utopias' from around the same time, including the famous collage of a technological grid superimposed on an endless desert. The critical irony of these images, reflecting a profound disillusion with modernist architecture and planning, was paired with visionary scenarios of a new anti-design culture in which everyone was given a sparse but functional allocation of space, free of superfluous objects (Lang and Menking 2003). These allusions to a happier 'natural state' – in confrontation with late-modern capitalism and the technocratic bureaucratic state – were paralleled by Marshall Sahlin's theories on 'the original affluent society', first presented at a symposium in 1966 and later published as *Stone Age Economics* in 1974. Drawing on the work of Richard B. Lee, itself based on prolonged co-habitation with one of the few remaining hunter-gatherer tribes in the Kalahari, Marshall claimed that, far from suffering a state of near-starvation in constant struggle against nature, our primeval ancestors were able to enjoy a lifestyle of leisure and affluence with minimised effort.

Escaping the city into the desert is therefore a familiar theme, a trope in urban narratives. Evidently those imaginaries of the late 1960s and 1970s exerted influence on Deleuze and Guattari in how they envisaged the desert and the figure of the nomad in *Mille Plateaux*. In an article published in 1962, Deleuze had problematised Rousseau's conception of the natural state as ultimately good for humanity. Presumably without the violence presupposed by social and economic structures, the natural state entails not only independence and self-sufficiency, Deleuze notes, but also isolation: 'need [for Rousseau] is not a factor which brings people together: it does not unite, it isolates each of us' (Deleuze 2004: 52). In reconceptualising production as desire rather than being based on need, and in reconfiguring the relationship between nature and the state, Deleuze and Guattari depart from the individualism inherited from Rousseau *and* from the impasse of orthodox Marxism that erupted in the 1970s. Emphasising the co-constitutive and relative function of their binary concepts – 'they function as a pair, in alternation' – Deleuze and Guattari advanced a non-dialectic way of thinking by which the simple opposition between the smooth and the striated gives rise to 'far more difficult complications, alternations, and superpositions' (Deleuze and Guattari 2004: 388, 531). Not everyone followed them, however. Perhaps the most significant outcome of May '68 lay latent in the beach beneath the pavement; this particular configuration of freedom carried the seed for the intensification of individualism that the following decades would bring.

My escape into the desert is therefore an attempt to escape from myself, from the subjectivity of the 'employable', 'adaptable' and 'flexible' researcher forged by neoliberal capitalism that brings on 'the fatigue of being oneself' (Malabou 2008: 50). Because as part of an urban imaginary, the desert is already embedded in the city – a city that has grown ubiquitous in global capitalism, working its way into our brains. But in order to challenge this immensely powerful abstract machine we must retain the *thought* of an exteriority, which for Deleuze and Guattari means situating thought in a smooth space, a thought 'for which there is no possible method, no conceivable reproduction, but only relays, intermezzos, resurgences' (Deleuze and Guattari 2004: 416).

2.

The little cottage where I spend the night is a sound machine. Something is moving about on the tin plate roof. The quick scuffling noises are amplified by the room; it acts like a drum, dislocating the source to generate an impression of repeated attacks coming from all sides. I am here to follow the Sevilla Trail on the property of Haffie Strauss, a white middle-aged woman who sits with her family on the porch drinking iced rooibos tea. It's been a long day's drive up from Cape Town, following the N9 highroad to Namibia through the vast, dusty landscapes of mono-industrial agriculture, passing the rows of people asking for rides with crumpled bank notes in their hands. But everybody knows that stopping your car in this part of the world is potential death. Haffie and her relatives express surprise to see me travelling alone – in a cheap rental car at that. Again I can't help but enter into a conversation about my accident the week before, and as ever the reaction proves significant for my cartography[2] of post-apartheid South Africa. Still overwhelmed by the structural violence that hit me in the shape of starving, drug-powered children, telling the story to whites has generated responses ranging from aggression to blame and denial. Most seem to think that violence is the price that has to be paid 'for democracy'. But Haffie's mother shrugs with the gesture of what-do-you-expect. 'Oh, it is Africa', she says.

This is Boer country. Land estates are vast with next to nothing in between, fences criss-cross the desert, trespassers are warned. Issues of *Farmer's Weekly* left in the cottage carry editorials arguing the right of landowners to armed defence. I set out on track in the hazy morning light, following the white footprints painted on the ground that show the way to the San rock art sites on the Travellers' Rest estate. Little animals scurry over the ridges. Hundreds of kinds of bushes and plants fill every possible fertile spot, endowed with their own special means for dealing with danger and opportunity: kraalbos, stapeliad, oxalis, vygies, kabong, kuni-bush, kruidjie-roer-my-nie, katbos, wild clove, milk bush, botterboom, sugarbush, amaryllis and the daisies for which the region is renowned. The average annual rainfall is less than 250 mm – according to the guidebook it's a 'transition area of mixed Fynbos and Strandveld with many Karoo elements' (Slingsby 2013: 10). The San must have had detailed knowledge of these plants in order to make use of their properties for food, medication, carrying devices, clothing, tools and weapons.

Hunting and gathering relies on an intense connection with the environment. Not only in a spatial sense – occupying and holding a smooth space, territorialising the land and extending its boundaries (Deleuze and Guattari 2004: 452) – but also in terms of temporality. It's a constant assessment of resources – nutritional value versus volume, carrying effort and the hands available – with respect to the location of the camp and the access of water (Parkington 2012: 1521). Based on his extensive studies of the !Kung San tribe, the Marxist anthropologist Richard B. Lee emphasises hunting and gathering as a mode of economic production. This includes not only the availability of raw materials – wild game and plants, nuts, fruits, fish and shellfish – but also the means for securing them, and the forms of distribution 'according to the principle of *generalized reciprocity*' (Lee 1979: 117). Its dynamic interactions in complex ecologist, social and informational networks of relations (1979: 5) make hunting and gathering rich with implications for the present. Suggestive of a way of life in tune with the Earth, it's a source of inspiration not only for survivalists and anarcho-primitivists, but also for ecological economists (Gowdy 1998). Reliant on attentiveness, immersion and speculation, hunting and gathering resembles the complex manoeuvres of the African urban poor – the 'hunter economy' defined by opportunities and kinship that Filip de Boeck observes in Kinshasa (de Boeck 2004) – but it also overlaps with the circulations of intensity and affect characterising the global financial trade (Simone 2011).

From what may be gathered from the archives,[3] the San way of life revolved around incessant negotiations between the spiritual world and everyday existence, between time and space, male and female, culture and nature, human and animal. There is ample material evidence left of their culture: dispersed across vast stretches of *trekkers* land, and to a large extent unregistered on maps, sub-Saharan Africa is believed to hold some 15,000 sites with tracings, marks and paintings. If the 'discovery' of the painted caves in Europe was a dramatic and contested event, almost immediately fraught with ideology (Rosengren 2012), the recognition of San rock art has been a longer process of gradual disengagement from colonial sources. Archaeological excavation of shelters points to a tradition going back some 27,000 years and maintained until the late nineteenth century, as shown by depictions of horses, ox-wagons and people with guns, indicative of contact with Europeans (Deacon 1998: 16). Although the bulk of San rock art is believed to be the work of pre-colonial hunter-gatherers, the increasing complexity of their identities due to the 'creolisation' of the region is transmitted through their paintings (Le Quellec 2008: 98). Already some two thousand years ago, with the emergence of pastoralist tribes and sedentary farmers, the Western Cape was supporting a range of intermediary and competing economies.

If the nomad is defined by occupying, inhabiting and holding a smooth space – 'a mode of distribution without division into shares, in a space without borders or enclosure' (Deleuze and Guattari 2004: 420) – San rock art complicates this scheme in providing materialist substance. Hidden in cracks and hollows, placed under ridges and cliff hangings and featuring processions of human figures carrying weapons or tools, frequently accompanied by anthropomorphic forms, animals and monsters, it is primarily characterised by its ubiquity across the terrain. Understood as territorial markings, it bears witness to how 'the nomad is one who does not depart, does not want to depart' (Deleuze and Guattari 2004: 420). Embedded within an economic mode of production, however, inseparable from its corresponding mythology, San rock art must be conceived as a more complex weaving of factors. The notion of becoming-animal, for instance, may be taken literally here since figures merging between human and animal traits – animals with human legs, humans with animal heads – are a common feature in these paintings. The recurrent motif of the *therianthrope* has contributed to pinning down the 'meaning' of this art within a hermeneutical framework of shamanism. Although highly contested, this 'single reading key' (Le Quellec 2008: 99) maintains its grasp as the dominant theory of interpretation. Conversely, to simply 'appreciate the art' by means of an emphatic 'immersion' (Skotnes 2008: 75) is equally problematic in that it fails to take into account the micro-assemblage involved – a territory 'made up of decoded fragments of all kinds', constituted by signs, actions and passions (Deleuze and Guattari 2004: 555). Any singular encounter with San enunciations is shaped and affected by a multitude of forces and conditions, most of which are below the borders of perception – post-colonial identities, pre-formed ideas, fences criss-crossing the desert.

But already the sun is too hot. I suffer moments of acute fear – a frequent experience during my stay in South Africa – as I lose track of the white painted footprints that only lead outwards and disappear in the other direction. For some time I wander around aimlessly in the bush before I recognise the rift of a dried out river and am able to find my way back to the road. There is a fundamental inconsistency between my ambulant, subjective positioning and the milieu of the San. Surely these paintings, tracings and markings were more than points in a nomadic trajectory, 'subordinated to the paths they determine', points reduced to relays, 'reached only in order to be left behind' (Deleuze and Guattari 2004: 419). These are but *consequences* of nomadism, Deleuze and Guattari say, whereas the nomad *in principle* is defined in relation to the Earth. The nomad is a vector of deterritorialisation, making the desert 'no less than being made by it', turning it into 'an extraordinarily fine topology that relies not on points or objects but rather on haecceities'. It is in this way that 'the land ceases to be land, tending to be simply ground (*sol*) or support' (Deleuze and Guattari 2004: 421). Surely these paintings, traces and markings must be regarded as so many haecceities – 'modes of individuation [. . .] different from that of a thing or a subject' (Deleuze and Guattari 2004: 287f.) – that in their diversity and visual complexity once formed a plane of consistency, the particular *nomos* of the San. For us it constitutes the folded ground in which we now have to find our bearings.

I do not trespass by crawling under a hole in the barbed wire fence, as someone suggests, but manage to enter the legal way to the adjoining estate of Bushmans Kloof.[4] The dusty red track on the other side of the gates leads to an oasis in the desert: peacocks on brilliant green lawns clipped with scissors, black servants dressed in white offering drinks under huge thatched roofs, guests brought in by helicopter from Cape Town. Graciously invited as a 'scientist', I take my place next to a British lawyer on the Safari Four-Wheel Jeep. We stop by the wayside after a little while to have safari-style coffee and rusks. From here, it's only a few minutes' walk to the rock art site, hidden under a shelter that's invisible from the road. The guide is very sceptical about the whole shamanistic thing. The quality of his guiding, crafted for the immensely rich, is infinitely superior to that of the unemployed taxi driver who took me on a tour the day before. During our scrambles he demonstrated the unfathomable click sounds of Khoisan language that is one of the few living legacies of the Cape San. Notwithstanding this, by now I feel I know about as much of these paintings as either one of them.

3.

Like me, the San were hunters and gatherers, setting out for an eland but content with a dassie (Lee 1979: 209), filling the bag with whatever seems useful, if not now then later perhaps. Quick decisions made on the go, negotiating between risks and opportunities – is that worth pursuing, is this worth holding on to? The various carrying devices used by the San were of crucial importance, constituting a technology that is regularly overlooked as hunting takes priority over gathering. For me, the significance of the antelope stomach sack is transposed to the space on my computer, the luggage restrictions of international airlines and a general assessment of how much material I can ever hope to make sense of in writing. Research is not a linear process. Incessantly skidding across the categories, I'm driven by an intuitive sense of necessity rather than rational thinking. By South African reckoning, I am conducting *surface work* – the work of the amateur, the naturalist, the adventurous explorer – in distinction to the professional archaeologist digging for certainty underground. Surface work involves moving from one site to another, sampling materials scattered on the ground, comparing findings from disparate sources and making connections through a combination of insight and chance. It's predominantly a horizontal practice, driven by affect and intensity, whereas professional archaeology is vertical and hierarchical, founded on the delimitation of site, the procurement of legal permits and scientific analysis. Disengaging from centuries of surface work, the institutionalisation of archaeology came late to South Africa and was a violent and tormented process.

Ione Rudner, now over ninety years old, sits in her bungalow surrounded by *Strandloper* pottery, mourning events in the 1970s: 'so much scathing towards surface work!' (Rudner et al. 1973). She and her husband Jalmar Rudner – a Swedish architect who immigrated to South Africa after the war – used to pack their *bakkie* and go out to the bush whenever time allowed. During a period of over thirty years, they travelled across sub-Saharan Africa exploring and tracing San culture. Ione tells me stories of setting up camp in the middle of the desert, falling asleep under the stars with Jalmar softly playing the mandolin. Life was so different back then in Cape Town: an endless swing of parties with a fun-loving crowd employed by the Swedish exporting industries. After Jalmar's death in 2003, Ione has continued working on their translations of notes and diaries by eighteenth-century Swedish explorers in Africa. I understand that the Rudners were very important in instituting San rock art studies at the South African Museum. Part of their collection of San ethnography has a permanent placement at the Bushmans Kloof, enhancing its unique status as a world-class resort – 'it's not a donation, we sold it to them,' Ione asserts. The bungalow is filled with their documentations, palaeolithic relics and copies of their books, and there is a loom and a small printer's press in what used to be the house servants' shed. I'm amazed at their proficiency across so many different and parallel professions. Jalmar's principal occupation was that of an urban planner, though, leaving as his legacy the freeway system in Cape Town: a massive entanglement of eight-lane drives encircling and fragmenting the historical urban fabric. I venture to ask what it was like working as a planner during apartheid. Ione does not like the question. 'It was never about politics,' she retorts. Jalmar did not impose on anyone, and District 6 was a slum[5] – it had to come down anyway. 'But once that was done he was free to design the beautifully undulating curve, what they now call the Nelson Mandela Highway.'

Surface work emanates from centuries of white supremacy, colonial exploitation and ruthless appropriation. Yet, as a 'prescientific or parascientific or subscientific agency' it holds more than a passing resemblance to the minor science put forth as nomad thought (Deleuze and Guattari 2004: 405). Carried out by legwork transversing the terrain, disregarding concepts and rationality, both are 'itinerant, ambulant sciences that consist in following a flow in a vectorial field across which singularities are scattered like so many "accidents" (problems)' (Deleuze and Guattari 2004: 411). The need for distinctions now imposes itself with violence. How is my own forage into the field, the practice of explorative, 'curious-driven' and interdisciplinary research, different from that of surface work? Essentially involved with claiming and bringing back findings as investments at 'home', what makes such research 'nomadic'? The notion of 'nomadic theory' has been used to the point of exhaustion to reconceptualise resistance, to subvert subjectivities, to establish a link between post-colonial theory and the politics of dislocation in late capitalism. Rosi Braidotti, for one, asserts that 'nomadic thought amounts to a politically invested cartography of the present position of mobility in a globalized world' and that her project on nomadic subjectivity 'constitutes an act of resistance against methodological nationalism and a critique of Eurocentrism from within' (Braidotti 2011: 4, 7). But for a project centred on identifying lines of flight, coined in terms of 'creative alternative space[s] of becoming', the component of violence this involves seems significantly underrated. In a similar vein, Dimitris Papadopoulos, Niamh Stephenson and Vassilis Tsianos have stressed escape as a creative and productive mode, endowed with the capacity to alter 'the very conditions within which struggles over existence are conducted' through 'everyday, singular, unpretentious acts of subverting subjectification and betraying representation' (Papadopoulos et al. 2008: 61). But it takes violence to break loose, to discontinue, to resist – and when trauma makes people strangers to themselves, it is precisely because 'no transcendence, flight or escape is left', when there is no other than 'being other to the self' (Malabou 2012: 11). Nomadic thought, to me, is not just about criticality: it necessitates a rupture that makes thought exterior to itself.

Scenes of violence are few and far between in San rock art. Lee describes hunter-gatherers as a radically egalitarian society, employing a variety of 'humility techniques' to avoid self-aggrandisement and to channel energies into socially beneficial activities (Lee 1979: 246 f.). In a mobile society based on sharing, with little sense of private property, dealing with disagreement is easy: some merely leave and set up their own camp, adhering to mechanisms that 'inhibit[s] the installation of stable powers, in favour of a fabric of immanent relations' (Deleuze and Guattari 2004: 395). The *nomos* of the San was not the war machine,[6] but it was brought into conflict with others as the social landscape in which they lived grew increasingly complex. This constitutes one possible key for understanding one of the most enigmatic San rock art paintings, known as *Veg en Vlug* ('Fight and Flight'). Located in a shelter under an overhanging rock, it's inaccessible to and held secret from the general public. I'm led here by a combination of random occurrences, tracing an incidental comment to a context, if not a source: a decolonising reading group from the university out here on a weekend trip.

We're now taking turns to squeeze under the shelter to look at the delicate brushstrokes of red, white and black that spread over the rock surface. What we see centres on a group of 'defenders' sheltered by a cave-like interior, anticipating an outside group of monster-like 'attackers' approaching along parallel lines. Some figures seem to be running away from the action along similar lines and there are other lines leading to less discernible figures in the margins of the composition. Constituting an anomaly in San rock art, *Veg en Vlug* is normally interpreted literally as depicting a scene of conflict. Drawing on the archives, however, John Parkington stresses the significance of the parallel lines. They cannot be footprints or a path because on closer inspection they are seen to emanate from bows or bowstrings and connects to the mouths or faces

Fig. 14.1 *Veg en Vlug*, Sevilla, Pakhuis region, Cederberg, South Africa (photograph by the author)

of the figures (Parkington 2005: 63). He suggests that the lines represent 'strings', a metaphor used by the San to express the relationship between their thoughts and their habitat. The system of lines surrounding the cave scene would thus refer to *attachments*; 'the intangible connections between people and the land' or, alternatively, the power of rituals to 'influence the behaviour or impact the wellbeing of others at a distance' (Parkington 2005: 64).

The cave is striated. It vibrates with transversality, with how Guattari emphasises the effects of ideas over matter. An entwinement of intensive and extensive space, *Veg en Vlug* furthermore resonates with Deleuze's ideas on the Fold. Centred on a division between interiority and exteriority, connected by thought strings, the image points to a correspondence, even a communication between 'the coils of matter and the folds of the soul'. Within a baroque conception of complexity, where each part is separate yet affected by and affecting all the others, 'there is always a cavern in the cavern: each body, however small it may be, contains a world insofar as it is perforated by uneven passageways' (Deleuze 1991: 229 f.). The intensified state of affective reciprocity and coexistence in

Fig. 14.2 *Veg en Vlug*, Sevilla, Pakhuis region, Cederberg, South Africa (tracing by Peter Slingsby)

this scene makes it an urban setting. The conflict and violence so explicitly conveyed by its central motif – frightful intruders advancing towards the cave – conjures up struggles over land ownership, the threat of eviction, the fragility of a mortgaged home. But what about the figures at the margins of the composition, merely mentioned by Parkington, whose possible significance only becomes apparent *in situ*? One of these figures is a nondescript, looming monster-like shape. Many of the lines connect here – the figure appears to be grasping at the lines and reeling them in. Who holds this determination over existence, what singular power or entity does it represent? A decentred source of absolute power, it's reeling in lines of flight. Whatever it signifies – be it God, Capitalism or the State – clearly, here, there is no escape from coping with an existence defined by reciprocal relationships and substantial connections. There is only fight, awaiting 'that final force', that decisive support of a people to come that is integral to desert thought (Deleuze and Guattari 2004: 416).

5.

Returning back to the city the front tyre of my car explodes, damaged from my driving on uneven desert roads. The car starts jerking from one side of the road to the other as I descend from the steep mountain pass. I narrowly escape crashing into oncoming cars and manage to pull over. It's close to 40°C and the battery of my phone is dead. A car runs up behind me, a man gets out and approaches. Without saying much he immediately grasps the situation and goes about changing the tyre, grunting at my stuttering thanks and shaking his head at my money. 'Be careful on the road,' he says, and escorts me until we get to the crossroad where he has to take off in his rusty old car packed to the brim with assorted bits and pieces. The folded ground shifts once again, as produced by correspondences and interaction – at once stable and evolving, defined by plasticity: the ability to create and to destroy.

Notes

1. The current population of San in southern Africa is estimated at 100,000, most of them living in Botswana and Namibia (http://www.kwatthu.org, accessed 15 May 2015). The few remaining tribes of hunter-gatherers are under severe pressure by governments and private developers, acting on behalf of wildlife conservation interests and the tourist trade (http://www.survivalinternational.org/, accessed 15 May 2015).
2. Cartography, here, refers to my body defined as 'the sum total of the material elements belonging to it under given relations of movement and rest, speed and slowness (longitude); the sum total of intensive affects it is capable of at a given power or degree of potential (latitude)' (Deleuze and Guattari 2004: 287).
3. Research on the San is enabled by the extensive documentation of their language, tradition and belief collected by Wilhelm Bleek and Lucy Lloyd in the late nineteenth century. The archive is held by the University of Cape Town library and constitutes an invaluable source for interpreting San rock art, in parallel to archaeological and anthropological investigations.
4. For a record of Bushmans Kloof, including video footage of the terrain, see http://www.bushmanskloof.co.za (accessed 21 March 2015).
5. The case of District 6, Cape Town, was a slum clearance of an inner-city, historic neighbourhood carried out in the late 1960s, an implementation of the Group Area Acts issued by the apartheid government. The forced eviction of its non-white population involved the obliteration of entire streets and houses while people were dumped into unplanned and informal settlements on the city's outskirts.
6. In discussing the concept of the nomad in relation to real nomadic practices, Ronald Bogue argues that the concept is *de jure* in kind; it captures a qualitative difference as regards the sedentary, but is de facto only present in a mixed-up state (Bogue 2004: 173). The effort of Deleuze and Guattari is not to fix categories or identify essences in nature, he asserts, 'but to make something pass *between* the terms of a binary opposition and thereby to foster a thought that brings into existence something new' (2004: 178).

References

Bogue, R. (2004) 'Apology for nomadology', *Interventions: International Journal for Postcolonial Studies*, 6 (2): 169–79.

Braidotti, R. (2011) *Nomadic Subjects: Embodiment and Sexual Difference in Contemporary Feminist Theory*. New York: Columbia University Press.

De Beock, F. (2004) *Kinshasa: Tales of the Invisible City*. Ghent and Amsterdam: Ludion.

Deacon, J. (1998) *Some Views on Rock Paintings in the Cederberg*. Cape Town: National Monuments Council.

Deleuze, G. (1991) 'The fold', trans. J. Strauss, *Yale French Studies*, 80: 227–47.

Deleuze, G. (2004) 'Jean-Jacques Rousseau: precursor of Kafka, Céline, and Ponge', in *Desert Island and Other Texts*, ed. D. Lapoujade, trans. M. Taormina. Los Angeles and New York: Semiotext(e).

Deleuze, G. and Guattari, F. (2004) [1980], *A Thousand Plateaus: Capitalism and Schizophrenia*, trans. B. Massumi. London and New York: Continuum.

Gowdy, J. M. (ed.) (1998) *Limited Wants, Unlimited Means: A Reader on Hunter-Gatherer Economics and the Environment*. Washington, DC: Island Press.

Guattari, F. (1995) *Chaosmosis: An Ethico-Aesthetic Paradigm*. Bloomington: Indiana University Press.

Lang, P. and Menking, W. (2003) *Superstudio: Life without Objects*. Milano: Skira.

Le Quellec, J.-L. (2008) 'Rock art research in Southern Africa', in P. Bahn, N. Franklin and M. Strecker (eds), *Rock Art Studies: News of the World III*. Oxford: Oxbow Books, pp. 97–111.

Lee, R. B. (1979) *The !Kung San: Men, Women and Work in a Foraging Society*. Cambridge: Cambridge University Press.

Malabou, C. (2008) *What Should We Do With Our Brain?*, trans. S. Rand. New York: Fordham University Press.

Malabou, C. (2012) *Ontology of the Accident: An Essay on Destructive Plasticity*, trans. C. Shread. Cambridge and Malden: Polity Press.

Papadopoulos, D., Stephenson, N. and Tsianos, V. (2008) *Escape Routes: Control and Subversion in the 21st Century*. London: Pluto Press.

Parkington, J. (2003) *Cederberg Rock Paintings*. Cape Town: Krakadouw Trust.

Parkington, J. (2005) 'Rock art research, conservation and social transformation', in J. Deacon (ed.), *The Future of Africa's Past: Proceedings of the 2004 TARA Rock Art Conference Nairobi*. Nairobi and San Francisco: Trust for African Rock Art, pp. 62–5.

Parkington, J. (2012) 'Mussels and mongongo nuts: logistical visits to the Cape West Coast, South Africa', *Journal of Archaeological Science*, 39: 1521–30.

Rosengren, M. (2012) *Cave Art, Perception and Knowledge*. New York: Palgrave Macmillan.

Rosenqvist, J.-O. (1981) 'Theodore of Sykeon and his biography', *Meddelanden från Svenska Forskningsinstitutet i Istanbul*, 6 (1): 5–18.

Rudner, J. et al. (1973) 'Review article: end of an era? A discussion', *South African Archaeological Bulletin*, 28 (109/110): 13–26.

Sahlins, M. (1974) *Stone Age Economics*. London: Tavistock.

Simone, A. M. (2011) 'Deals with imaginaries and perspectives: reworking urban economies in Kinshasa', *Social Dynamics: A Journal for African Studies*, 37 (1): 111–24.

Skotnes, P. (2008) *Unconquerable Spirit: George Stow and the Landscapes of the San*. Athens: Ohio University Press.

Slingsby, P. (2013) *Sevilla Rock Art Trail*. Muizenberg: Slingsby Maps.

Chapter 15

Sociability and Endurance in Jakarta

AbdouMaliq Simone

Instead of devolving into chaos or becoming more proficient copycat imitations of their northern counterparts, could it be that the big metropolitan areas of the so-called Global South are concretising new ways of 'becoming' cities – ones which make broader and more judicious use of the varied actors who inhabit them? Is it possible that even as the familiar tropes of collaboration, autoconstruction and informality are fading, new formations of collective life, less readily discernible, are coming to the fore, and in ways that alter the social arrangements and subjective experiences of being in the city? These questions inform an exploration that will focus largely on Jakarta but also touch implicitly on other metropolitan areas across the 'majority world'.

Cities of this 'majority world' share an important sense of the 'afterwards' – after apartheid, colonialism, authoritarian rule or partition – but this common disjuncture, while important in accounting for particular trajectories of spatial and economic organisation, does not in itself point to shared horizons. Most cities of Africa, Asia and Latin America have been subjected by and articulate subjectivity through the simultaneous application of highly contradictory, contentious, experimental and formularised modalities of city making. This means that social and material formations are always being undone as they are being remade and then undone again.

These oscillations give rise to different forms of collective life, sometimes operative through discernible associations and social movements, at other times through more implicit, provisional modalities of collaboration. Here, households ensure that they are surrounded by and embedded in heterogeneous relational fields which compel them to negotiate the practicalities of everyday life with different walks of life, affiliations and networks. Local economies were built from small initiatives undertaken by households to incite collaboration from others. A continuous process of adjustments ensued as residents tried to make their own initiatives fit together or sidestep each other in order to attain larger scales or decentralise larger operations into more specialised production or service. But often these efforts did not aim for specific objectives charted in advance.

As in Deleuze's (1989) notion of the missing people, sociality is always yet to be completed, always inclusive of conjunctions of all kinds. Related directly to the very structuration of language with its plurality of references and specificity, that which is yet to be built is reliant upon the impersonal that need not identify a specific subject. Thus an assemblage of residents, for example, do not conjoin activities or their proximity to each other in order to attain the status or experience of a 'community', some coherent whole that explains and accounts for their coming together. Rather, the conjunction becomes the possibility of 'saying something' that need not be summed up, saying something that need not have specific parameters of efficacy or objectivity, something that 'keeps people going' in and through transformations that are without precedent in the sense that they need not represent the culmination of a goal or necessity.

Given these insights of Deleuze, what are the practices that keep the people of Jakarta 'going'? What are the terms of endurance, the mixtures of games, moves and orientations that produce sociability? Much of the interaction among the residents of Jakarta never went anywhere, often never accomplished anything. But instead of this apparent failure acting as a deterrent, it tended to keep the game going.

The difficulties of everyday life in places like São Paulo, Lagos, Jakarta or Karachi feed an intense hunger for justice and equity. But there is also a general wariness of pinning things down too much, of instituting policies where capacities and conditions are calculated and compared. There is often a preference for keeping things incomplete. Everyday life may be full of antagonisms, misconstrued behaviours, evasions, tricks and manipulations, but they are also the conditions that give inhabitants something to work with, something to try and put right, something that brings people together who otherwise would keep their distance, and thus a platform for the incessant rehearsal of different ways to 'work things out'. Now, of course, this can be labour-intensive and a strain for residents already overwhelmed with trying to make ends meet. But it is in these rehearsals that residents often feel that new vistas are opened up, where at least they are exposed to worlds otherwise inaccessible, even though there are no guarantees that they can take advantage of them.

Experimental Enactments of Everyday Life

Cities are arenas where the proximity of differences is often stark. Take, for example, the relatively new Kalibata City complex in central Jakarta. Part replication of the now standardised middle- to upper-middle-class all-in-one apartment blocks combining residences, shopping mall, leisure zones, schools and social services and part low-cost, densely packed towers of small flats, social class divisions are built into the very spacing and composition of dwelling. Class divisions are also reinforced by the availability of parking spaces and other amenities. Roughly 30,000 people live in the complex and, unlike many other similar developments, there has been some effort made to landscape ground levels with scores of small shops, restaurants, coffee houses and public spaces. As residents are thrown together in an environment with limited history and situated in a context where relations of authority and civility can no longer rely upon the mores and practices of long-honed, thickly enmeshed residential/commercial districts, those who live in Kalibata are still trying to figure ways of working with and around each other. Lower-income residents (in the 'lower' zone) find ways to take advantage of their proximity to those middle-class residents (in the 'upper' zone).

Here, residents enact various performances, not so much to anchor themselves in specific positions and reputations, but rather they use the nascent character of the complex as a platform for opportunist ventures across the surrounds. Young men pay particular attention to various items of equipment carried by young women living in the 'upper zone' – phone chargers, pens, cell phones equipped with particular applications, books or laptops – as a means to initiate conversation, requesting the temporary use of such items for purported exigencies. Young women pay particular attention to gatekeepers, such as security guards, managers or maintenance personnel, offering cigarettes and conversation as a means of cultivating the ability to cross boundaries, particularly in order to gain access to the amenities or services of the 'upper zones'. There is particular attention paid to those who have some kind of power, and in the deployment of various games of facilitating proximity to opportunities, the nature of power itself changes. The powerful may continue to be those who have money, good jobs, the latest consumer goods. But they also include those who may not have direct access to them but know how to put others, whose identities and backgrounds may make them more eligible to affiliate with such resources, in touch with the people who control them, through duplicity, stealth or tact.

The small shops and cafes attract and curate niche groups and audiences at different times of the day, e.g. older men who live with younger women, older women who live with younger men, women in polygamous marriages who want to have 'legitimate' sex and children but don't particularly want the burden of living with a full time husband, and other couplings of various genders and sexual preferences. The commercial and public spaces are aligned in such a way as to separate out lifestyles and sexual performances that might clash, but to keep them in a mutual view sufficient to satisfy curiosities, permit tentative forays across thresholds or at least temper the inclination of any one constellation of actors to impose their codes of propriety upon the others.

These are filiations that seek no definitive reproductions; they are not intended to stabilise a genealogy, but rather to keep unravelling and refiguring strata of activity, continuously repositioning individuals in terms of each other so as to broaden horizons of opportunity and vantage point. They bring into play different actors, scales, niches and situations, but in ways that are not organised hierarchically, that do not accrete experience into an accumulative narrative of attainments. As Deleuze and Guattari point out in their discussion of the concept of involution as an intensification of growing difference:

> Becoming is a rhizome, not a classificatory or genealogical tree. Becoming is certainly not imitating, or identifying with something; neither is it regressing-progressing; neither is it corresponding, establishing corresponding relations; neither is it producing, producing a filiation or through filiation. Becoming is a verb with consistency on its own. (Deleuze and Guattari 1987: 239)

In many respects, Jakarta has opted for grandiosity, square footage, door-to-door automobility and the banal spectacles of mass consumption. But the bulk of its residents still try to eke out new, virtuous basins and pathways from the intensely punctured material environment that they have repeatedly distorted, generating new inclines and surfaces. The resultant curvatures roll things, people and opportunities their way, as they are rolled toward others in some tentative formulations of a project. This is what Levi Bryant (2014) calls a 'terraformation', a material and semiotic framework that enables disparate people and things to intersect and generate new trajectories of movement and becoming.

Despite the grandiosity and mass consumption, experimentation continues to thrive, perhaps just barely, and in a way that may exemplify Deleuze and Guattari's (1987: 238–9) notion of involution as a kind of striving that has no particular end in sight. Residential space in my Jakarta district, Tebet, can be described as a collection of projects. Even if the term 'project' has been overly tainted with neoliberal connotations, a popular sensibility remains that everybody has got to have a project. When people say they live in the 'projects', they are not talking about social housing; they are not talking about being warehoused in run-down areas. In some respects, a lot of Jakarta is run-down, but not because stuff is no longer happening. Too much might be going on, too many projects. Residents have their domiciles, their households and their stuff. But they mostly live elsewhere; they live large, in the sense that a person tries to turn whatever they have access to into something other than what it is at the moment. A house becomes part of something else, like part of a chain of making or distributing things, information or influence. A street is divided up, not into turf (although turf exists), but more often into particular concentrations or specialisations which then have the street as a conduit to each other, a physical medium of relationship.

Some projects rework long-term kinship, commercial and political 'lineages', extruding wide effects, problems and potentials. There are people who have known and worked with each other for a long time and have played off their different capacities in ways that are able to absorb new blood, which brings fresh ideas and momentum. Sometimes it is hard for people to remain 'solid' and avoid clashing with others, but competing projects are usually able to step 'sideways', again trying to do something different with what they have. Importantly, projects fold in the remains of depleted, overworked, under-utilised, practically disposed institutions, buildings and other facilities as points of reference, launching pads and frames of legitimacy.

Projects depend on investigation: you look to where people gather, wait, enter or exit, where there is a moment of hesitation, and you think about what you can put in front of them, what they could see and experience, and then buy or talk about to someone else. You step outside of your front door and you look at the different angles, lines of sight; you see how one thing leads to another, and how the different ways where you are standing are connected to a larger surrounding. You try and figure out ways to work the distance between you and all that could be gathered up by something you could do with others that you already know, some kind of coordinated operation. Because if you look inside people's houses, you realise just how much stuff has been 'locally sourced' by such operations, how many things have been fixed or invented. Some projects are about operating across various gaps and enclosures. Canals, intersections, administrative boundaries have to be crossed. Empty lots and vacant spaces can be filled in for the time being. While collaborative effort among residents may seem like putting together individuals in some mathematical set, it is usually more an intermeshing of projects. While norms, policy and law may guide the melding and coordinating of individuals and corporate entities, they may have little traction with projects that are imagined and enacted with shifting casts of characters, terrain, objectives and results.

Of course there are institutions whose functions are widely understood and which have clearly delineated rights and responsibilities. But how do you regulate a project that entails stringing together a bunch of cheap eating places on the slim verge between property fronts and the street for taxi drivers who take breaks along a small public park, places that operate as expansion businesses for those who are losing customers from their cafes in a nearby social housing project to a rash of fast-food chains around the corner? How do you link these projects to a thrice-weekly night market that a local Islamic school rents out to a group of itinerant preachers to sell cheap goods to young kids not old enough to take their motorcycles to the nearest shopping malls?

What holds a project together? Part of the 'holding' entails spatial impressions, as if particular 'pressings' of space create inclines which move people and projects toward or away from each other. In quite literal ways, any two steps you take in Jakarta will seldom be the same. Strides are interrupted by a ground that is dented and twisted from the propulsions of use and the turbulence of the surface. Space is twisted, folded, forced open and shut with structures both makeshift and permanent. There is stuff everywhere – carts, wheels, tyres, wood, metal planks, tiles, tools, shards, dirt that is pieced together as containers, stages, exhibitions, hiding places.

Another facet of holding involves propagating lures, eliciting or inciting attention and proximity, by which projects are lured toward meetings, toward a situation of unanticipated discovery and negotiation. Projects are also lured away from each other, into thinking that the 'real deal' is located somewhere else than it actually is, or lured into a position where a project may have only limited access and influence over another. Lures are often matters of gesture rather than discourse, a matter of performances that exude a kind of magic or mystery to be uncovered. Lures are conveyors of the elusive – what you see is not what you get – and thus the impetus for a mimesis where projects attempt to cloak themselves in the guise of another as a way of penetrating to the heart of things.

In this way, projects are always 'on the run'. Even if the same people, materials and objectives remain inextricably affiliated to them, projects move through each other, and sometimes duck and dive, avoiding undertows and onslaughts or riding the crests of waves. These are the interplays of those who aim to map themselves on the radar and those who wish to remain off it, those who attempt to spread out, expand, take over and those who enfold and insulate themselves. Expanding households and kin relationships, the consolidation of external resources inward, insertions into the slivers among contested or dominated areas, the keeping of everything in view and the selective veiling of events and bodies, the parcelling out of functions and places and the erasures of divisions – all are manoeuvres in the polyrhythmic composition of projects.

What is also important in all of these performances and manoeuvrings are the things that do not get done, do not take place. For the intermeshing and circumventions of projects do not take care of everything. They do not pick up all of the trash; they do not rescue or remove all of that which decays; there are not continuous updates and renovations. Traumas fester, some people and areas appear immobilised as if caught in some time warp; contiguous persons and structures may march completely out of step.

Yet sociability can exist among project situations where no one is pushed aside, where capacities unfold in tandem even where exchanges are marked by inequity. For example, subcontracting work involving manual labour to small, unregulated units is a common project for the medium-size commercial enterprises focused on printing, textiles, electronics and household goods. Sometimes exclusive relationships are forged, but more often these small units take piecework from wherever they can get it. Hours are long, wages are low and working conditions can be hazardous. While formally being exploited by and dependent upon big players, most of the 'small-time' workers know that the 'real' money, as well as innovation, comes from those instances when the small units gather themselves together to develop their own 'lines', and then feed them into parallel wholesale and retail circuits. Such projects have to take place under the radar, since the bigger enterprises are well connected to dominate the official circuits of marketing and exchange. Yet, these projects, which ebb and flow through shifting assemblages of the small, can turn out goods and services at cheaper prices and equivalent quality. Everyone seems to know this game of projects is taking place, and it continues as long as it doesn't draw too much attention to itself.

Intersecting the City

In my Jakarta neighbourhood, called Tebet, I live near a 'problematic' intersection. It is problematic in that it requires continuous assessment of how much time is needed to get out of the immediate surroundings into the larger city. The surroundings are replete with meandering roadways that empty out onto this intersection. It is a place of convergence for crowds of pedestrians and hawkers and for the loading and unloading of goods. It brings together the two main flow-through traffic pathways. Because of these features, the intersection is subject to oscillating gaps and closures, unpredictable rhythms of congestion and circulation.

Now think of all of the occurrences, activities, events and gestures that take place at any given time in a neighbourhood like Tebet. Think how we commonly explain the causes and effects of all of these occurrences. Think about how we assess the impact we have on other people's lives and the impact these lives have on our own. Much of what we think is possible in this regard has much to do with the infrastructure of how bodies, things and words are connected, what can be seen or heard, what kinds of arrangements of bodies and materials allow for things to circulate. But also think of the possibility that any of the things that take place at a given time in Tebet might have an effect on each other outside of any seemingly plausible or visible form of mediation. That somehow things intersect across distance and difference, coming together in all kinds of 'strange' constellations and circuits of causation.

So this intersection in Tebet is not just a physical feature of the neighbourhood. It also marks the frontiers of shifting basins of consolidation that fold in events and materials whose interactions would tend to ramify outwards, away from each other, or bring together occurrences and actors that would seem to have no basis to connect or connect only in arbitrary, chance encounters. Different kinds of residents and economic activities that might otherwise not pay attention to each other end up dealing with each other in unanticipated durations of time. This is not only because the transportation grid lends implicit structural definition to chunks of space, but also because the intensity and range of the activities and actors and their reverberations at the intersection are selectively incorporated as the impetus and content of more or less stabilised basins of residence and commercial and social activity within given chunks of local space. Local solidities take place not only because particular kinds of people and activities are next to each other or because they have histories and concepts that enable them to discern commonalities, but also because they rely upon alternating currents and patterns in the intersection of different streams and networks that provide food, services, materials repair, leisure time and information that are gathered up in changing bundles in a particular space. No small sub-neighbourhood can simply depend upon one particular way of doing things and getting things done, of accessing supports and services. There have to be many possible alternatives for enacting the solidity of a place if it is not to simply atrophy and fall apart.

The entirety of the city is in some sense enacted at the intersection in various durations and manifestations, and congestion is not just a matter of too much traffic. Congestion is also an indication of the plurality of linkages at work, which residents selectively pay attention to or withdraw from. It is evidence of all of the places people are going, as the area around the destination is both a point of arrival and a point of departure. These arrivals and departures are coated with intensities of aspiration, fatigue and the weight of influences of all kinds. The surroundings of this intersection in Tebet are particularly heterogeneous because they contain facilities for servicing the needs and aspirations of the very different kinds of residents who live in the area. These needs and aspirations are in turn inscribed in space, through the forms of property, design, consumption and exposure.

The availability of these surroundings to particular people and uses ensue from diverse histories of land consolidation and tenure, zoning, resettlement and legal frameworks which are tied to various documents, policies, political mechanisms, institutions, calculations of pricing and compositions of capital. The plurality of objects that have to be affiliated in 'working relationships' which follow from these histories, produce seemingly untenable densities when coupled with the sheer number of cars, trucks and motorbikes on road layouts not easily rearranged without substantially disrupting hard-won, yet constantly renegotiated, balances among intensely discrepant uses and users of the area. The pathways have to follow the documents and sentiments as the pathways also structure these documents and sentiments at the same time.

It is also conceivable that the congestion at the intersection could be replaced with a different kind of congestion. Lateral interchanges that could enable those who reside in this area to work and live with each other in radically different formats could be actionable through comprehensive detachments of a greater number of residents from their involvement in other parts of the city. This would require a realignment of resource allocation and a self-constituted web of affordances that maximise mutual care and synergies of skill and income. In other words, there exists the virtual potential for an intensification of residents working, socialising, administering, producing and distributing within the immediate surroundings themselves. If it is possible that anything that takes place in Tebet could register, and perhaps already is registering, an important impact on everything else outside of the visible infrastructures of cause and effect, why not actively use this as a way of making a different kind of everyday life for those who at least reside in Tebet?

Of course this is unlikely to happen, given the exteriorising deformations of intensive differentiation and the inclinations of people to put distance between themselves and others and as part of the entropic trajectories entailed in the amassing of effort and activity. But this plane of 'virtual consolidation' never ceases to exist as the substrate along which enacted linkages – explicit and implicit – take place to various degrees and in various forms within the different 'neighbourhoods' that mark and are marked by the intersection. What gets connected or remains apart, then, is a matter of ethical decisions, of the dynamics entailed in making the choice to actualise something that exists all along, even though that which has existed all along may not be available to human cognition or to extant forms of calculation and verification. The ethical decision is not based on the evidence, but rather on a conviction that the evidence of the viability of the choice, of the commitment to venture into new arrangements of living, will ensue from the decision itself, but not necessarily inform the capacity of the decision in the first place.

Sex of the City

In addition to many dilemmas of ethical decision, some processes of interconnection are also about sex. In Tanah Sereal, a particularly rambunctious district of Northern Jakarta, there seems to be a continuously intentional sense of sexual provocation. The district borders on being many things at the same time – slum, up-and-coming middle-class area, repository of sinister characters and a bastion of new found righteousness. It also borders on one of the city's largest small- and medium-scale textile production districts. While there have been significant spillovers in recent years, Tanah Sereal defies being 'turned over' to any dominant economic activity. A small river separates it from the hustle and bustle of Glodok, the historic centre of Chinese commerce. Despite the economic spillovers from other parts of the city, Tanah Sereal tends to accumulate the more 'dirty' and marginal jobs, as well as being known as the place where it is possible to buy all kinds of 'junk'. Painting buildings with an array of wild colours, bright pinks, greens and oranges is rampant; this tends to divert attention from the dilapidation on all sides, but it can also engender nausea in the casual observer. There are long thorough-fares that seem to go on forever without interruption, but behind these are emplaced tightly packed three- to six-storey buildings separated by narrow lanes that wind their way eventually to an opening where vehicles are able to pass.

Tanah Sereal is a district replete with signs – signs that advertise for non-existent job openings and signs that invite participation in activities that are clearly illegal but which are elaborated with such detail and bear what look to be the authentic signatures of the appropriate authorities so as to constitute some kind of official collective joke. Other signs are offered as warnings that some could even construe as invitations to indulge in the activities prohibited. For example, in the extremely slim frontage of a house painted with an image of red bricks – while a pile of real bricks stand neatly stacked by the front entrance – the owner had planted an orange tree some years back. On an adjoining wall an image of the same tree is painted with a sign that warns that anyone taking an orange will suffer from excruciating bouts of diarrhoea that have a 65 per cent chance of leading to the person's death, and advises that a relevant life insurance policy could be taken out at an address which is provided. On another wall a few minutes' walk away, there is another large sign in which residents are invited to register a mark whenever they have had a particularly 'good time' in bed, an invitation which seems to both be taken seriously and to elicit all kind of salacious comments; these sit alongside pasted announcements of lectures at the local mosque on the importance of morality.

Most districts similar in look and composition to Tanah Sereal in Jakarta are usually eager to participate in the frequent contests held by municipal authorities to beautify and green their areas. But some residents in Tanah Sereal respond to these invitations with graffiti that disparagingly point to the secret wish of power brokers to 'send the inhabitants back to the jungle'. Other signs conversely point to the fact that the district is 'already so far from civilisation that there is no turning back now'. Yet others observe that 'beauty is skin deep and it is only what is inside that counts', written in a slang that clearly points to the statement's sexual overtones. Most of the district leaders – the local headmen – are reluctant to talk to outsiders, but one headman, Hari, describes the area over which he presides as an 'Olympic competition for sexual gymnastics'. Hari is a former gangster who won a lot of money gambling, then built a well-equipped Islamic day school, went to make pilgrimage in Mecca and reports spending most of his day in the mosque because the local women otherwise just 'can't keep their hands off of me'.

Hari's district is a hodge-podge of mostly one- and two-storey small bungalows appearing to heave with the weight of too many people crammed into them. *You see how the buildings seem to sniff each other out; how they try to touch each other in every way possible; I mean we are mostly Muslims here, but looking around, you wouldn't know it.* Pointing to a house across the street from where we are talking, where a public phone booth is set right in the middle of the family's spot for washing clothes, Hari says, *I have no idea how that thing got there, but if someone wants to make a call, it looks like they have to inspect the family's underwear at the same time.* This is a prospect that gets even more daunting as a passing three-wheeled motorcycle cart carrying bottles of water is emblazoned with the sign, 'Daddy just got home and mama is wet'.

Setting aside the erotic dimensions of its construction, Tanah Sereal does participate in different 'collective projects'. Residents along two parallel roads, and the winding pathways that crisscross in the spaces behind them, have been putting up a building for the past several years. Almost the length of a football field and now five stories high, it is a rudimentary construction, slowly being assembled by mostly voluntary labour as the contributions come in. Some of those are financial, but most are in-kind, i.e. materials, labour and political connections to keep the project going. It is a project that would inescapably violate some codes, although residents are serious about it being viably occupied. The building has walls and interior floors, and the surface cladding is almost finished. But it remains to be seen what it will be used for. Individual residents have no shortage of ideas for possible uses, though everyone agrees that it should not be a rooming house to accommodate workers, as residents have already turned over part of their homes to this function. Everyone also agrees that the building should not be divided into individual apartments assigned to each of the residents that have participated in the project.

The headaches entailed in assessing the relative monetary value of different kinds of contributions, assigning volumes of space according to the quantity of assistance contributed or simply dividing up the space equally for all contributing residents are viewed as enormous. In addition, there are no clear ideas about what would constitute the end of the project, at what point the construction will be over. There have been discussions about different scales and temporalities of completion, about assigning specific uses now and getting them ready to be actualised and leaving more open-ended other parts of the building whose use would be worked out later. There is also recognition that, at some point soon, construction will have to come to an end given the likely onset of structural vulnerabilities that ensue when structures are not used. The conundrum brings out various displays from local power figures, who all want to declare the 'defining moment', but each instance tends to reveal an impoverishment of imagination which seems to act as an incentive for residents to keep on building.

As construction usually proceeds at a snail's pace anyway, the act of continuance does not hurry any irreversible horizon. Discussions remain open, as the building operates more as an occasion for an insistent exploration of options and next moves, most of which never materialise. In this way the building is a technical operation that connects residents to a series of ongoing potentialities. Its actualisation may mean that residents have to narrow their range of options, but since actualisation does appear imminent, another set of conundrums and possibilities is looming.

Amid the jumble of interstices, enclosures and openings that ensue from the interaction of materials and metabolisms, power is mobilised through efforts to posit architectures of possibility. These possibilities entail specific lines of association and distancing, gathering up things as mutually implicated and affected while separating off other possibilities and matters viewed as disallowed and irrelevant. The density of the city is not just that of human bodies but of the multiplicity of possible associations among bodies and various materials. While these associations have been subject to various political technologies of governance and control, there has always been something that slips through, leaks out, overflows or generates long shadows.

The possibilities of life, then, in cities such as Jakarta have depended upon a range of forces, neither virtuous nor demonic, productive nor anarchic, but which do entail 'dangerous' circulations of bodies through materials, atmospheres and transactions whose dispositions are not clear one way or the other. As such, experimentation is never easy, as it is an encounter with an anomalous form of life (Delpech-Ramey 2010).

To Do Justice

Density is not only about the proximity of bodies. It is also the intermixing of devices – measures, angles, calculations, impulses, hinges, screens, surfaces, soundscapes, exposures, folds, circuitries, layers, tears and inversions. All are instruments for bringing things into association, where things get their 'bearings' by having a 'bearing' on each other. City life is propelled by this possibility of creating sets of 'bearings', by things having a bearing on each other.

So in some ways all configurations of life and matter in the city are speculative. You can start with components as they 'move' toward something else – place-to-place, body-to-body, body-to-place and so forth. But there is nothing in their trajectories, characters or 'aspirations' that necessarily 'takes' them to each other. Or if there is some overarching 'need', it can only be accounted for from the multiple starting points of the elements themselves. But there is no overarching map which determines how these elements work together. If there is a core essence to the city it is a sense of its *plasticity*, to borrow the term from Catherine Malabou (2008, 2012). It is the incessant exchangeability of substances, where the entanglements of effort, body and stuff constantly reduplicate themselves in ways that do not have to be the same or different, but constantly move on, into and through strange syntheses. Constellations are torn apart and recomposed without relying upon any clear sense of what should have taken place or what must take place. Malabou's notion is important here because it circumvents a preoccupation with flexibility – the assumption that people's urban livelihoods and capacities to adapt exhibit an intensive flexibility, a capability to roll with the punches. This capacity may indicate reservoirs of strength, but also turns particular urban populations into objects of easy imposition. As Malabou indicates:

> To be flexible is to receive a form or impression, to be able to fold oneself, to take the fold, not to give it. To be docile, to not explode. Indeed, what flexibility lacks is the resource of giving form, the power to create, to invent or even to erase an impression. Flexibility is plasticity minus its genius. (2008: 12–13)

There is no ultimate substrate on which everything rests, on which clear trajectories of rightness or efficacy could be grounded. The city is replete with layer upon layer of how antecedent actions produced particular consequences. Cities cannot cover over the fact that they are repositories of decay, of rot and decomposition. For the ability to make things, to harness and consolidate the energies of dense interactions is, at the same time, always taking things apart, detaching them from their 'life support systems', digging and filling in land with enormous volumes of waste, as well as extracting from waste something that might live on.

If what the city 'just is' is something constantly mutable, it, nevertheless, has to show some kind of 'face', act as if it is a definitive culmination of specific histories and decisions. The form of that showing, borrowing once again from Malabou (2011) is fantastic, a phantasm. What presents itself as stable and unequivocal is always already moving on, in the process of exchanging the apparently critical elements of its coherence with a surround that is also 'shedding its skin'. Whereas urban modernity acted as if the intense deformations and recompositions – the plasticity – of urban life could be summed up once and for all with all the componential elements gathered up in clear calculations of mutual implication, a neoliberal urbanisation gives up on such conceit and simply turns the fantastic into the predominant marker (and market) of urban life.

As landscapes in cities like Jakarta become crowded with one showcase project after another, making the city a spectacular show becomes a critical organising principle of resources, attention and affective affiliation. Instead of a modernity of institutions, design and comportment acting to gather together the disparate facets of urban life, 'all-in-one' enclaves provide a fantastic proximity of residence, leisure, work, shopping, schooling, worship and socialising in highly circumscribed spaces that render larger swathes of the city irrelevant. Here both the solidly and the aspirant middle classes can feel assured that they need not waste their time with messy negotiations and collaborations. They can spend their time in incessant self-improvement, a process of continuous updated statuses and digital evidence of recognition – the thumbs-up status of being 'liked'. The phantom of self-sufficiency, the closing off the rest of the world in order that one might be part of a larger, abstract global space enjoins residents to a position where they occupy a world of homogeneous environments strewn across city and national borders. They don't know each other directly, but they don't need to, for what is important is an implicit collective affirmation of a kind of super-belonging, of not being left out or left behind.

This kind of phantom then turns the rest of the city, now viewed as increasingly dangerous, anachronistic or simply insignificant, into another phantom. For the all-in-one attempts to secure a seamlessness in the transitions between contexts – from home to work to school to clinic and so forth – that risks no interruption or interference. Without being subjected to the exposures of other atmospheres and navigational circuits, the residents, too, verge on being phantoms. They become ciphers and avatars in an intensive sedentariness meant to facilitate expansive mobility across social media, tourist destinations, and various convocations across the world.

But what of the ground underneath, what of the movement of physical, biochemical, infrastructural and animal processes? In exchange for the enclave-portal, the all-in-one, a wide range of facilities of engaging with different dynamics seems to go by the wayside. This is the long-term problem of multiplicities: the fact that the city highlights the existence of dangerous circulations, of arbitrary irruptions in the fabric of conjunctions that emanate from the sheer density of processes brought in close proximity. These are dispositions whose trajectories can be charted and anticipated but not always fully controlled. Even in contexts of continuous and successful adjustments and repairs, not only are tears, irruptions and malfunctioning compensated for but the very act of repair often has to delink and dismantle the familiar and relied-on, a process that generates untoward implications not always discernible in the present. Cities are the results of specific intentions and objectives, as well as the culmination of plans, management protocols, power struggles and both systematic and random selections of what to pay attention to, what to use and value. But the 'results' of the city are not most effectively composed simply from the viewpoint and instrumentality of human inhabitants, no matter how diverse their perspectives and capacities might be.

Since residents do not share their neighbourhoods only with each other but with a much broader range of entities, what kind of moral procedures are applicable to these extensions of hospitality? The exigencies of hosting, of improving livelihoods, of being able to discover new potentialities within what a person is as well as to become something completely different means that people largely 'circle' each other, come at each other from different angles, even when subject to all of the devices of calculation and location which orient them. This circling is a willingness to engage the people or events at hand knowing they can never be grasped or known definitively. It is also a means of prolongation. One does not have to know who one is dealing with for sure in order to keep the game of collaboration going; it is always possible to look at things from new angles, to recalibrate relationships. At the same time, collaborations need not always be prolonged; they can be momentarily occupied and then let go of without the fear of experiencing debilitating loss. This circling means that many things are going to intersect accidentally and precipitate their own energetic transformations that will register some kind of impact, even as the circling continues. This circling is the necessary ingredient for just and information-rich environments, if not necessarily the guarantee of political mobilisation that can defend such environments from those forces which refuse or see no need to be hosted, let alone deflected or reshaped.

References

Bryant, L. (2014) *Onto-Cartography: An Ontology of Machines and Media*. Edinburgh: University of Edinburgh Press.

Deleuze, G. (1989) *Cinema 2: The Time Image*. Minneapolis: University of Minnesota Press.

Deleuze, G. (1995) *Difference and Repetition*. New York: Columbia University Press.

Deleuze, G. and Guattari, F. (1987) *A Thousand Plateaus: Capitalism and Schizophrenia*. Minneapolis: University of Minnesota Press.

Deleuze, G. and Guattari, F. (1994) *What Is Philosophy?* London: Verso.

Delpech-Ramey, J. (2010) 'Deleuze, Guattari and the "politics of sorcery"', *SubStance*, 39 (1): 8–23.

Flaxman, G. (2012) *Gilles Deleuze and the Fabulation of Philosophy*. Minneapolis: University of Minnesota Press.

Malabou, C. (2008) *What Should We Do With Our Brain?*, trans. S. Rand. New York: Fordham University Press.

Malabou, C. (2011) *Changing Difference*, trans. C. Shread. Cambridge: Polity Press.

Malabou, C. (2012) *Ontology of the Accident: An Essay on Destructive Plasticity*, trans. C. Shread. Cambridge: Polity Press.

For an Urban Machinic Ecology

Gary Genosko

Félix Guattari wrote impressionistically about the cities that fascinated him, such as the Tokyo he imagined would become the northern capital of the emancipation of the global south, and his writing about São Paulo is dotted with references to street scenes, some involving himself, his dreams and recollections. Other street haecceities allow certain places and times to enter into an assemblage with Guattari and his companions. Guattari often mentions the most economically depressed and socially marginalised areas of cities, such as the south Bronx in New York City and Sanya in Tokyo, as exemplary sites for novel self-organising solutions to the challenges of their populations, sometimes in unlikely forms such as the good work of gangs despite their reputation for violence. Trouble may stir in the strata of many cities, but it can be productive given the right conditions. In China Miéville's novel *The City and the City* (2009), the cities of Beszel and Ul Qoma are crosshatched together, yet it is illegal to see one while in the other, and any such fleeting visions must be unsensed. 'Breach' is the word that is uttered when transgressions occur, and one is forced to appear before a kafkaesque tribunal after the alleged fact. Cities overlap like quantum waves. One serves as substratum for the other and vice versa, with interstratic mixes in the middle, the so-called third city of Orciny, that may or may not exist. Miéville gives new meaning to the unseen of our cities.

A Guattarian investigation of urban subjectivation passes through his conception of a 'subjective city' that is defined through a machinic ecology and urban enunciations (architecture, infrastructure, populations on the move). That is, an ecosophical approach to cities that focuses on the dependency of processes of subjectivation on the vast phylum of technological, informational, chemical, biogenetically engineered infrastructures that support human existence. The question is whether these can promote new singular and incomparable subjectivations. Ecosophy, with its three registers, is counterpoised by pathosophy, the vectorial city of viruses, plagues and pestilence in our new era of pandemics. Cities of rats and feral cats, of birds whose migratory paths bring them into collision courses with skyscrapers, bird flu epicentres and the like.

Given that Guattari relies on the concept of the megamachine borrowed from Lewis Mumford in order to describe large machinic assemblages at the scale of urban agglomerations, he has a specific usage in mind: to discover the ways that cities produce subjectivities. He writes:

> The material infrastructure, communications and services of cities cannot be separated from functions that may be described as existential. Megamachines model sensibility, intelligence, inter-relational styles, and even unconscious phantasms. Hence, the importance of bringing about a transdisciplinary collaboration between urbanists, architects, and all the other disciplines of the social, human, and ecological sciences. (Guattari 2015: 105)

Guattari wanted to influence the production of subjectivities within contemporary cityscapes and he took a Braudelian route, of sorts, to do so. He extended Braudel's invocation of the multidisciplinary requirement expressed in *A History of Civilizations* (1994: 9) – that all the social sciences must be marshalled to study civilisations – adopting the term transdisciplinary (of his own making) to indicate it would be more than a multitude of experts that he called upon. The creation of vibrant microspaces of experimentation, in which Guattari engaged throughout every phase of his career, would be brought to bear upon the urban ecological predicament in a global context. Such a predicament required non-technocratic solutions to industrial pollution and the invention of a non-polluting transportation system in order to influence the urban machine's collective self-elaboration and the development of an ecological consciousness attuned to ethically responsible negotiations of collective actions at large scales.

A new Guattarian megamachine requires the creation of collective assemblages of enunciation based on eco-political and aesthetic principles that promote resingularising subjectifications. The overlapping registers of the mental, social and environmental ecologies entail that any environmental efforts aimed at global warming or species extinction must be accompanied by a change in collective consciousness and social relations; otherwise, fighting pollution is just 'remedial' (2015: 106). For Guattari, it is the city that is at the centre of the tri-ecosophical problematic because 'the urban phenomenon has changed nature. It is no longer one problem among many. It is problem number one: the problem sitting at the crossroads of economic, social, cultural and ideological stakes. The city forges the destiny of humanity . . .' (2015: 107).

If there is only one machine in the future, it is a planetary city whose 'diverse components are scattered over every surface of a multipolar urban rhizome encircling the planet' (2015: 101). Drawing on the existing north/south divide and rich/poor distinctions, Guattari moves in the direction of a subjectivity that has escaped from capitalist valorisations employing these and other similar binaries and answers to other values based on solidarity, emancipation of oppressed groups, social reinsertion of the aged, etc. He rejects the universalist presumptions of architectural modernism in the manner of Le Corbusier for a more non-specialist attention to the qualities of the subjectivities they aspire to produce through particularities of sites and inhabitants. These qualities themselves carry proto- and partial-subjective functions and cannot be abandoned to the whims of gentrification, market forces, consensual tastes and so-called democratic processes of decision-making easily manipulated by financial interests: 'This partial subjectivation, in a sense, will have a tendency to cling to the past, to some cultural influences and reassuring redundancies but, in another sense, it will remain attentive to elements of surprise and innovation in its way of looking, even if that is a little destabilizing' (2015: 114).

Guattari uses the megamachine as an establishing shot of the city that inaugurates the humans–machines interfaces that define his posthumanism. The megamachine is 'a node at the core of a multidimensional network' (Guattari 1986: 460) in which we are machinically enslaved as component parts. This is not a megamachine that Mumford would have accepted. It is perhaps easier to grasp Guattari's recourse to the network figure if a few provisos are added: that the network of nodes and lines is multidimensional or perhaps multiscalar. Yet visibility and functionality fall short of Guattari's insights into the complexity of urban experience. This is how architects, for instance Helene Furján, understand Guattari's urban eco-logic, as a subjectivation machine engaging global and molecular dimensions (Furján 2008: 297), to which may be added Guattari's sense of the spatial and temporal dynamics of urbanisation, conceived as web-like, but in terms of differential speeds of technical, scientific and aesthetic advances on a planetary phylum. Guattari (1981: 39) was once asked about his ideal city and replied by noting his experiences in Japan. He viewed the emergence there of 'machinic mutants . . . *for the best* and for the worst! You asked me how I see future cities, ideal cities? From the perspective of the best noted above.' Obviously, this is no simple valorisation of unambivalent machinism, despite Guattari's obsessive attachment to machines of all kinds, but a recognition of how urban environments subjectivate animistically, absorbing, calling, manipulating their denizens concretely and abstractly, corporeally and incorporeally, from the smallest details (a hallway) to the largest infrastructural features (bridges, highways, skyscrapers). These highly charged features are partial enunciations that catalyse the amassing of components into a consistent assemblage of subjectivation, with all of the nuances of a polyphonous and emergent formation. Within these infrastructural and, of course, architectural transferential phenomena, Guattari considers pathic apprehensions of partial enunciators and provides as the simplest spatial example that of an ambience, which is without mediation and without reference to distinct, parcelled information: for example, 'as soon as one enters certain primary schools, one feels anguish oozing from the walls' (Guattari 1993: 146). Further, Guattari (2015: 82) described the overall objective of Japanese architect Shin Takamatsu's practice as 'arriving at a point where the building becomes a nonhuman subject capable of connecting with individual and collective human subjectivities'. Such partial enunciators infuse the material infrastructure, and their pathic apprehension draws transversal lines between them, sometimes slowly, sometimes in a flash, perhaps as the institutional paint applied to cement blocks in a barracks-style school is mocked by the traces left upon it by the ball games played against it. The 'objectity' of the partial enunciators entails that subjectivation, at least its extra-human parts, is objective, or that objectity and subjectity overlap. Guattari's renewal of Mumford can be put succinctly: megamachinic animism redefines the city as a talcum-like dusting of partial-enunciators and hence proto-subjectivations in all strata (Melitopoulos and Lazzarato 2012). This megamachinic animism is temporary like the cityscape itself. Machinic species like proto-subjectivations are fragile and their evolution is uncertain. All it takes is a little breeze for the assemblage to mutate.

The overlapping cities that Miéville imagined help us to grasp the description Guattari provides of how overlapping objectities and subjectities 'incarnate themselves as an animist nucleus' (1995: 102). They work by mutual invasion, that is breaches, half-one and half-the-other. Strange alterities grasped pathically. The scattered objectities and subjectities cling to human bodies and machines alike, and form a film, a mineral dusting, that is moistened by peculiar liquids of indeterminate origins and alien viscosities, like ticker-tape and confetti, these most urban of life-giving showers.

References

Braudel, F. (1994) *A History of Civilizations*, trans. R. Mayne. London: Allen Lane/ Penguin.

Furján, H. (2008) 'On eco-logics', *Artforum*, November, pp. 295–7 and 374.

Guattari, F. (1981) 'Quelle est pour vous la Cité idéale?', *La Quinzaine littéraire*, 353: 39.

Guattari, F. (1986) 'Questionnaire on the city', trans. B. Benderson, *Zone*, 1/2: 460.

Guattari, F. (1993) 'Space and corporeity', *D: Columbia Documents in Architecture and Theory*, 2: 139–49.

Guattari, F. (1995) *Chaosmosis*, trans. P. Bains and J. Pefanis. Bloomington: Indiana University Press.

Guattari, F. (2008) *The Three Ecologies*, trans. I. Pindar and P. Sutton. London: Bloomsbury.

Guattari, F. (2015) *Machinic Eros: Writings on Japan*. Minneapolis: Univocal.

Melitopoulos, A. and Lazzarato, M. (2012) 'Machinic animism', *Deleuze Studies*, 6 (2): 92–101.

Miéville, C. (2009) *The City and the City*. New York: Ballantine Books.

Notes on Contributors

Ronnen Ben-Arie is a Research Fellow at the Minerva Humanities Center at Tel-Aviv University and teaches at the Department of Architecture and Town Planning at the Technion Institute. His PhD studies explored the concepts of resistance in the political thought of Gilles Deleuze and Michel Foucault as a basis for thinking about possibilities for the transformation of political order. He has published on the spatio-political dimensions of the Israeli regime and his current research explores modes and practices of control, resistance and cooperation in heterogeneous urban spaces in Israel-Palestine.

Marc Boumeester is the Dean of AKI Academy of Art and Design, Enschede. He lectures and publishes in the fields of media philosophy and design theory. His research focuses on the liaison between affect, non-anthropocentric desire, socio-architectural conditions and instable media, in particular cinema. Previously he was a researcher at the Delft University of Technology, Delft School of Design, Faculty of Architecture, and co-founded the department of Interactive/Media/Design at the Royal Academy of Art in The Hague.

Magnus Eriksson is a PhD candidate in Sociology of Law at Lund University and the University of Macerata, writing on the relation between digital and urban space. He also holds a position as design researcher at the Interactive Institute in Gothenburg. Outside of research he is active in the hackerspace movement, the art collective Fatlab as well as having been a co-founder of Piratbyrån (2003–9) and Telecomix (2009–12). Currently he resides in Gothenburg, Sweden.

Ignacio Farías is a Sociologist and Assistant Professor of the Munich Center for Technology in Society (MCTS) and the Faculty of Architecture at the Technische Universität München. Ignacio works on science and technology studies, urban studies and cultural sociology, with a focus on infrastructural transitions and participation. He is co-editor of *Urban Assemblages: How Actor-Network Theory Changes Urban Studies* (Routledge 2009) and *Urban Cosmopolitics: Agencements, Assemblies, Atmospheres* (Routledge, forthcoming).

Hélène Frichot is Associate Professor and Docent in Critical Studies in Architecture, KTH School of Architecture, Stockholm, Sweden, and Adjunct Professor in the School of Architecture and Design, RMIT University, Melbourne. She co-curated the Architecture+Philosophy public lecture series with Esther Anatolitis in Melbourne, Australia between 2005 and 2014 (http://architecture.testpattern.com.au). Between 2004 and 2011 she held a tenured academic position in the School of Architecture and Design, RMIT University. Her research examines the transdisciplinary field between architecture and philosophy, and while her first discipline is architecture, she holds a PhD in philosophy from the University of Sydney (2004).

Catharina Gabrielsson is an architect, researcher and writer. She holds a position as Assistant Professor in Urban Theory at the School of Architecture KTH (Stockholm) and is Director of Art, Technology and Design, a doctoral programme in collaboration with Konstfack (University College of Arts, Crafts and Design). Her practice combines fieldwork explorations with considerations in art, architecture and philosophy to address spatial production in different registers. She is a contributor to *Deleuze and Architecture* (Edinburgh: Edinburgh University Press, 2013), *Field/Work* (London: Routledge, 2010) and *Curating Architecture and the City* (London: Routledge, 2009), an editorial member of *Architecture and Culture* and *Arkitektur*, and Research Fellow at the Swedish Research Institute of Istanbul.

Gary Genosko received his BA in Philosophy at the University of Toronto and his MA in Philosophy at the University of Alberta. He received his MES at York University and completed his PhD in Social and Political Thought at York University. He held a Canada Research Chair from 2002 to 2012 in Technoculture Studies and has received SSHRC funding for a number of projects since 2001, as well as participating in a McConnell Foundation grant for community service learning. His most recent books are *When Technocultures Collide* (WLUP 2013) and *Remodelling Communication* (UTP 2012), and he recently edited a special issue of the journal *Deleuze Studies* on 'Felix Guattari in the Age of Semiocapitalism' (2012). Recent articles by Dr Genosko have appeared in *Cultural Studies, Parallax, Cultural Politics* and *Ctheory*, as well as chapters in *The Cambridge Companion to Deleuze, Valences of Interdisciplinarity, The Guattari Effect* and *Transforming McLuhan*. His previous books include *Félix Guattari: An Aberrant Introduction* and *Félix Guattari: A Critical Introduction*. He has also contributed many entries to the *Deleuze and Guattari Dictionary* (Bloomsbury).

Maria Hellström Reimer is Professor in Design Theory at Malmö University, School of Arts and Communication, and Director of Studies at the Swedish Design Faculty for Design Research and Research Education. She was trained as an artist and holds a PhD and Readership in Landscape Architecture. Her research is interdisciplinary concerning the aesthetics and politics of design, including questions of criticality and methodological experimentation. Hellström Reimer has been affiliated with several research environments in Europe and the US during 2014: as Visiting Professor at Université de Paris 8 Vincennes/Saint-Denis and during the autumn at Parsons The New School for Design in New York.

Jean Hillier is Professor of Sustainability and Urban Planning at RMIT University, Melbourne, Australia. Her research interests include Deleuzian-inspired planning theory and methodology for strategic practice in conditions of uncertainty and the problematisation of cultural heritage practices and public art in spatial planning. Books include *Gilles Deleuze and Félix Guattari* (2013), *Stretching Beyond the Horizon: A Multiplanar Theory of Spatial Planning and governance* (2007) which applied Deleuzian concepts, the *Ashgate Research Companion to Planning Theory: Conceptual Challenges for Spatial Planning* (2010) edited with Patsy Healey and *Critical Essays in Planning Theory* (2008) in three volumes, edited with Patsy Healey. Jean also guest edited the Special Issue on Poststructuralism and Planning in the Chinese-language *Urban Planning International* (2010), and the special issue of *Town Planning Review* on Planning in Uncertainty (2011).

Stefan Höhne is a postdoctoral research fellow at the Center for Metropolitan Studies at TU Berlin. In 2011 and 2012 he was a teaching and research fellow at the Institute for Cultural History and Theory at Humboldt University, Berlin. From 2008 to 2010 he was a member of the Transatlantic Graduate Research Program Berlin–New York at the Center for Metropolitan Studies, TU Berlin and a visting scholar at Columbia University. His research interests include the historical anthropology of technology, urban studies and cultural theory. In his dissertation, he explored the subjectivities of the passenger in the New York Subway in the first half of the twentieth century. Recent publications include 'Tokens, Suckers und der Great New York Token War', in *Zeitschrift für Medien- und Kulturforschung* (1/2011) and 'An Endless Flow of Machines to Serve the City – Infrastructural Assemblages and the Quest for the Machinic Metropolis', in *Thick Space: Approaches to Metropolitanism* (Transcript, 2012).

Louise Beltzung Horvath is a PhD candidate at the Austrian Academy of Sciences and research assistant at the Vienna University of Technology. Since October 2012 she has been working with a quantum physicist and literature scientist on how to rethink spaces in view of the deployment of automated and autonomous technologies within philosophy of technology and urban studies. The project 'Thinking Space' is mentored by the post-phenomenologist Peter-Paul Verbeek (http://www.thinkingspace. eu). Relevant publications include 'Extremely Small and Incredibly Close' (*Handbook for Ambient Intelligence*, Springer, 2012), as well as a paper on 'Actual and Virtual Matters' (accepted, to be published) in a new book on materialism by New York University which focused on working with DG and Simondon on reconceptualising matter. At the Deleuze Conference 2013 she presented an approach to rethink the urban by the example of tracking and the city. (Both publications and the presentation resulted from the DOC-team work.)

Michele Lancione is an urban geographer and ethnographer interested in issues of marginality and diversity, activism and continental philosophy. He is currently based at the Department of Geography, University of Cambridge, as a Research Fellow of the Urban Studies Foundation. Michele is also Book Reviews Editor of the journal *City*. His new edited book is entitled *Rethinking Life at the Margins* (Ashgate, forthcoming). You can follow him @michelelancione and download his publications at http://www.michelelancione.eu.

Janet McGaw is a Senior Lecturer in Architectural Design at the University of Melbourne. She is a qualified architect and has a PhD by Creative Works (University of Melbourne). Her research work, teaching and creative practice investigate ways to make urban space more equitable. Janet uses methods that are discursive, collaborative and sometimes ephemeral. She led an ARC Linkage Grant exploring Indigenous placemaking in Melbourne (2010–14) with Anoma Pieris and Emily Potter. The project was supported by the Melbourne City Council's Indigenous Arts Program, the Victorian Traditional Owners Land Justice Group and Reconciliation Victoria. Recent publications include *Assembling the Centre: Architecture for Indigenous Culture, Australia and beyond* (London: Routledge, 2015), co-authored with Anoma Pieris, and 'Mapping "place" in southeast Australia: crafting a possum skin cloak', *Craft Research*, 5: 1 (2014), pp. 11–33.

Markus Maicher studied in the cities of Graz, Brussels, Madrid, Copenhagen and Vienna at sociology, geography as well as cultural theory institutes. Currently he works as a university assistant and PhD candidate at the Sociology Institute of the Vienna University of Technology, where he does research on spatial theory, public space and technological mediation. He is interested in 'Intensive Spaces' and the relation between smooth/striated space and intensity/extensity in the work of Deleuze and Guattari and has presented a paper at the 4th Inter-Disciplinary.Net 'Space & Place' conference in Oxford.

Jonathan Metzger is Associate Professor and Docent of Urban and Regional Studies at KTH. Metzger has a broad social scientific background and concrete experiences from working as a planning practitioner. He is a member of the board of editors of the international scholarly journals *Planning Theory*, *Planning Theory and Practice* and *Environment and Planning A*. His research interests include spatial theory, posthumanism and political ecology, particularly in relation to issues concerning spatial planning and territorial development practices. Among his recent publications are the edited volumes *Planning Against the Political* (New York: Routledge, 2014) and *Sustainable Stockholm: Exploring Urban Sustainability in Europe's Greenest City* (New York: Routledge, 2013).

Karl Palmås is Associate Professor in Innovation, Entrepreneurship and Social Change at Chalmers University of Technology. From his doctoral studies in sociology (LSE) and onwards, Palmås has studied how notions of innovation, entrepreneurship and creativity – all key imperatives of contemporary economic life – relate to issues of politics and activism. He is also working on a new project that charts how the so-called 're-invention of invention' is actualised in the context of initiatives that aim to harness creativity among citizens. More specifically, the project explores different modes by which urban space is used as a laboratory for the generation of innovations.

Mark Purcell is a Professor in the Department of Urban Design and Planning at the University of Washington where he studies urban politics, political theory, social movements and democracy. He is the author of *Recapturing Democracy* (2008), *The Down Deep Delight of Democracy* (2013) and numerous articles in journals including the *International Journal of Urban and Regional Research*, *Urban Geography*, *Environment and Planning A*, *Antipode*, *Urban Studies*, *Political Geography*, *Review of International Political Economy* and *Planning Theory*.

Andrej Radman has been teaching design and theory courses at TU Delft Faculty of Architecture since 2004. A graduate of the Zagreb School of Architecture in Croatia, he is a licensed architect and recipient of the Croatian Architects Association Annual Award for Housing Architecture in 2002. Radman received his Master's and Doctoral degrees from TU Delft and joined the Architecture Theory chair as Assistant Professor in 2008. He is on the editorial board of the peer-reviewed journal for architecture theory *Footprint*.

AbdouMaliq Simone is an Urbanist and Research Professor at the Max Planck Institute for the Study of Religious and Ethnic Diversity and Professor of Sociology at Goldsmiths College, University of London, as well as Visiting Professor at the African Centre for Cities, University of Cape Town, Research Associate with the Rujak Center for Urban Studies in Jakarta and Research Fellow at the University of Tarumanagara. For three decades Simone has worked with practices of social interchange, cognition, local economy and the constitution of power relations that affect how heterogeneous African cities are lived. In the past six years he has re-examined some of these issues in urban Southeast Asia. Simone has not only required a substantial understanding of urban processes and change in Africa and Southeast Asia as a body of academic knowledge, but he has worked on the concrete challenges of remaking municipal systems, training local government personnel and designing collaborative partnerships among technicians, residents, artists and politicians. The focus of these efforts has been to build viable institutions capable of engaging with the complexities of life across the so-called 'majority world'. For further research and project activities see http://www.abdoumaliqsimone.com/.

Fredrika Spindler is an Associate Professor of Philosophy at Södertörn University, Stockholm, Sweden. She holds a PhD in philosophy from the Université de Montpellier, with the dissertation title, *Philosophie de la puissance et détermination de l'homme chez Spinoza et chez Nietzsche* (1996). Fredrika has published extensively on Spinoza, Nietzsche and Deleuze and is also the translator of works by Deleuze, Derrida, Hardt and Negri, among others. Her current research is devoted to the question of temporality and subjectivity in Deleuze's thought. Recent publications are: *Spinoza. Multitud, affekt, kraft* (Göteborg: Glänta Produktion, 2009); *Nietzsche. Kropp, konst, kunskap* (Göteborg: Glänta Produktion, 2010); *Deleuze. Tänkande och blivande* (Göteborg: Glänta Produktion 2013); 'Multitude and Democracy', in Marcia Sà Cavalcante Schuback and Luiz Carlos Pereira (eds), *Time and Form* (Stockholm: Axl Books 2014); 'Foreword', in Spinoza, *Politisk-teologisk traktat* (Göteborg: Daidalos 2014); and 'Affektivitetens ekonomi', in Magnus Halldin (ed.), *De Nios Litterära – Kalender* (Stockholm: Norstedts 2015). Forthcoming in 2015 are: *Att läsa Spinoza* (ed. with Carl Montan); 'Time and Eternity', in Andre Santos Campos (ed.), *Spinoza. Basic Concepts* (Exeter: Imprint Academic); 'Deleuze: om identitet, fascism och motstånd', in Stefan Johnsson (ed.), *Samtida politisk teori* (Stockholm: Tankekraft).

Sven-Olov Wallenstein is Professor of Philosophy at Södertörn University, Stockholm, and editor-in-chief of Site. He is the translator of works by Baumgarten, Winckelmann, Lessing, Kant, Hegel, Frege, Husserl, Heidegger, Levinas, Derrida, Deleuze, Foucault, Rancière and Agamben, as well as the author of numerous books on philosophy, contemporary art and architecture. Recent publications include *Biopolitics and the Emergence of Modern Architecture* (2009), *Svar på frågan: Vad var det postmoderna?* (ed. 2009), *Swedish Modernism: Architecture, Consumption and the Welfare State* (ed. with Helena Mattsson, 2010), *Nihilism, Art, Technology* (2011), *Edmund Hussserl* (ed. 2011), *Aisthesis: Estetikens historia del 1* (ed. with Sara Danius and Cecilia Sjöholm, 2012), *Translating Hegel: The Phenomenology of Spirit and Modern Philosophy* (ed. with Brian Manning Delaney, 2012), *Foucault, Biopolitics, and Governmentality* (ed. with Jakob Nilsson, 2013) and *Heidegger, språket och poesin* (ed. with Ola Nilsson, 2013). Forthcoming in 2015 are: *Architecture, Critique, Ideology: Essays on Architecture and Theory* and *Madness, Religion, and the Limits of Reason* (ed. with Jonna Bornemark).

Index

Page numbers in *italics* refer to illustrations and page number followed by an 'n' refer to the page on which a note appears.